AA

explo

TURKISH COAST

Christopher and Melanie Rice

AA Publishing

2

Page 2: Worry beads
Page 3: Pigeon food vendor with an interested audience
Page 4: Waiting at Erdek harbour
Page 5: (top) The lagoon at Ölüdeniz
Page 5: (bottom) Traditional house at Erdek
Pages 6–7: (top) Statuary and reliefs on display at Selçuk Museum
Page 6: (bottom) Fish seller at Akçay
Page 7: (bottom) *Gulet* cruise at Marmaris
Page 8: Bazaar at Kaş
Page 9: The dramatic costline at Alanya

Written by Christopher and Melanie Rice
Edited, designed and produced by AA Publishing
Maps © The Automobile Association 1998

The contents of this publication are believed correct at the time of printing. Nevertheless, the publishers cannot be held responsible for any errors or omissions or for changes in the details given in this guide or for the consequences of any reliance on the information provided by the same. Assessments of attractions, hotels, restaurants and so forth are based upon the author's own personal experience and, therefore, descriptions given in this guide necessarily contain an element of subjective opinion which may not reflect the publishers' opinion or dictate a reader's own experiences on another occasion. We have tried to ensure accuracy in this guide, but things do change and we would be grateful if readers would advise us of any inaccuracies they may encounter.

Some material in this book has been previously published by AA Publishing in various publications

A CIP catalogue record for this book is available from the British Library.

ISBN 0 7495 1718 2
Published by AA Publishing (a trading name of Automobile Association Developments Limited, whose registered office is Norfolk House, Priestley Road, Basingstoke, Hampshire RG24 9NY. Registered number 1878835).

Colour separation by Fotographics Ltd
Printed and bound in Italy by Printer Trento srl

Titles in the Explorer series:
Australia • Boston & New England • Britain
Brittany • California • Caribbean • China • Costa Rica
Crete • Cyprus • Egypt • Florence & Tuscany
Florida France • Germany • Greek Islands • Hawaii
Indonesia • Ireland • Israel • Italy • Japan • London
Mallorca • Mexico • Moscow & St Petersburg • New York
New Zealand • Paris • Portugal • Prague • Provence
Rome • San Francisco • Scotland • Singapore & Malaysia
South Africa • Spain • Tenerife • Thailand • Turkey
Venice • Vietnam

AA World Travel Guides publish nearly 300 guidebooks to a full range of cities, countries and regions across the world. Find out more about AA Publishing and the wide range of services the AA provides by visiting our Web site at www.theaa.co.uk.

How to use this book

This book is divided into five main sections:

❏ Section 1: *Turkey Is*
discusses aspects of life and living today, from Atatürk's legacy to puddings and pastries

❏ Section 2: *Turkey Was*
places the country in its historical context and looks at past events influencing Turkey to this day

❏ Section 3: *A to Z Section*
covers places to visit arranged by region, with suggested walks, boat trips and drives. Within this section are Focus-on articles, which cover a range of topics in greater detail

❏ Section 4: *Travel Facts*
contains the practical information that is vital for a successful trip

❏ Section 5: *Hotels and Restaurants*
lists recommended establishments with a résumé of what they offer

How to use the star rating
Most places described in this book have been given a separate rating:

▶▶▶   **Do not miss**

▶▶   **Highly recommended**

▶   **Worth seeing**

Not essential viewing

Map references
To make the location of a particular place easier to find, every main entry in this book is given a map reference, such as 46C1. The first number (46) indicates the page on which the map can be found; the letter (C) and the second number (1) pin-point the square in which the main entry is located. The maps on the inside front cover and inside back cover are referred to as IFC and IBC respectively.

Contents

5

Quick reference

This quick-reference guide highlights the elements of the book you will use most often: the maps; the introductory features; the Focus-on articles; the walks, the drives and the boat trips.

Our Turkey

by Christopher and Melanie Rice

Christopher and Melanie Rice have travelled extensively in Europe and the Near East and enjoy sharing their experiences with others. Over the last 10 years they have written numerous guidebooks and travel articles. Their titles for the AA include: *CityPack Istanbul, Berlin; Essential Prague, Budapest* and *Explorer Moscow and St Petersburg.* They now live in London with their two children.

As we wander contentedly back to the hotel, still savouring our first encounter with Turkish cooking (a selection of *meze* followed by grilled sea bass), we are hailed from across the street by Abdülgani (Charlie to his friends) and invited in for a glass of apple tea. Like thousands of tourists before us, and no doubt many since, we have been lured into a carpet showroom. Three hours later we emerge, fully conversant with the mysteries of the flat-weave kilim, the significance of the Ghiordes double knot and the use of a handkerchief in detecting synthetic dyes. We are also carrying a carpet, having somehow been induced to part with 27 million *liras* (we wonder just how much that is in pounds!).

At 5am we are awake again. The experience of the muezzin calling the faithful to prayer from the local mosque is one we will come to treasure but on this, our first morning, his throaty baritone is an alarm call we can do without. We drag ourselves down to breakfast where we decide to spend the rest of the day recuperating by the sea. There are more than a dozen caiques lined up along the harbour front advertising a bewildering variety of trips around the locality. We try negotiating for the best deal until it slowly dawns on us that there is only one itinerary and that all the boats are owned by the same enterprising businessman.

But thankfully this is the last decision we will have to make. After staking a claim to a place on deck, disentangling the headphones and applying the sun block, we can lie back at last and enjoy the day. And what a day! Diving from the side of the boat into the clear turquoise waters of the Aegean; snorkelling over the ruins of a classical city, surrendered thousands of years ago to the sea; filming a school of dolphins; making a facepack out of the mud produced by hot springs issuing from a shoreline cave.

And tomorrow – who knows? If we are feeling energetic, we may decide to try tandem paragliding over the bay; or we could join an excursion into the mountains to visit a traditional Anatolian village; or spend a leisurely day shopping in the bazaar…

TURKEY IS

■ **While Turks look back with pride to the age of Süleyman the Magnificent, when the power and wealth of the Ottoman empire were the envy of the West, they are also aware of the humiliations they were forced to endure at the hands of the European powers in the 19th century. Today their country's strategic importance, straddling the Balkans and the Middle East, is a bargaining chip that may help them to gain entry to the European community of nations.** ■

Image For centuries the Turks were seen through Western eyes as the scourge of Christendom and a threat to the European order. The word Turk came to symbolise everything that was savage or barbaric, and in popular medieval imagination Turks took their place in the litany of plagues, floods, earthquakes, Tartars and comets sent by the Almighty to punish the wicked. In the 16th century, for example, Martin Luther prayed for deliverance from 'the world, the flesh, the Turk and the Devil'. During the Western European Renaissance it was Europe's historic ties with Greece that fanned the flames of prejudice. For most Western thinkers, the Greek civilisation stood at the dawn of their own – all that was classical was therefore considered noble and pure. In the 19th century, poets such as Lord Byron eulogised Greece with its classical ideals and romantic associations. Byron died in 1824 fighting against Turkey for Greek independence. In the minds of most Westerners, the Ottoman Empire still conjured up images of decadence, blood-lust, harem intrigue and perfidious paşas.

Such prejudices and stereotyping tend to linger: it is perhaps not surprising that when the

Contrasting images of Turkish women: (above) Muslim visitors to the Pool of Abraham, a religious shrine at Şanlıurfa; and (below) a villager wearing the traditional dress of the Aegean region

Greeks and Turks fought over Cyprus in the 1950s and 1960s, leading to the island's partition in 1974, Westerners were inclined to side with the Greek Cypriots, simply because they seemed more 'European'.

❑ At critical moments in their history the Turks have had a habit of doing the unexpected. After suffering military defeat in World War I, they fought back, ousting the Allies and going on to achieve recognition as an independent nation. In 1945 President İnönü turned Turkey from a dictatorship into a democracy overnight; and in 1961 the military, after seizing power in a coup 18 months earlier, handed it back in an orderly manner to a parliamentary regime. In each of these cases, Turkish actions ran contrary to the confident predictions of the experts. ❑

A busy street near the Grand Bazaar in Istanbul's Eminönü district. With a population of nearly 12 million, Istanbul is one of the world's most crowded cities

Reality Following World War II, Turkey was elected to the Council of Europe and, in 1952, was admitted to the North Atlantic Treaty Organisation (NATO) – although it was military considerations, as well as self-interest, that lay behind these decisions as far as the Western powers were concerned. Turkish NATO bases provided a potential launching pad for strategic air strikes against the Soviet Union and, more recently, for direct military action against Iraq during the Gulf War.

In the post-Communist era, Turkey's foreign policy took a new direction, as her influence extended to the 100 million Turkic speakers in the former Soviet republics of Central Asia and to the Muslim populations of the Balkans, for whom Turkey provides a model, combining Islamic beliefs with modern social and economic policies. Turkey's role as the strategic link between Europe and the Asian world has never been more crucial to the prospects for a peaceful 21st century than it is now.

Young Turks today are more open and relaxed in their behaviour than their elders

■ **Modern Turkey is largely the creation of one man, Mustafa Kemal, later known as Atatürk, Father of the Turks. To achieve his reforms, Atatürk formed the Republican People's Party in 1923, intending that its members should constitute the local leadership in every town and village throughout the country.** ■

Kemalism According to Kemalist philosophy, civilisation assures freedom, while happiness lies in personal independence, that is a life without political, social or religious constraints. Kemalism especially abhors religious extremism for creating inequalities, for excluding women from playing an active role in society and for stirring up international conflict. It is opposed to the class system and scornful of

Atatürk's stirring speeches to the nation he founded still have a resonance today

intellectual élites, believing passionately in the need to educate workers and peasants in order to deliver them from capitalist oppression. By promoting literacy and culture (especially literature and music) it aims to bring civilisation closer to the ordinary Turk. The final keystone is patriotism, considered essential for the defence of a people's independence. In its application, this remarkable philosophy demonstrated that, through disciplined education, it was possible to achieve in one generation what could otherwise have taken ten or more.

World War II By the time Atatürk died in 1938, 15 years of autocratic leadership had won for Turkey a credible place in the international arena. That the regime he left behind him was able to withstand the stresses and strains of World War II so soon after his death is perhaps the best testimony to his achievement. Turkey managed to stay neutral during the conflict, despite pressure from the Western powers, but at a price – economic hardship combined with the risks involved in maintaining a policy of armed neutrality gave rise to a more authoritarian

❏ Atatürk's unbendingly stern, eagle-like countenance is omnipresent in Turkey, looking down from statues placed outside every public building, hanging from picture frames in schoolrooms and staring out from posters in cafés and restaurants. Each year on the anniversary of his death in 1938, a minute's silence is observed. ❏

12

Atatürk's mausoleum is a powerful symbol of the personality cult his memory inspired

government than Atatürk had intended and ultimately led to the imposition of martial law.

Struggle for secularism In the years since Atatürk's death, Turkey has been dominated by the struggle between secularism and religion. Supporting the former are the army officers, teachers and bureaucrats who form the back-bone of the Republican People's Party, while the cause of Islam has considerable backing from the rural population, including migrants to the towns. After three coups in the space of 20 years, the election of Tansu Çiller as Turkey's first woman prime minister in 1993 seemed to indicate that the country would continue along the secularist path. However, politics in Turkey is never what it seems and within three years Çiller's True Path Party had formed a coalition government with the pro-Islamic Welfare Party of Necmettin Erbakan. Erbakan's reluc-tance to promote secular education at the expense of religious schools and his diplomatic overtures towards overtly Islamic regimes, led the army to react to what it saw as the danger of creeping fundamentalism. After

12 months of political stalemate and increasingly weak government, Erbakan was forced to resign as prime minister, vowing to return after the 1998 elections.

Turkey's first woman prime minister, Tansu Çiller

■ **It is important to distinguish between Turkey as a state and the Turks as a people, for while the Turks are Muslim, Turkey is no longer an Islamic state. Orthodox Muslims regard the secularisation of Turkey as an apostasy from Islam and Atatürk as a heretic.** ■

14

Turkish Islam Muslims in Turkey welcome foreigners into their mosques, except during their prayers, allowing them to stroll about freely and to linger at will. In the rest of the Islamic world such tolerance of outsiders is rare and many countries, even those used to foreign visitors such as Morocco and Tunisia, will not permit non-Muslims to enter their mosques at all.

When you cross the border from Greece or Bulgaria into Turkey, you will find it is not the appearance of

Men performing their ablutions before entering the Süleymaniye mosque in Istanbul. Ritual is an important part of the Islamic faith

the people, or their dress – almost everybody wears Western clothes – that makes the country visibly different from its neighbours, but the prevalence of mosques and minarets. Worship, however, is by no means confined to the mosque: on hearing the call to prayer five times a

day, Muslims everywhere – gardeners in parks, peasants in fields, businessmen in their offices, – stop what they are doing and drop to their knees to perform the ritual obeisances laid down in the Koran. During these 10-minute periods of prayer, nothing is allowed to intrude or distract and even telephones and doorbells are left unanswered.

Europeanisation Most of Atatürk's radical reforms of the 1920s and '30s were concerned with religion, for Islam was seen to be a major obstacle in the path of Westernisation.

Religious education in schools was outlawed, while the Latin alphabet replaced the Arabic script. This was a double blow for Islam, since Arabic is the language not only of the Koran but also of the sacred calligraphy that adorns all mosques. The reform of the alphabet almost completely alienated the younger generation of Turks from their Islamic cultural background, while strict Muslims regarded the Latin alphabet as being synonymous with the infidel. For modern travellers arriving from other Islamic countries, such as Iran or Syria, the Latin script outside shops and on road signs is an immediate reminder of Turkey's pro-Western affiliations.

The law No other Muslim country has abolished Koranic law and this is a remarkable departure from Islamic tradition, where the law is held to be an essential part of religion. The word Islam was erased from the constitution of the Turkish Republic when it was proclaimed in 1923, and from that point Turkey effectively withdrew from the Muslim world.

Atatürk's aim, it should be said, was not to abolish religion but to free the people from what he believed to be Islam's oppressive and backward-looking influence. This he considered to be a necessary step on the road towards modernisation. The effect, however, has been to cause a division in society between strict Muslims and Turkey's educated élite, which is more or less avowedly agnostic in outlook.

Praying five times a day is one of the main tenets, or pillars, of Islam

❏   The Islamic belief that all things are pre-ordained lies behind orthodox Islam's rejection of insurance. How can one insure against dying prematurely, or the collapse of a building, when such things are the will of God? Insurance is therefore seen as indicating a lack of trust in the supreme power of God. ❏

■ **Turkey lies at the meeting point of three different climatic zones: the Euro-Siberian, the Mediterranean and the Irano-Turanian. The result is a tremendous variety of topography and vegetation, far greater than in most countries of a similiar size, with deserts, high mountains, coastal plains, forests and pastures. This diverse environment, where nearly 9,000 species of wild flower flourish, is a paradise for naturalists and botanists. ■**

Climate By far the largest of Turkey's climatic zones is the Irano-Turanian. This is the steppeland of the central Anatolian plateau, which is very dry in summer and bitterly cold in winter, when temperatures drop to minus 40°C and snow lies for up to 120 days. The Euro-Siberian zone includes the Istanbul region and the Black Sea coast, where European-type deciduous forests of ash, oak and beech flourish in summer temperatures that rarely exceed 28°C. The Mediterranean coast is different again; here the fertile Cilician plain, with cotton fields, palm trees and orange groves, experiences temperatures as high as 43°C in the summer. The seasonal variation in temperature – sometimes as much as 50°C – is one of the most extreme in the world.

Anamur – an unspoilt stretch of coastline in the east Mediterranean

❏ Birds known in Europe, Asia and Africa are all to be found in Turkey, where the unusually wide range of climatic conditions allows for the diversity. May is probably the best bird-watching month and, on a typical two- or three-week touring holiday, even the inexperienced will spot over 100 species. The easiest to spot are the storks, who make their nests on minarets, rooftops and telegraph poles, while around rivers and lakes grey herons are equally difficult to miss. ❏

Geology Turkey's geological structure is extremely complex: the country consists largely of several old plateau blocks, against which masses of younger rock series have been squeezed to form fold mountain ranges of varying sizes. These fold mountains run in many different directions with considerable irregularity as one range unexpectedly gives way to another, or turns

equally abruptly to plain or plateau. In the north and west of the country, seismic activity has led to enormous cracking and disturbance of the rocks. Faulting is responsible for the long, indented Aegean coastline with its numerous oddly shaped islands and estuaries, and for two of Turkey's most distinctive geological features, the Bosphorus and the Dardanelles Straits.

Flora Turkey's extensive national parks have encouraged plant life to flourish in a protected environment, but many colourful flowers also grow wild on the hillsides and even at the roadside in the Aegean and Mediterranean regions. The Turks adore flowers and are inspired gardeners: April and May are the most impressive months, when the pink oleander bushes, red anemones, poppies and white irises abound. Tumbling white jasmine and purple bougainvillaea bloom throughout the summer in many gardens.

Wild flowers are one of the chief delights of Turkey's south Aegean region

17

■ **Turkey is a potentially rich country: its mountains are full of minerals; its land and climate are perfect for a wide range of agricultural produce; the seas all around are full of fish. There is no shortage of manpower, but the country is burdened with huge foreign debts and the struggle for growth has not been easy.** ■

Farming on the slopes beneath Yılanlıkale ('Castle of Snakes'). Snakes are still found here in great numbers

The problems The scale of Turkey's recent economic problems is the legacy of the dynamic but extravagant Menderes government (1950–60; see page 40), which incurred debts that will not be cleared until 2014. Another hangover from the past is the continuation of Atatürk's policy of exempting agriculture from taxation, a move initiated in the 1920s to encourage expansion. However, currently at least half the population works in agriculture, producing 35 per cent of the gross national product (GNP) but contributing less than 5 per cent of total taxation. Although this policy is clearly outdated, no government dares to impose taxes on the big farmers and landowners whose support is critical to them. Major landowners, known as *ağas*, often have no actual title to their lands, but have somehow managed to acquire

it, often from peasants who have since migrated to the cities. In much of central and eastern Anatolia, these *ağas* 'own' as many as 100 villages and for thousands of peasants their word is law. At election time, the landowner is therefore in a position to deliver thousands of votes to whichever party he chooses to support.

Population increase is a further problem: the population of Turkey, estimated in 1996 at 63.2 million, has more than doubled in the last 25 years, and, at 3 per cent net increase annually, has one of the highest rates of growth in the world. This is partly accounted for by a fall in the death rate following the eradication of diseases such as malaria, but the birth rate is extremely high and attempts to introduce family planning have encountered substantial opposition. Inevitably this has placed enormous pressure on Turkey's resources, leading to a rise in unemployment and a widening of the trade gap as agricultural produce intended for export is diverted to feed new mouths.

The solutions Land reform, essential for any real economic recovery but never seriously attempted in the past, is now being implemented to a limited extent, together with reforms of the tax system.

There has also been a concerted attempt to privatise state-owned agricultural enterprises, traditionally responsible for producing Turkey's main raw materials, cotton, wool,

Fishermen at work in the harbour at Akçakoca on the Black Sea

mohair, beet-sugar, olive oil and tobacco. It is hoped that market forces will increase the efficiency of the public sector as a whole, which currently swallows a staggering 40 per cent of GNP.

Current position Inflation, still running at about 70 per cent annually, is the main economic problem facing Turkey today, although domestic debt also continues to increase and the trade deficit is widening. However, exchange reserves are high, company profits are buoyant, there are no shortages of commodities and labour costs remain low. Both the International Monetary Fund (IMF)

and the World Bank have promised large loans (in excess of $3 billion) on condition that the Turkish government introduces further measures to reduce inflation to around 10 per cent per annum and continues privatising the state sector. (So far only Turkish Telecom has been fully privatised.) These measures should also help Turkey in the currently protracted negotiations to integrate with the European Union.

Basket weaving and other cottage industries are still a mainstay of the village economy in Turkey

❏   There is a long tradition of tax evasion in Turkey, aggravated by inefficient book-keeping and incompetent collection methods. As a result, some of Turkey's richest citizens contribute little or nothing to the exchequer. ❏

■ **'Ne mutlu Turkum diyene' ('How happy is he who can say he is a Turk')** was one of Atatürk's great sayings, still seen all over Turkey proclaimed on banners and carved into hillsides. Another favourite slogan, **'We resemble ourselves',** was designed to endow Turks with a sense of pride in their identity. ■

Who are the Turks? The Turks were nomadic tribesmen from the steppelands of Central Asia who began making raids on Byzantine territory early in the 11th century. The vexed question, which still puzzles historians today, is how was it that this relatively small band of invaders succeeded in stamping their Turkish identity on Anatolia in such a short period of time, without being absorbed by the ethnic mix of Jews, Greeks, Kurds, Armenians and numerous tribal peoples already there? Part of the answer surely lies in the Turks' shrewdness, flexibility and tolerance – there were after all no massacres or mass deportations

The Kurds of eastern Turkey have always been nomadic. This woman stands outside a traditional goat-hair tent known as a yurt

of the indigenous population and Christians were allowed to continue worshipping as before.

The Turkish perspective
The Turk's view of history, still taught in schools today, is that the original Turkish homeland, from the Caspian to Mongolia, was the cradle of world civilisation. From here successive waves of migrants swept eastwards into China in around 7000 BC, while others invaded the Indian sub-continent, northern Europe (the Celts), the Middle East and North Africa. Some Turks regard the Greek and Roman civilisations as successors to the (Turkic) Phrygians, Lydians and Hittites.

Personality The Turkish character is one of contrasts and contradictions: Turks are thrifty and hard-working,

Private enterprise flourishes on the streets of Istanbul. Impoverishment has led many Turkish villagers to seek casual work in the major cities

yet realise the futility of worrying about tomorrow; although outwardly dour (their reserved manner led them to be dubbed 'the Englishmen of the East' by early travellers), they appreciate a good sense of humour – Nasreddin Hoca, a comic character, is their favourite folklore hero. Turks have a reputation for being patient but have a capacity for violence when pushed too far. They are fiercely proud of their country and its history, but coupled with this there is a belief in a Turcocentric universe and an extreme sensitivity to slight and external criticism.

Ethnic minority
The Kurds form the largest ethnic minority in Turkey with a population estimated at 10 million (about 17 per cent of the total); the majority live in the country's eastern

provinces. Like the Turks, most of the Kurds are Muslims but they are fiercely jealous of their own language, culture and traditions and have been fighting for independence for about 80 years. Since 1984 the undeclared war in the south-eastern provinces has cost up to 10,000 lives and shows no signs of abating since the Turkish authorities regard Kurdish aspirations as a threat to the unitary Turkish state.

One of Adana's more colourful inhabitants

■ **Turkish religious festivals, including Ramadan and Kurban Bayramı, are identical in character to those observed throughout the Islamic world and, like other nations, the Turks also commemorate important dates in their country's history on specially designated public holidays. For foreigners the most enjoyable celebrations are the cultural festivals, usually lasting a week or more, that take place in regions throughout the country.** ■

City festivals Istanbul has a rich variety of international festivals, including the Music and Arts Festival from mid-June to early July, a jazz festival in July, film in April, theatre in May – as well as an ever-increasing

The 24,000-seat theatre in the former Greek city of Ephesus has been adapted to accommodate the festival-goers who flock here every summer

number of festivals throughout the year, many of which feature artists of world renown. İzmir holds an international fair from the end of August to the end of September, which includes commercial exhibitions as well as cultural and folklore events. Samsun, on the Black Sea coast, holds a similar fair in July. Bursa's annual festival, from mid-June to mid-July is entirely cultural, attracting international singers and musicians.

A proud camel-owner leads his beast into the arena at Selçuk

Festivals in ancient settings Turkey is blessed with numerous magnificent venues for festivals, including Graeco-Roman theatres, Byzantine churches and medieval fortresses. In April and May each year Ephesus hosts an excellent culture and art festival, with folk dancing in the theatre. The ancient medical centre known as the Asklepeion is the setting for plays and dancing during the entertaining Pergamum Festival, which takes place in May/June. The Çanakkale Festival uses the site of Troy as a setting for folk dances and other musical performances. The Antalya Film and Art Festival, which takes place annually in October, makes creative use of the splendid Roman theatre at Aspendos.

Wrestling Camel wrestling can be seen throughout the province of Aydın, especially in the town of Germencik, throughout December

and January. The camels go at each other with no holds barred, but, while vicious, it is not usually a blood sport. Grease-wrestling between male human contestants is popular throughout Turkey. The major festival is held near Edirne on the little island of Saray İçi in the first week of July. Up to 1,000 contestants take part, clad in leather trunks and greased all over with olive oil. Gypsies arrive in force to provide the entertainment, which includes drum and oboe music to accompany the warm-up exercises.

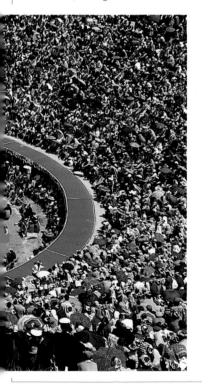

❏ Each region in Turkey has its own special folk dance and costume. Around the Black Sea for example, the men, dressed in black with silver trimmings, perform the famous 'Horon' dance. The sword and shield dance at Bursa – again an all-male affair – celebrates the Ottoman conquest of the city; here the performers wear early Ottoman battle dress. The male and female participants in the spoon dance (popular everywhere from Konya to Silifke) tap out the infectious rhythms with pairs of wooden spoons carried in each hand. ❏

■ The abundance of *pastahanes* (pastry shops) in Turkey, positively bursting with every conceivable gooey concoction, betrays the national sweet tooth, while the names – 'nightingale's nest', 'lady's navel', 'lips of the beautiful beloved' – say something about Turkish attitudes to desserts. Milk, nuts, honey, eggs and pastry are the basic ingredients of the local puddings, of which the best known are *baklava* and *kadayıf*. ■

Pastries *Kadayıf* uses long, finely shredded strands of dough to enclose a mixture of ground hazelnuts and honey. Even the Turks buy *baklava* from the *pastahane*, as it takes an expert to prepare these sticky, syrup-sodden triangles of flaky pastry filled with ground walnuts. *Dilber dudağı* ('lips of the beautiful beloved') are small oval-shaped pastries, soaked in oil, with fresh cream added, and with crushed pistachio nuts tumbling from a small slit down the middle.

Milk puddings and jellies The classic Turkish milk puddings are *muhallebi*, a type of rice pudding with cinnamon, sometimes flavoured with rose water, and *keşkül*, a smooth mixture of milk, ground almonds and pistachios, garnished with dried coconut. *Aşure* is a rose-water jelly, filled with chickpeas and dry beans and decorated with dried figs and apricots, raisins, walnuts, pine nuts and pistachios. When using fresh fruit in their puddings, the Turks create such delights as black cherry and peach bread, pumpkin with nuts and banana rice pudding.

Of all Turkish sweets the best known is undoubtedly Turkish delight, *lokum*, made from solidified sugar and pectin, flavoured with rose-water, lemon or pistachio and dusted with icing sugar.

Halva and baklava *are just a few of the temptations awaiting visitors with a sweet tooth*

24

TURKEY WAS

■ **The most ancient relics found so far in Asia Minor date to the seventh millennium BC. Remains from the early second millennium BC reveal the existence of Assyrian trading colonies in Cappadocia and an important Copper Age culture in central Anatolia. Later in the second millennium, most of Asia Minor fell under the rule of the Hittites, whose empire flourished from about 1750 BC–1200 BC, reaching its peak in the 14th and 13th centuries BC. ■**

Mystery of the Hittites Three thousand years ago the ancient Hittites rivalled the Egyptians as the greatest power on earth, yet until a century ago they remained a mystery race, with the only documentary evidence of their existence being in the Old Testament, where they are mentioned as a tribe living in Palestine. When Egyptian

❑ The elaborately wrought bronze 'sun discs' found in the graves at Alacahöyük are unique to Hittite art. They appear to have been endowed with mystical properties, and their unusual criss-cross pattern was perhaps intended to symbolise the sun and its rays. Sometimes an antlered stag appears at the centre of the design, indicating that they are the work of a mountain people. ❑

These two stone lions, which gave the Lion Gate its name, have been guarding the Hittite fortress at Hattuşaş (now Boğazkale) for over 3,000 years

hieroglyphs were first deciphered, an inscription was found to relate to a defence treaty between Rameses II and Hattusilis, king of the Hittites. To cement the treaty, Rameses married the Hittite king's daughter.

No further clue to the mystery of the lost Hittite Empire was found until 1834, when a Frenchman,

Charles Texier, discovered the ruins of the Hittite capital, Hattuşaş, at Boğazkale. In 1906, German excavations on the site uncovered thousands of cuneiform tablets. These were finally deciphered in the 1940s, revealing the full history of the Hittites, an achievement heralded as one of the greatest archaeological triumphs of the 20th century. Since most of the research and decipherment was carried out by German and Czech scholars, Hittite culture remains less well known in the English-speaking world than perhaps it should be.

Mountain culture The Hittites were the only ancient civilisation to exist and develop in inhospitable mountainous country. While their military strength, necessary to their survival, was awesome, they were humane in the treatment of conquered enemies (unlike the Assyrians), and in peacetime were governed by statesmen with sound

Many powerful stone sculptures (left and right) survive from the Hittite empire era

and well-developed policies. A practical and intellectually unpretentious people, they lacked the sophistication and graces of their Near Eastern neighbours.

Scholars, intrigued that the fall of Troy coincided roughly with the disintegration of the Hittite Empire, have found evidence recently that may suggest a link between ancient Troy (Truva) and the Hittite kingdom.

Tutankhamun link One of the cuneiform tablets found at Boğazkale indicates a curious link between the Egyptian boy-king Tutankhamun and the Hittites. According to the inscription, the Hittite king, Shubbililiuma, was encamped by the Euphrates when a messenger arrived from the Egyptian queen, begging him to send her one of his many sons for her to marry, because her own husband Tutankhamun had died. Shubbililiuma eventually sent one of his sons: on his arrival in Egypt he was put to death on the orders of an ambitious official who went on to marry the queen himself.

❏ The most memorable relics left by the Hittites are their simple but powerful rock-cut sculptures, to be found on some sites, depicting their gods and ceremonies. The figures – broad, heavy and squat, with none of the grace and subtlety associated with Egyptian or Babylonian art – indicate a tough, warlike mountain people, used to a harsh climate and conditions. Hittite culture stands in sharp contrast to the valley cultures of Mesopotamia and the Nile, where the inhabitants were able peacefully to pasture their flocks beside the great rivers, without the need for defences or fortifications. ❏

Storage amphorae excavated at the site of the ancient Hittite capital of Hattuşaş

■ After the break-up of the Hittite Empire, Asia Minor disintegrated into a number of dynasties and peoples – Phrygians, Cimmerians, Lydians and others – who remain largely obscure. At this time the Greeks began to invade the eastern seaboard of the Aegean, known as Ionia. ■

Alexander and Hellenisation A long period of struggle followed which encompassed the Trojan War recounted by Homer in his epic poem *The Iliad*. Successive waves of Greeks displaced the western Anatolian peoples and established flourishing cities along the Aegean coast. Their success attracted the attention of their powerful neighbours, the Persians. When, in the spring of 334 BC, the 21-year-old Macedonian Alexander crossed the Hellespont into Asia Minor at the head of some 35,000 soldiers, determined to drive out the Persians for once and all, he was heralding the dawn of an era that was to last 1,000 years, to be eclipsed only by the rise of Islam.

Sweeping triumphantly through western and southern Anatolia, by 333 BC Alexander 'the Great' stood poised at Issus, in the easternmost corner of the Mediterranean, where his army routed a Persian force three times its size. The cultural consequences of these great military exploits were immeasurable, since by opening up a corridor for cultural interaction and fusion between East and West, Alexander was initiating the process that was later to become known as Hellenisation.

The Hellenistic age is characterised by an extreme competitiveness of spirit on all levels: cities rivalled each other for power and trade, while their citizens competed to amass great fortunes, flaunting their wealth by financing the construction of splendid monuments. This was also a period of marked cultural activity and scholastic innovation. The two outstanding centres of learning, Alexandria in Egypt and Pergamum (see page 104), bequeathed a vast intellectual legacy, the influence of which cannot be overstated.

The Roman age The Romans were at first drawn with reluctance into Asia Minor, crossing the Hellespont in 190 BC to crush the ambitious Seleucid ruler Antiochus III. When in 133 BC Attalus III, King of Pergamum, bequeathed his entire kingdom to Rome, western Asia Minor became a Roman province. Problems with troublesome Cilician pirates and the Pontic kingdom of Mithridates in the 1st century BC later drew the Romans eastwards to take over the whole of Anatolia, which then

enjoyed 200 years of peace and prosperity.

The Romans recognised the cultural achievements of the Greeks who were now subject to them: Roman artists, writers and architects gradually began to imitate all forms of Greek art. All over the eastern empire there sprang up cities inspired by Greek models, with a distinctive Roman provincial city architecture, often including splendid theatres such as the one at Aspendos. While landowners and the ruling élite lived lives of opulence, peasants were tied to the land. This

The amazingly well-preserved Roman theatre at Aspendos

Statue of the goddess Serapis in the temple at Ephesus

period of stability lasted until the late 2nd century AD, when a succession of barbarian invasions caused havoc and weakened the economic structure of the Empire.

Even during times of prosperity, Christianity had been troublesome to the Roman Empire, and its devotees were brutally persecuted for their refusal to comply with the emperor cult. Gradually opposition to the new religion waned, however, and in 312 Emperor Constantine was himself converted. The following year he proclaimed Christianity the official religion of the Roman Empire.

❑ Christianity was introduced to Asia Minor by St Paul during his three missionary journeys. From AD 47 to 57 he sailed along most of the Aegean and Mediterranean coastline, proselytising in major cities such as Antioch, Attaleia (Antalya), Miletus and Ephesus. ❑

■ The name Byzantium is derived from Byzantion, a Greek trading colony said to have been founded in 657 BC by a Greek named Byzas. In AD 330, some 50 years after the Emperor Diocletian had divided the Roman empire into two parts, his successor, Constantine, moved the capital of the eastern empire to Byzantium, which was renamed Constantinople in his honour. ■

❑ The name Constantinople survived until the Ottoman invasion of 1453, when the city became Istanbul. ❑

Eastern Empire After the collapse of Rome's western empire, its Byzantine rival acquired immeasurable political prestige and untold wealth. Cultural and artistic life blossomed.

Byzantine art At first sight, Byzantine art bears little resemblance to its Greek and Roman antecedents, being static, icon-like and rather formalised. Classical influences survive, however, in such

One of the superb 14th-century mosaics in the Kariye Camii

figurative details as the folds of the drapery, the modelling of the faces and in certain conventional gestures. The Byzantine artist was bound by a strict code of rules: only certain subjects – Christ, the Holy Virgin, the saints and episodes from the scriptures – were permissible; while the perfect remoteness of the heavenly world was suggested by rejecting perspective in favour of two-dimensional images.

Doctrinal divisions Byzantine civilisation developed around a distinctive Christian tradition, centring on the notion of the emperor as representative of God's will on earth. The early years of Byzantium were racked by doctrinal divisions, and successive councils of the Church were convened to clarify

matters. The first, held at Nicaea (İznik) in 325, denounced the Arian heresy, proposed by Arius of Alexandria, according to which Jesus Christ was not the Son of God. The outcome was the Nicene Creed, a formal statement of Christian belief and still an important part of Christian worship. The same council declared the emperor head of the Church.

Justinian the Great (527–65)
Under the dynamic rule of Justinian, Byzantium flourished as never before. While his generals recovered much of the western Roman empire, including Italy, North Africa and southern Spain, the Emperor presided over the reconstruction of the capital, Constantinople, commissioning numerous architectural masterpieces, including Aya Sofya.

Break up of the empire
After Justinian's death, the empire suffered a series of irreversible setbacks: the western provinces were lost to the Goths and Lombards; Persian and Arab raiders (the latter inspired by the new religion of Islam) harried the south; and the empire was further weakened by serious internal conflicts and feuding.

Delacroix's interpretation of the taking of Constantinople in 1204

The Crusades
The Byzantines were willing to support any movement that might help them re-establish their own political control in Asia Minor. The Crusaders volunteered their support, but, as the emperors were soon to discover, the Christian knights and their European backers had their own agenda. The shocking rapacity of these 'soldiers of God' was brutally revealed during the Fourth Crusade, which culminated in the sacking of Constantinople in 1204 and the murder of thousands of its people.

❑ The historian Steven Runciman observed: 'There was never a greater crime against humanity than the Fourth Crusade. Not only did it cause the destruction or dispersal of all the treasures of the past that Byzantium had devoutly stored, and the mortal wounding of a civilisation that was still active and great; but it was also an act of gigantic folly... It upset the whole defence of Christendom.' ❑

The Seljuks

■ **The Seljuk Turks formed the first wave of the Turkic peoples who were eventually to make themselves masters of the Byzantine Empire. With their arrival, the culture of Anatolia saw a dramatic change as many of the Greek inhabitants fled westwards. By the 15th century almost all of Asia Minor was Turkish-speaking.** ■

Origins Originally nomads from the region of Samarkand and Bukhara, the Seljuks were descended from the Tu-Kin people of the Mongolian steppes (hence the name Turk). In the 11th century, waves of Seljuks descended on Persia, Iraq, Syria and Palestine, where they were converted to Islam. Led by Alp Arslan, they advanced from Antioch (modern Antakya) into Anatolia, bringing their new religion with them.

Although the Seljuks were effective fighters, renowned for their physical prowess, once the fighting was over their greatest sultans, notably Alp Arslan, Malik Shah, Keykâvus I and Keykubad I (Alâeddin), proved to be enlightened rulers who laid the foundations for commercial prosperity and the development of education and the arts. The Seljuks

The 13th-century Seljuk fortifications at Alanya

evolved a remarkable form of welfare state, in which medical schools were linked with hospitals, orphanages, poor-houses, mental homes, baths and religious schools, all offering free services to the needy.

❑ The network of caravanserais established along trade routes by the Seljuks was a great encouragement to commerce. The services they offered to travelling merchants were remarkable: around the central mosque and ablution fountain were arranged sleeping quarters, baths, cafés, blacksmiths' and leatherworkers' workshops, and areas for listening to music. The most remarkable feature of all was that these services were offered free by the State. ❑

Art The 13th century was the high point of Seljuk civilisation in Asia Minor. The Seljuks brought from Persia the exquisite art of tile-making, which was unknown to the Greeks and Romans. They developed their own distinctive designs in plain colours and geometric patterns, still seen today on mosques, tombs and *medreses* all over Turkey (see page 63). The other great Seljuk art, carpet-weaving, has its origins in the domestic furnishings of the Turkic nomads (see page 90).

The single pointed arch (here at Aspendos) is a distinctive feature of Seljuk bridge architecture

The dome of the Mevlana Dervish monastery at Konya

Architecture Characteristic architectural forms include the cylindrical mausoleum (*türbe*), built on a square base with a conical roof (the most famous being the Mevlana Tomb in Konya, the Seljuk capital, where the Mevlana order of Whirling Dervishes was founded). This characteristic design is thought to recall the pointed tents of early Seljuk encampments. The double-headed eagle, symbol of the Seljuk state, can still be seen on many of their buildings, which were usually plainly constructed in red brick or stone. Typical of the elaborate external decoration (reflecting Persian influence) is the honeycomb, or stalactite, carving over doorways in the surviving caravanserais and *medreses*. The latter were charitable foundations similar to the gymnasiums of the ancient world, with theology, the arts, sciences and sport all on the curriculum.

The Seljuks were also prolific and skilled builders of bridges and many of these, solidly built in stone with a single pointed arch, remain in use today. Also used to great effect in windows and doorways, the pointed arch may have been introduced by the Crusaders into Europe, where it later inspired the Gothic arch.

■ In the 13th century the Seljuk sultanate of Konya fell into decline, to be succeeded by a number of smaller principalities. One of these was ruled by a certain Osman Gazi (1288–1326), who gave his name to a small tribe known as the Osmanlı Turks or Ottomans. ■

Expansion Under Osman, the Ottomans embarked on a great movement of expansion and by 1400 they controlled most of the Balkan peninsula and Anatolia. In 1453, after a seven-week siege led by Sultan Mehmet II, they captured Constantinople and made it their capital, renaming it Istanbul. Ottoman rule was to last for almost 500 years. While retaining many

❏ Founded by Murat I (1362–89), the Janissaries formed the backbone of the Ottoman army. Chosen from Christian families on the basis of physical prowess, they were converted to Islam and trained to exceptionally high standards of discipline in the palace schools. By the 18th century, however, this élite army had become something of a law unto themselves and they were abolished in 1826. ❏

❏ On the death of Murat I in 1389, his son Beyazıt I had his own brother, Yakub, murdered to avoid any argument about the succession, thus initiating the Ottoman sultans' practice of having all male relatives killed on the day of their accession. The Koranic verse 'rebellion is worse than execution' was cited in their justification. ❏

aspects of the Byzantine administrative system the Ottomans also made innovations, introducing such institutions as the corps of Janissaries (see box) and *vakıfs*. The latter were religious trusts, set up on captured land to provide revenues for the funding of caravanserais (baths, hotels and other public amenities).

Traditional Ottoman costumes, 1825. Shortly after this the Court adopted Western dress

Süleyman the Magnificent

The 46-year reign of Süleyman the Magnificent (1520–66) was unquestionably the zenith of the Ottoman age. A contemporary of Henry VIII of England, the Habsburg emperor Charles V, François I of France and Ivan the Terrible of Russia, Süleyman was an outstanding leader, legislator and patron of the arts. Under his rule the Ottoman Empire doubled in size. While his armies entered Belgrade in 1521 and Buda in 1526 (and almost captured Vienna in 1529), the Ottoman navy evicted the Knights of St John from Rhodes in 1522, ravaged the French, Spanish and Italian coasts and in 1538 defeated the combined navies of Europe at Preveze. Thus it gained

almost total control of the Mediterranean. Süleyman's victories were made possible not only by the quality of his troops and generals, but also by their superior weaponry, the superb financial organisation of his armies, and, above all, by their discipline, the envy of Western rulers. Meanwhile Süleyman's architects, notably Sinan (see page 55), were transforming the skylines of the great cities of the empire: Istanbul, Edirne, Damascus, Baghdad, Jerusalem and Mecca.

*One of the Ottoman Empire's most dynamic rulers, Sultan Süleyman II
Below: Extent of the Ottoman Empire in 1676*

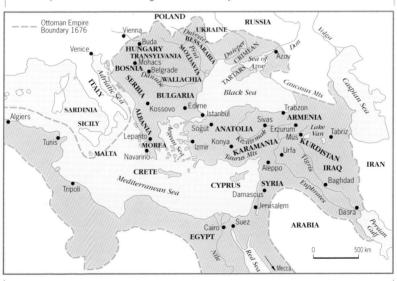

■ **Süleyman's successors, incapable of emulating his great powers of leadership, found themselves increasingly unable to control his vast and disparate empire and only five years after his death, in 1571, the once invincible Ottoman navy was destroyed by Venice and her allies at Lepanto, off the Greek coast.** ■

Harem politics Süleyman's marriage to Hürrem Sultan, known as Roxelana in the West – the first time in two centuries that a Turkish ruler had committed himself to a single wife – helped to forge the first link in a chain of events that would eventually bring about the downfall of the Ottoman Empire. Roxelana's obsessive lust for power and taste for political intrigue shifted the centre of decision-making from the *selâmlık* (sultan's quarters) to the harem. Another crucial factor was that the administration of the empire had never been in Turkish hands, but was entrusted instead to a vast, mainly Christian, slave community, trained in the palace schools.

Thus the seeds of the empire's demise were already sown, to be hastened by the ineffectual rule of a string of sultans, starting with Roxelana's feeble and incompetent son, Selim 'the Sot'. Selim's disastrous reign ended when, in an alcoholic haze, he stumbled on the way to the bath and cracked his skull. His wife, Nur Bana, had shared

Roxelana's ambition and from then on policy was implemented through murder and intrigue. Thus the empire decayed gradually from within.

The Turkish minister Nazim Bey is assassinated on an Istanbul street during the Young Turk Revolution

❏ In her book *Beyond the Sublime Porte* (1931), Professor Miller wrote of Süleyman: 'Between him and his immediate successors, who ceased with surprising suddenness to be either soldiers or statesmen, there was no graduation whatever. Enervated and enfeebled by seclusion and idleness, filled with ennui, they sought pleasure and diversion in every conceivable form of extravagance, self-indulgence and vice.' ❏

The Young Turks and World War I The first stirrings of a new spirit among the Turks (prompted by political developments in western Europe) came during the reign of Selim III (1789–1807), and for much of the 19th century sultans and ministers worked on a programme of modernisation and reform. This process came to an abrupt halt in

❏ German influence, which was already beginning to grow under Sultan Abdül Hamid II, increased further under the Young Turks. German officers reorganised the army, German businessmen and technicians extended their hold on the country's economy, while German engineers and financiers began the construction of the Tehran–Baghdad railway, which was to provide a direct link between Germany and the Middle East. ❏

1876 with the accession of the reactionary Abdül Hamid II. In 1908 a liberal opposition group, the Young Turks, led a revolution that temporarily overthrew Abdül Hamid, but quickly degenerated into a dictatorship, rent by internal dissension and plagued by foreign wars.

When, in 1914, Turkey entered World War I on the side of Germany, the alliance was of immense military value to the Central Powers but disastrous for the Turks. Having held out against Allied attacks on the Dardanelles and Mesopotamia, they were finally isolated by British advances from Egypt and India, and forced to sign an armistice in 1919.

After the débâcle of World War I, the victorious Allies arranged for the dissolution of the Ottoman Empire, 'the Sick Man of Europe'. Under the terms of the Treaty of Sèvres, the death warrant of the Ottoman Empire, the Turks lost most of their territory, excepting Istanbul and part of Anatolia. So harsh were these conditions – far more severe than those imposed on Germany – that they inspired a nationalist uprising under a bold new leader, Mustafa Kemal, later known as Atatürk.

Sultan Abdül Hamid II (above) was finally deposed by the Young Turks in 1909 (below) after ruling for more than 30 years

Le Petit Parisien

Vingt-et-unième année - N. 1038   Supplément Littéraire Illustré   Dimanche 16 Mai 1909

CINQ CENTIMES   CINQ CENTIMES

A YILDIZ-KIOSK
Lecture au Sultan Abdul-Hamid de l'acte de déchéance

■ **So complete was Turkey's defeat at the end of World War I, and so abject its humiliation under the Treaty of Sèvres, that the spirit of its people might well have been crushed and the Allied subdivision of Ottoman lands have continued unhindered, had it not been for the exaggerated territorial ambitions of Greece.** ■

Mustafa Kemal Pasha (left), leader of the Turkish War of Independence

War of Independence Opposed by all the Allied powers except Britain, Greece landed an invasion force at İzmir in May 1919. This was the catalyst needed by the budding Turkish nationalist movement, based in Anatolia with Ankara as the provisional capital. The Turkish forces were led by the young commander Mustafa Kemal who, at the height of the War of Independence (1919–1922), routed the Greeks at the Battle of Sakarya and eventually expelled them from Turkey. Kemal's efforts were crowned by the terms of the Treaty of Lausanne in 1923, which recognised Turkish sovereignty within approximately its present-day borders.

Westernising reforms During the remaining 15 years of his life,

Mustafa Kemal, who took the name Atatürk (Father of the Turks) in 1934, ruled Turkey as a dictator at the head of a single-party state. The Republican People's Party implemented his radical new policies, founded on a series of far-reaching reforms that sought to Westernise Turkey and integrate it into the modern world.

The last ruler of the House of Osman, Mehmet VI, left Istanbul on a British warship bound for Italy in March 1920 and the sultanate was abolished. Atatürk then turned to the reform of Islam, issuing a series of edicts doing away with the Ministry of Religious Affairs and with religious orders such as the Mevlana (Whirling Dervishes). At the same time he replaced the Koranic law with a legal code based on European models, and finally, in 1928, disestablished Islam, amending the constitution to make Turkey a secular state. Not content with these sweeping changes, Atatürk abolished the

❏ **Atatürk's words:**
'There are two Mustafa Kemals. One is the man sitting before you, the Mustafa Kemal of flesh and blood, who will pass away. But there is another, whom I cannot call "Me". It is not I who this second Mustafa Kemal personifies, it is you – all of you who are present here, who go into the furthermost parts of the country to inculcate and defend a new ideal, a new mode of thought. I stand for these dreams of yours. My life's work is to make them come true.' ❏

Crowds circle the new Turkish flag after the capture of İzmir in 1922

Arabic alphabet, the language of the Koran, giving a body of academics a mere six months to devise a new Latin alphabet for Turkish. Introduced virtually overnight, the new script resulted in instant chaos in the printing world: only one book was published in the whole of 1929. All this is not to say that Atatürk was opposed to religion itself: in the new secular state the right of every citizen to practice as a devout Muslim in private was guaranteed. What was not permitted was religious interference in public and political life.

Anxious to improve the position of women, whom he wanted to see accepted as equals, Atatürk encouraged them to cast off the veil, denouncing it as an oppressive device used by men to subjugate women. In 1934 women were given the vote and the right to stand for parliament. Atatürk's own wife was a model for Turkish women – emancipated and independent in spirit (perhaps too independent for the Turkish leader, who dissolved the partnership!).

Although undoubtedly an autocrat, Atatürk was not only an outstanding leader but a man with a great appetite for life, renowned for his sense of humour, charm and sheer stamina. His early death at the age of 57, from cirrhosis of the liver, was a tragedy for Turkey.

Turkish war memorial at Gelibolu (Gallipoli), where the Allies were routed by Atatürk's forces

❑   The word 'civilisation' occurs again and again in Atatürk's speeches: 'We shall live as a progressive, civilised nation. We shall follow the road to civilisation and get there. We must prove that we are capable of becoming active members of the society of civilised peoples.' By civilisation, he meant the secular civilisation of the West, as opposed to the religious civilisation of Islam.   ❑

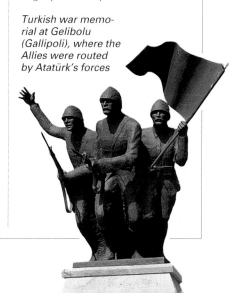

■ Turkey is ranked as a 'developing country' by economists and sociologists, but her recent political history does not fit the standard model implied by this description. For, unlike other modern developing nations such as Nigeria, India and Brazil, the Turkish state has inherited many of the bureaucratic and militaristic features of the former Ottoman regime. ■

The Reaction Following World War II, the secularist ideology of Atatürk (see pages 38–9) lost favour as rivals to his Republican People's Party, notably the Democratic Party, made rapid political headway. One consequence of the growing liberalisation was that Islam began to reassert its right to play an active role in Turkish life. Ever since, all the Turkish political parties have felt compelled to make concessions to religion in order to secure votes. Religious schools had already begun to reappear in the 1940s and in 1950 Prime Minister Adnan Menderes decreed that the call to prayer should again be in Arabic rather than Turkish. Today, increasing numbers of Turks make the pilgrimage to Mecca and observe Ramadan.

The 1960 coup Initially popular with the electorate, Adnan Menderes quickly fell out of favour thanks to his gross mishandling of the economy, which resulted in massive inflation, huge foreign debts, increasing budget deficits and falling exports. He responded to criticism by introducing a series of repressive measures aimed at muzzling the press and intimidating journalists, many of whom were imprisoned. At the same time, he managed to antagonise the army and alienate Kemalist intellectuals and writers. In 1960, after a decade of highly controversial rule, the army intervened, staging a near-bloodless coup: subsequently Menderes was tried and executed. Democracy was restored shortly afterwards and survived the following two decades, always under the watchful eye of the military.

The 1980 coup Unfortunately, the economic weaknesses of the Menderes period were never really ironed out, provoking an alarming growth in political violence and an accompanying rise in Islamic fundamentalism. It was this that finally persuaded the armed forces, under General Evren, to seize power in

Two portraits: (above) former Prime Minister Adnan Menderes...

...and (below) General Kenan Evren, head of the military junta

Turkish voters go to the polls in Erzurum (north-eastern Anatolia)

September 1980. Law and order was re-established at the expense of human rights as thousands of 'extremists' were detained and many tortured. The West's response was to ban Turkey from the Council of Europe and to suspend EEC aid. Elections were reintroduced in 1983, but the army continues to play an interventionist role in Turkish politics.

Following the appointment of a pro-Islamic Prime Minister, Necmettin Erbakan, in June 1996, immediate tensions appeared between the new government and the army, suspicious that Erbakan was taking the country down the fundamentalist road. His shaky coalition with Tansu Çiller's True Path Party finally collapsed in June 1997, but there are indications that Erbakan may be able to stage a political comeback when the next elections are due, some time in 1998. Meanwhile action against the Kurds continues in the south-east of the country, maintaining the spotlight on Turkey's poor human rights' record and damaging the prospects of her eventual entry into the European Union.

Necmettin Erbakan, pro-Muslim leader of the Turkish Welfare Party

❑ İsmet İnönü, Atatürk's successor as President of the Turkish Republic, was a man of brilliant intellect who inspired the observation: '40 foxes go round in his head and the muzzle of one never touches the tail of the next'. ❑

7500 BC First Stone Age settlements in existence at Çatalhüyük – the earliest known urban society, with religious shrines and frescoes.

1900–1300 BC The Hittite Empire, with Hattuşaş (Boğazkale) as its capital, and roughly contemporary with ancient Egypt and Babylon, thrives as a mountain culture with storm and weather gods.

1259 BC The Treaty of Kadesh between the Hittites and the Egyptians – the earliest recorded peace treaty.

1250 BC The Trojan War between the Greeks and the Trojans, culminating after ten years' fighting in the famous ploy of the Trojan horse and the subsequent Fall of Troy (Truva), at the time the foremost trading city of the north-west Aegean.

1200–700 BC The migration of Greeks to Aegean coastal regions. The kingdoms of Phrygia, Ionia, Lycia, Lydia, Caria and Pamphylia grow up in the western Aegean and Mediterranean regions. The Urartian civilisation flourishes in eastern Anatolia.

700 BC The birth of Homer in Smyrna (İzmir) coincides with the beginnings of Hellenistic culture in Aegean Turkey.

546 BC Cyrus the Great of Persia invades. Anatolia is under Persian rule, with local Persian governors (known as *satraps*) ruling areas.

334 BC Alexander the Great conquers Anatolia, freeing it from the Persians. Hellenistic culture takes hold.

130 BC Anatolia becomes the Roman province of Asia with its capital at Ephesus (Efes); a long period of peace and prosperity.

40 BC Anthony and Cleopatra marry at Antioch (Antakya).

AD 47–57 St Paul's missionary journeys; the first Christian community at Antioch.

AD 313 Christianity is accepted as the official religion by the Roman Emperor, Constantine the Great.

330 Byzantium is renamed Constantinople by Emperor Constantine and becomes the new capital of Byzantine Empire, the eastern half of the Roman Empire; Rome remains the capital of the western part.

527–65 The reign of Justinian and the height of Byzantine power; an enormous building programme goes on throughout the Byzantine empire.

636–718 Muslim Arabs (in the Holy War of their young faith, Islam) defeat Byzantines and besiege Constantinople.

1054 The schism between the Greek and the Roman churches.

1071–1243 Seljuk Turks from Central Asia conquer Anatolia; Konya becomes their capital. They establish the Sultanate of Rum, convert the population to Islam and establish Turkish as the dominant language of Anatolia.

1096–1204 The Crusades: Latin armies enter Anatolia for the first time. Constantinople is sacked in the Fourth Crusade of 1204. The Byzantine Empire is effectively dismembered.

1288 The birth of the Ottoman Empire, founded by the Muslim Osmanlı (Ottoman) tribe from eastern Anatolia; its capital is Bursa.

1453 Sultan Mehmet II conquers Constantinople and renames it Istanbul as the new capital of the Ottoman Empire. Aya Sofya in the capital, like many other churches throughout Turkey, is converted to a mosque.

1520–66 The reign of Süleyman the Magnificent and the Golden Age of the Ottoman Empire, which now extends from the Danube to Aden and Eritrea, and from the Euphrates and the Crimea to Algiers. The Ottomans are the leading world power.

1682–1725 The reign of Peter the Great in Russia begins a new phase of Russo-Turkish rivalry.

1717–30 The 'Tulip Period', so-called because of Sultan Ahmet III's obsession with tulips, a century after Germany, France and Holland had been seized by a passion for these Turkish bulbs.

1839–76 The 'Tanzimat Period', a programme of reforms in the Ottoman Empire.

1854 The Crimean War; Ottomans are supported by the British and French against the common enemy, Russia.

1895–6 The Armenian massacres, in which some 150,000 Armenians die.
1909 Sultan Abdül Hamid, the last Ottoman sultan, is deposed by the revolutionary group known as the Young Turks.
1914 Turkey enters World War I as an ally of Germany.
1915 The Gallipoli Campaign. Allied landings on Turkish soil are repulsed.
1918 The end of World War I; the Allies propose the division of the Ottoman Empire.
1919 Atatürk leads Turkish resistance in the fight for national sovereignty. The War of Independence against the Greeks and the British begins.
1923 The Turkish state is proclaimed, with Atatürk as president. Minority populations are exchanged between Greece and Turkey in order to prevent future outbreaks of inter-communal conflict. Half a million Greek-speaking Muslims are sent from Greece to Turkey, and 1.3 million Turkish-speaking Christians from Turkey to Greece. Reforms to modernise and secularise the state are set in motion: the Islamic faith is disestablished; the Arabic script is replaced by the Latin alphabet; the Turkish language is revived; veils and the fez are banned.
1938 Atatürk dies unexpectedly at the age of 57.
1939–45 Turkey remains neutral throughout World War II.
1946 Turkey becomes a charter member of the United Nations.
1950 The first free nationwide elections, in which Adnan Menderes is elected prime minister, are held. A massive national debt builds up following many highly ambitious building programmes.
1952 Turkey joins NATO in a new, pro-Western stance.
1960 An almost bloodless military coup is followed by successive inefficient governments.
1964 Though geographically 97 per cent in Asia, Turkey becomes an associate member of the European Economic Community (EEC). The emigration of 'guest-workers' to Germany begins.
1974 Turkey intervenes in (or invades, depending upon your point of view) Cyprus to protect the Turkish Cypriot community, seizing the northern third of the island. It is condemned by the international community, notably the EEC, but the island remains divided, and its border is patrolled by soldiers from the United Nations.
1980 Another bloodless military coup under General Kenan Evren is followed by three years of military rule.
1983 Turkey again returns to civilian rule with Türgüt Özal elected prime minister, moving to the presidency in 1984, the first civilian president of Turkey for 30 years.
1985–90 Disputes with Greece over Cyprus and over Aegean territorial waters damage Turkey's continuing attempts to join the EEC, as does its human rights record in handling the Kurdish insurrection in the south-east.
1991–3 Süleyman Demirel is elected prime minister, forming a coalition government. He forms the post of Minister for Human Rights and promises a thorough review of policy towards the Kurdish uprising. Stringent economic reforms are introduced to combat levels of inflation of between 70 and 125 per cent.
1993–5 President Türgüt Özal dies. Veteran politician Süleyman Demirel becomes his successor and Tansu Çiller is appointed Turkey's first woman prime minister. Turkey accepts IMF (International Monetary Fund) economic reforms. Kurdish rebels carry out attacks on a few tourist sites in an attempt to discourage tourists. During the campaign of violence a British tourist dies after a bomb explodes on the beach at Fethiye.
1996 Turkey enters the European Customs Union. The pro-Islamic leader of the Welfare Party, Necmettin Erbakan, becomes Prime Minister and immediately faces hostility from the armed forces.
1997 After less than 12 months in power, Erbakan is forced to resign. The Kurdish war continues as more than 30,000 Turkish troops attack bases in northern Iraq.

43

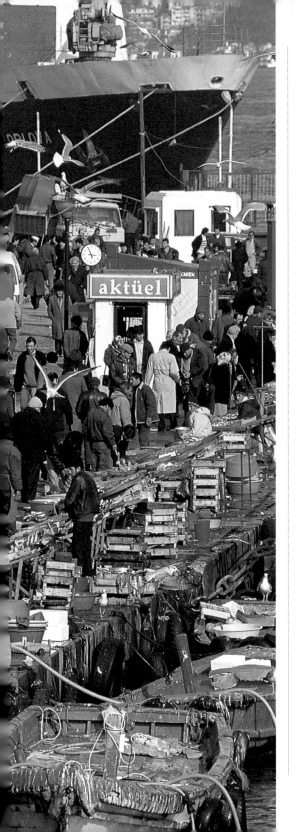

ISTANBUL A to Z

CITY HIGHLIGHTS ◄◄◄◄◄◄

EXCURSION HIGHLIGHTS ◄◄◄◄◄◄

ISTANBUL

Pages 44–5: the view
from Galata Bridge,
Istanbul

Sunset over Sultan
Ahmet Mosque

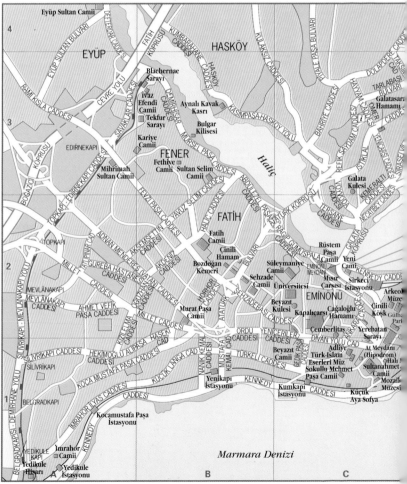

Istanbul The port is the lifeblood of this maritime city; Istanbul lies on the Bosphorus, a narrow stretch of water 30km long that acts as a natural frontier between Europe and Asia. (The ease with which one can cross continents here is something that takes some getting used to.) In the 4th century, the strategic importance of Byzantium, as Istanbul was then called, induced the Emperor Constantine to make it the new capital of the Roman Empire (it was renamed Constantinople in his honour); and, when the Byzantine Empire succumbed more than 1,000 years later, the Ottoman conquerors saw no reason to move elsewhere (but changed the name to Istanbul). Today the Bosphorus, linking the Mediterranean to the Black Sea via the Sea of Marmara, is one of the world's busiest shipping lanes. Look out from the terrace of Topkapı Palace and you will see oil tankers from Russia, Bulgaria and Azerbaijan massing like warships at the mouth of the Marmara, or snaking their way towards the open sea, while sleek white cruise ships from Venice and Odessa line up along the shores of Beyoğlu.

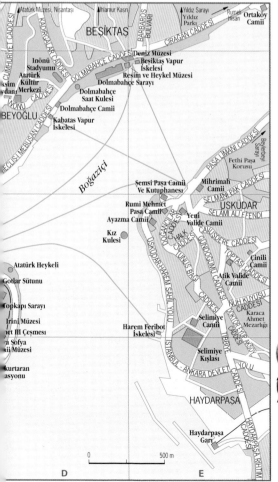

47

One of Istanbul's army of street traders

ISTANBUL

Famous skyline
'...it must look more splendid than any other city one comes to by sea. Even Father Chantry-Pigg, who did not think that Constantine's city and the Byzantine capital ought to have had all those mosque-domes and minarets built on to its old Byzantine shape... thought that the famous outline climbing above the Bosphorus and the Sea of Marmara, with all its domes and minarets poised against the evening sky, was very stupendous.'
Rose Macaulay, 1956

Old Istanbul
The area of old Istanbul known as the Beyazıt–Sirkeci–Eminönü triangle has a remarkably transient population. Each day an estimated 800,000 people arrive for work in the handicraft shops, government offices, small businesses and tourist sights. At night, however, the district is all but deserted as the workers return to their homes in the suburbs, leaving the visitors to drink in the numerous bars and restaurants.

Beyoğlu is where Istanbul's shops, banks and offices are concentrated and where the city's vast army of commuters heads for work each morning. The dominant landmark is the conical Galata Tower, built by Genoese merchants in the 14th century. Washing hangs out to dry in congested streets that cling precariously to the hillside below; locals with no business here avoid the steep climb by taking the tiny underground railway, known conveniently as the Tünel. They emerge on İstiklâl Caddesi, one of Istanbul's few genuine avenues; here Western influence, always conspicuous, is most in evidence at night when the restaurants, cinemas and nightclubs are bathed in garish neon.

Back now to Eminönü waterfront and the smell of fried fish as the fishermen, some dressed in fezes and embroidered jackets for the tourists, hand up steaming rolls of mackerel to passersby – lunch for some busy Istanbullers, a mid-morning snack for others. Stop even for a moment and you will be besieged by shoe-shine boys, spur-of-the-moment tour guides and dealers in boat tokens and combs, postcards and penny whistles, evil eyes and cigarettes, the sales pitch invariably prefixed by a hopeful 'Yes, please'. For the 300,000 new citizens arriving each year from the impoverished villages of Anatolia, street trading is the only way to eke out a living and maybe send something to help out the family back home.

At night they will return to where they came from: the wretched *gecekondu* (shanty towns) on the outskirts, but, by day, their haunts are the main tourist sights: Aya Sofya, the Sultan Ahmet Mosque, Topkapı. Visitors are amazed at the friendliness, patience and boundless optimism of these people but are impressed above all by their courtesy. Very rarely will a polite refusal to buy result in pestering and never

Shoeshines are part of the fabric of every-day life

in harrassment; for its size, Istanbul is one of the safest cities in this part of the world.

Istanbul's 4,000 taxi drivers seem as thick on the ground as the street traders: this must be the only city in the world where the cab driver will flag you down for custom rather than the other way round. Lost in one of the back-streets behind the Covered Bazaar or the Süleymaniye Mosque? Don't worry. You can bet that waiting just around the corner will be one of Istanbul's ubiquitous yellow cabs and the door will already be opening. In a city with such a chaotic public transport system this, with the honorable exception of the ferry, is the only way to get about: fares are reasonable, the drivers know their way around and are adept at avoiding the snarl-ups. Rather than ask you not to smoke, they are more likely to ask you for a cigarette, but there's no more reliable person to get you safely (and quickly) back to your hotel at night.

But it is the ferry that you will fall in love with, and it will take you anywhere for no more than a pound or so. There's nothing better for a case of sightseeing blues (a rare affliction in Istanbul, admittedly) than to hop on a ferry – any ferry, it's hard to get really lost. You can take a short hop to the mosque at Üsküdar; have lunch in one of Ortaköy's legendary fish restaurants or take a stroll through Yıldız Park, a lovers' lane for young Istanbullers. At least once during your stay, however, you should allow for a full day's cruise up the Bosphorus. You won't need a seat for the outward leg of the journey because you'll be too busy taking photographs and admiring the spectacular views, not forgetting the grandiose Ottoman palaces, ruined medieval castles and charming fishing villages.

Tea vendor on Eminönü Meydani, considered to be the hub of the city by Istanbullers

Blue charms to protect against the evil eye

Byzantine Istanbul

▶ **Aya İrini (Church of Divine Peace)** *46C2*

First Courtyard, Topkapı Palace

This sturdy brick church is one of the oldest religious buildings in Istanbul. It was commissioned by Emperor Justinian in AD 537, about the same time as Aya Sofya. In Ottoman times it served as the Janissaries' arsenal. Of the once lavish interior decoration, only a stunning mosaic of Christ on the cross survives. The church is usually open only for concerts or exhibitions.

New roles
Most churches in Istanbul were converted into mosques in the 15th century by the conquering Ottomans, who added minarets externally and *mihrabs* (prayer niches) and *minbers* (pulpits) internally. Other churches were used as warehouses, arsenals or grainstores.

▶ **Hipodrom** *46C1*

At Meydanı, Sultanahmet

Originally a racecourse for charioteers, the Hippodrome was laid out on the site of the present park by Emperor Septimius Severus in AD 203 and enlarged by Constantine in the 4th century. The leading chariot teams, the Blues and the Greens, evolved into political factions and, in AD 532, rioted against Emperor Justinian, provoking General Belisarius to storm the Hippodrome with the loss of 30,000 lives. The amphitheatre, which could hold 100,000 people, was destroyed during the Fourth Crusade and the Ottomans plundered the ruins for the Sultan Ahmet Mosque. From the 16th century the square was known as At Meydanı or Horses Square – the sultan's pages played a game resembling polo here. Among the surviving monuments in the Hippodrome is the sharply etched Egyptian Obelisk, commissioned by Pharaoh Thutmose III in the 16th century BC.

▶ **Küçük Aya Sofya**
    (Saints Sergius and Bacchus) *46C1*

Mehmet Paşa Sokak, Kadırga

Little Aya Sofya is even older than the great Byzantine church that it resembles. It was commissioned by Emperor Justinian in about AD 527 as part of a comprehensive rebuilding programme. The architect, Anthemius of Tralles, also worked on Aya Sofya. The church was converted to a mosque early in the 16th century, in the reign of Beyazıt II, by the leader of the Black Eunuchs, Hüseyin Ağa, who is buried in a tomb north of the apse. Damaged by earthquakes in 1648 and 1763, the mosque is currently suffering from subsidence, although restoration work should be complete by the year 2000.

The astonishingly lifelike figures in the Mosaic Museum are more than 1,500 years old

Look out for the intricately carved decoration on the column capitals, some of which bear Justinian's monogram, and the frieze under the gallery which, in Greek verse, honours the Emperor, his consort Theodora and St Sergius, though curiously not Bacchus. There are also tell-tale traces of the original gold leaf and marble revetments that once adorned the church.

The magnificent remains of the former imperial palace known as Tekfur Sarayı

►   **Mosaik Müzesi (Mosaic Museum)**   *46C1*
Arasta Çarşısı, Sultanahmet
Open: daily except Tue 9.30–5.
The mosaics in this small museum were discovered during excavations in the Arasta Bazaar in the 1930s and 1950s. They are thought to date from the 6th century and belong to the first imperial palace. Very little of the palace remains today apart from the ruined loggia at the entrance to the emperor's private harbour and these superb mosaic friezes and pavements (the largest of which covers an area of 170sq m). Set in a background of white marble tesserae, the cubes of glass, stone and terracotta radiate colour, while the action-packed scenes open a fascinating window onto everyday life in Byzantium. In one of the most vivid depictions an elephant is shown strangling a lion with its trunk – a scene that may have been acted out in the Belgrade Forest more than 15 centuries ago.

►   **Tekfur Sarayı**   *46B3*
    (Palace of the Porphyrogenitus)
Şişhane Caddesi Avcı Bey
The Palace of the Sovereign (Porphyrogenitus) is a late-13th-century Byzantine ruin, a three-storey shell with huge arched windows that once contained imposing ceremonial halls. In the courtyard take a closer look at the intricate geometrical patterns of red brick and white marble, typical of the late Byzantine period. The owner of the house in the grounds, who describes herself as the museum 'director', may ask for a tip in return for a hand up the ladder to the ramparts.

Iconoclastic zeal
In the 8th and 9th centuries much religious art of the Byzantine world was destroyed by zealots known as Iconoclasts (from the Greek 'image breakers'). Fearing that the veneration of images would lead to idolatry, some emperors not only prohibited the creation of religious art, but also authorised the wholesale destruction of church images already in existence.

Interior of Aya Sofya Mosque, now a museum

Pilfering and plundering

To ensure the new basilica was the most magnificent in existence, precious materials, fine marbles and sculptures were plundered from the most celebrated temples of the ancient world. The eight green breccia columns were taken from the Temple of Artemis at Ephesus, and others were pillaged from temples in Baalbek (Lebanon), Athens and Delos.

The greatest internal damage the basilica has sustained throughout its long history occurred in 1204 when the Catholic armies of the Fourth Crusade stormed it, stripping it bare and hacking the altar to pieces.

Sultans' gifts

The gigantic alabaster urns on either side of the entrance were donated by Sultan Murat III, and were once used as ablutions fountains, while Süleyman the Magnificent gave the candelabra on either side of the *mihrab* (the prayer niche facing towards Mecca). The great chandelier hanging from the centre of the dome was donated by Sultan Ahmet III.

The Sweating Column

Near the entrance to the gallery stairway stands the porous 'Sweating Column of Saint Gregory'; for centuries the moisture exuded by this column has been said to cure eye diseases and infertility.

▶▶▶ **Aya Sofya Müzesi**   *46C1*
(Haghia Sophia Basilica)

Aya Sofya Meydanı, Sultanahmet
Open: daily except Mon 9.30–5. Admission charge: expensive.

More than any other building in Istanbul, this extraordinary masterpiece of Byzantine architecture embodies the different phases of the city's history. The first church on this site was consecrated by the Emperor Constantine in 360 to Divine Wisdom (Haghia Sophia in Greek), and was enlarged by his son Constantius to become the episcopal church of the capital. In 404 and 532 this building and the church that succeeded it were burned down during revolts, and it was in February 532 that the Emperor Justinian ordered work to begin on the current structure, which became the largest church in Christendom at that time. In 1453, on the very day that Constantinople fell to the Turks, Mehmet the Conqueror entered the basilica and ordered it to be converted to a mosque named Aya Sofya. The building remained a mosque until the early 1930s when, in recognition of its unique and pivotal role in Byzantine and Ottoman history, Atatürk turned it into a museum.

Earthquakes have taken their toll on the over-ambitious dome, which several times had to be shored up by increasingly large buttresses. These make it difficult to work out the groundplan of the basilica from the outside, and the minarets, added by various sultans along with yet more buttresses, serve to disguise the original still further.

The interior Internally, Aya Sofya remains as stupendous as it must have been in Byzantine times. Entrance to the precinct is through an attractive courtyard garden; on the right are scattered various tombs of Ottoman sultans; on the left the old kitchens and ablutions fountain.

In the vestibule, look out for the 9th-century bronze-covered doors into the narthex, and for the 10th-century mosaic showing the Virgin Mary holding the baby Jesus with, on one side Constantine I offering her the city, and on the other, Justinian presenting a model of the basilica. Another notable mosaic is to be found above the main door to the basilica itself. Dating from the late 9th century, it depicts Christ enthroned and holding out his right hand in blessing.

Inside, the colossal green and purple columns supporting the dome, the walls sheathed in marbles of all colours and, above all, the sheer scale of the interior space combine to take the breath away. The tops of the columns are dominated by huge discs bearing the names – in Arabic script – of Allah, Mohammed and key figures of Islamic history.

On the left-hand side of the nave as you enter is the stairway to the cobbled ramp which zigzags up to the galleries just below the dome. The south gallery contains the celebrated Gates of Heaven and Hell, false doors of marble decorated with elaborate reliefs. It is here that the most magnificent of the basilica's mosaics are concentrated, inadvertently preserved in the 18th century by the Ottomans, who covered them with a thick layer of whitewash. The most famous is the 13th-century Deesis, or Prayer, mosaic: against a gold background, the figure of Christ is flanked by an expressive Virgin and an agonised John the Baptist.

■ **The distinctive artistic style that we now think of as characteristically Ottoman began to develop after the Turkish conquest of Constantinople in 1453, and reached its peak in the reign of Süleyman the Magnificent (1520–66). The buildings considered to be most typical of the Ottoman style are the grand imperial mosques such as the Fatih (see page 51), the Süleymaniye and the Sultan Ahmet (Blue Mosque) (see page 53).** ■

Below: decorative feature on the Kaiser Wilhelm II Fountain erected in the Hippodrome in 1895

Ottoman institutions These mosques lay at the centre of huge complexes (*külliyes*) established by religious, educational and philanthropic foundations. *Külliyes* consisted of *medreses* (theological schools), *mekteps* (primary schools), a *darüşşifa* (hospital), a *han* (caravanserai), and an *imaret* (public kitchen), which gave free food and lodging to travellers for three days after their arrival in the city and which also distributed food to the poor. The *hans*, built round a courtyard like most Ottoman buildings, provided all services necessary to travelling merchants, even blacksmiths, and they were the key to Istanbul's thriving commerce during Ottoman times. Recently, some of these remarkably advanced Ottoman institutions have been restored to serve again as libraries, student residence halls and clinics. Two other notable Ottoman foundations were the *hamams* or public baths, over 100 of which function today, and the *çeşmes* or public fountains, more than 700 of which are still standing. In Ottoman times attendants would have handed out free cups of clean drinking water to passersby.

The typical Ottoman mosque has a large central dome with cascades of smaller domes clustered around, all offset by tall thin minarets. The basilica of Haghia Sophia (Aya Sofya) (see pages 60–1) is thought to have provided the inspiration for the dome, but the other elements are original to the Ottoman style.

The great Sinan
The greatest and most prolific of all Ottoman architects, Sinan built an astonishing 81 large mosques, 50 smaller ones, 55 *medreses*, 19 mausoleums, 15 public kitchens, 3 hospitals, 6 aqueducts, 32 palaces, 22 public baths and 2 bridges. No fewer than 84 of his buildings remain standing in Istanbul. His achievement is all the more remarkable in view of the fact that he did not build his first mosque until he was 50; he completed his masterpiece, the Selimiye Mosque at Edirne at the age of 85.

Süleyman's patronage The arts flourished under Süleyman the Magnificent, and the hallmark of this period was its scrupulous attention to, and delight in, detail. This is evident in the superbly illustrated and decorated copies of the Koran, as well as in ceramics, textiles and paintings. Ottoman rulers such as Süleyman were not only connoisseurs and patrons of bookbinding, calligraphy and illumination, but were also prolific authors themselves, especially of poetry. The art of calligraphy was highly esteemed, and its techniques were applied both to books and to the design of monumental inscriptions for mosques in Istanbul. Calligraphy even appeared on garments, such as the talismanic shirts, decorated with victorious verses from the Koran, which were worn for protection on the battlefield. All court costumes were elaborately decorated with leaf and flower patterns, with

lavish use of gold and silver thread and costly materials and jewels – Süleyman's parade helmet and mace, for example, were encrusted with turquoises, rubies and gold. The Habsburg ambassador to the Sultan's court was spellbound: '...everywhere the brilliance of gold, silver, purple, and satin...No mere words could give an adequate idea of the novelty of the sight.'

Sinan The name of a single architect, Mimar Sinan, is virtually synonymous with the architecture of the Ottoman era. A protégé of Süleyman, he was born to Christian parents in Kayseri, Cappadocia, and was recruited into the Sultan's service at the age of 20. Having served in the Janissaries as a military engineer, he was promoted in his late 40s to the position of Chief of the Imperial Architects. By the time of his death in 1588, at the age of 100, he had changed the skyline of Istanbul for ever. This contemporary of Michelangelo and Leonardo da Vinci is little known in the West, where non-figurative art is less commonly appreciated.

The Sultan Ahmet Mosque, one of Istanbul's finest sights

Exotic drinking water
The fountain house of Ahmet III, built in 1728 at the entrance to the Topkapı Palace, is Istanbul's most magnificent. It is a perfect example of Turkish rococo architecture and its every surface is elaborately decorated in rich golds, greens and reds.

Detail of the Ahmet III fountain outside Topkapı Palace

Istanbul mosques

*Interior of the
mosque at Eyüp*

►   **Beyazıt Camii (Beyazıt Mosque)**   *46C1*
Beyazıt Meydanı
The architect of this magnificent complex, Yakub Şah, clearly had an eye for detail and an instinct for geometric proportion. He used these gifts to brilliant effect in the courtyard, where the columns of contrasting red, grey and green marble are crowned with stalactite decoration. Yakub Şah modelled this interior on the Aya Sofya. The *minber* (pulpit), *mihrab* (prayer niche) and the beautifully sculptured balustrade are original 16th-century features, as is the sultan's *loge*, to the right of the *minber*.

Beyazıt Square, which contains the ceremonial gateway to Istanbul University and the mosque *medrese* (theological college), now the Museum of Calligraphy (*Open* Tue–Sat 9–4), is one of the best places to take the pulse of this tumultuous city. You will find students and hawkers rubbing shoulders with the devout, while small boys kick footballs – and beg from tourists.

►►   **Eyüp Sultan Camii (Eyüp Mosque)**   *46A4*
Camii Kebir Caddesi, Eyüp
Open: daily except Mon 9.30–4.30.
Eyüp Ensari, standard-bearer and close companion of the prophet Mohammed, fell in battle during the Arab siege of Constantinople in AD 674–8. His burial place was rediscovered in 1453 by Akşemseddin, tutor of Mehmet the Conqueror; the sultan was delighted and erected a shrine on the site. The best time to visit Eyüp is on holy days (including Friday prayers), when crowds of pilgrims gather to make their devotions. The market stalls do a brisk trade in evil eyes, koranic plates and other religious ephemera.

Terrace with a view
From the Eyüp Mosque, take the path up through the famous Ottoman cemetery to reach the Pierre Loti Café, which has a terrace giving fine views over the Golden Horn, especially attractive at sunset.

57

The original mosque was destroyed during the earthquake of 1766 and rebuilt by Selim III. A fine example of Ottoman baroque, the interior is highlighted with gold leaf on white marble and graced by a sumptuous turquoise carpet. After praying at the mosque, pious Muslims make their way to the octagonal mausoleum of Eyüp Ensari. Dating from 1485 the *türbe* (tomb) is decorated with blue, white and henna-red tiles from İznik and Kütahya.

► **Fatih Camii (Fatih Mosque)** 46B2
Tophane Sokağı, Fatih
Named after the conqueror of Constantinople, Sultan Fatih Mehmet, this important mosque complex actually dates from 1767–71. Its predecessor, built to a different plan, was destroyed in an earthquake in 1766. The exterior features are most appealing; the attractive courtyard has cypress trees surrounding the central ablution fountain. You can see Fatih's tomb in front of the *mihrab* wall.

Minaret technology
Mosques are always recognisable by their minarets, the tall thin towers from which the call to prayer is made. The muezzin used to climb the stairs to the balcony to summon the faithful, but nowadays his voice is recorded and broadcast by loudspeaker.

► **Mihrimah Camii (Mihrimah Mosque)** 46A3
Fevzi Paşa Caddesi, Fatih
The patron of this beautiful mosque, Mihrimah Sultan, was the favourite daughter of Süleyman the Magnificent and the richest woman in the world at the time. Both she and her husband, Rüstem Paşa, shared a passion for architecture, particularly the work of Sinan (see page 55).

The centrepiece of Mihrimah Camii is the enormous cuboid prayer hall, entirely covered by a dome 37m high and 20m across. Light floods in from all directions, as row upon row of stained-glass windows throw beams of turquoise, pink, blue and gold across the spacious interior.

While the terrace overlooking the Edirne Kapı, Istanbul's highest hill, conceals a bustling street bazaar, the garden courtyard, in complete contrast, is a haven of quiet.

The glorious Süleymaniye Mosque presides over the Golden Horn

▶ **Rüstem Paşa Camii**   46C2
(Rüstem Paşa Mosque)

Ragip Gümüspala Caddesi, Eminönü

Dating from 1561, this mosque was designed by Sinan (see page 55) for Süleyman the Magnificent's son-in-law, the Grand Vizier, Rüstem Paşa. He never lived to see it completed, but his widow, Mihrimah Sultan, spared no expense on the decoration and every available space on the walls, piers, pillars, galleries, *minber* and *mihrab* is set with exquisite İznik tiles. The predominant theme is the paradise garden, with delicately painted tulips, hyacinths and carnations. The presence of 'Armenian red' in the colour scheme is indicative of the high point of İznik tile production, about 1555–1620.

▶ **Sokullu Mehmet Paşa Camii**   46C1
(Sokullu Mehmet Paşa Mosque)

Şehit Mehmet Paşa Yokuşu, Kadırga

Often overlooked by tourists, this small masterpiece by Mimar Sinan was commissioned by the Grand Vizier, Sokollu Mehmet Paşa in 1571–2. The entrance is through a courtyard framed by the *medrese* (theological school) where you may well hear the rhythmic hum of schoolboys reciting the Koran, as they have done for centuries.

The prayer hall of this beautifully proportioned building is a model of taste and refinement. A low gallery around three sides of the hall rests on slender marble columns with characteristic Ottoman lozenge capitals. The chief glory of the mosque is the tiled *mihrab* wall, where swirling patterns of green and red tulips and carnations on a turquoise ground are set against the pure white stone. Other outstanding features include some of the original painted arabesques under the gallery, fragments of black stone from the Kaaba in Mecca (above the entrance and in the *mihrab* wall) and the tiled crown on the *minber*, the only one of its kind in Istanbul.

Minaret counting
The Sülemaniye has four minarets with a total of ten balconies – symbolising Süleyman's position as the fourth sultan after the conquest and the tenth Ottoman sultan overall, whereas Sultan Ahmet is the only mosque outside Medina to have as many as six minarets.

▶▶ **Süleymaniye Camii**   *46C2*
(Süleymaniye Mosque)

Süleymaniye Caddesi, Mercan

With the construction of the Süleymaniye mosque in 1550–9, the architect Sinan finally emancipated himself from the Byzantine influence of Aya Sofya to reveal his astonishing originality. Süleyman the Magnificent was so delighted that he handed him the keys at the official opening ceremony. The mosque reveals a passion for architectural symmetry. The prayer hall is a perfect square, while the diameter of the dome is exactly half its height. All the other elements in the composition – semi-domes and cupolas, window-lit tympana, galleries and pillars – dance in attendance around this crowning feature. There is little sculptural decoration but Sinan allowed his artists free rein, especially on the *mihrab* wall.

▶▶ **Sultan Ahmet Camii (Blue Mosque)**   *46C1*

Sultanahmet Meydanı, Sultanahmet

Known as the Blue Mosque because of the light that reflects from the cobalt tiles in the prayer hall, this awesome building was designed by Sedefkar Mehmet Ağa. Completed in 1616, it immediately became the focus of religious activities in the city – every Friday the Sultan's procession would make its way here in silence from Topkapı Palace. Within the inner courtyard are an ornamental fountain and a beautifully proportioned portico of 26 porphyry columns surmounted by 30 domes, while the view from above is of domes and semi-domes cascading in an apparently unbroken sequence. Inside, more than 20,000 İznik tiles decorate the walls and galleries. Delicately painted with floral and geometric designs, they are the work of the master craftsman, Çinici Hasan Usta. Look closely at the ivory, tortoiseshell and mother-of-pearl inlay on the wooden doors and window frames, and at the beautiful carving on the *minber* and the sultans' *loge*.

Delicately sculpted arches in the inner courtyard of the Blue Mosque

Ottoman climax
Tucked into the walled garden behind the Sülemaniye are the impressive octagonal *türbes* (tombs) of Süleyman and his wife Roxelana, decorated inside with wonderful İznik tiles in far greater numbers than in the whole vast space of the mosque itself. Sinan's own *türbe* stands a short distance to the north-east of the complex, just past the caravanserai.

■ **Islam originated in the early 7th century in Mecca on the Arabian peninsula, with the charismatic figure of Mohammed. It spread to Turkey in the 11th century with the arrival of the Seljuks from Persia and remained the state religion until 1923, when Atatürk officially secularised the Turkish Republic. ■**

Women and Islam
Muslim men are allowed to take up to four wives, but it is rare for them to do so nowadays, especially in Turkey, and most have only one. Traditionally a man may divorce a woman but not vice versa, though the law has now been reformed in many countries including Turkey. The Koran exhorts women to cover all parts of the body that might be a temptation to men, but again this is very loosely interpreted: most Turkish women, especially in the cities, now wear the Western style of dress.

60

Studying the Koran in the mosque at Eyüp. Eyüp is an important centre of Islamic pilgrimage

Cleanliness is next to godliness
'He who performs the ablution thoroughly will extract all sin from his body, even though it may be lurking under his fingernails.'
The Prophet Mohammed

Later called the Prophet, Mohammed proclaimed himself the mouthpiece of Allah: in no way divine himself, he was simply the medium through which Allah had chosen to reveal his word. Mohammed was illiterate, but the Koran (literally 'Recitation') was revealed to him in bursts over a period of 22 years ending in 632, the year of his death at the age of 62. The text of the Koran consists of God speaking to man, offering divine instruction and guidance in the Arabic language; because of this, Muslims all over the world, whatever their nationality or language, pray and recite the Koran in Arabic, having learnt it by heart. One consequence of this is that classical Arabic has altered less over the last 1,300 years than any other language.

Islam, meaning 'submission to the will of God', spread rapidly from the Arabian peninsula as a result of the exhortation to jihad (holy war), imposing an obligation on all believers to spread the word to unbelievers. Within ten years Arab armies had conquered Syria, Egypt, Mesopotamia and the Persian Sassanid Empire. The tolerance shown by Muslims to Christians and Jews was frequently in stark contrast to the persecution they had suffered previously, and won Islam many converts.

Relationship with Christianity and Judaism Christians and Jews are referred to in the Koran as 'People of the Book' (that is, of the Bible), a separate category from straightforward unbelievers. This is because Islam regards Allah as being the same god as the one worshipped by Christians and Jews. Its main point of

ت سعادت غازئ صاحب رامتنر ولّ پاک خصلت علم و حلم و لط

contention with Christianity lies with the Christian doctrine of the Trinity and the belief that Jesus was the Son of God, rather than merely a prophet like Mohammed. The Koran affirms the righteousness of previous prophets and revelations: 'Surely, We sent down the Torah full of guidance and light', and 'We caused Jesus son of Mary to follow in their footsteps...and We gave him the Gospel'. Mohammed is claimed to be the 'seal' of the prophets, however – the last one with the final word.

The Five Pillars The five basic tenets of faith as laid down by the Koran are known as the Five Pillars. The first is the declaration of faith that 'There is no God but God and Mohammed is the Messenger of God' (proclaimed in the calls to prayer from mosque minarets). The second is the act of prayer, made five times a day – at dawn, noon, mid-afternoon, sunset and before bed. Ritual ablution of hands, feet and face is compulsory before prayer. The third is *zakat*, or alms tax, a yearly charitable donation. The fourth is fasting during Ramadan, the month in which the first revelation of the Koran was given. The 30-day fast during daylight hours applies to food, drink and smoking; the old, the sick and children of up to about eight years are exempt. The fifth is the pilgrimage (*hajj*) to the Kaaba, the House of Allah at Mecca, to be undertaken at least once in a lifetime by any Muslim who can afford it.

Islamic culture When it was at its peak, between the 7th and 13th centuries, Islamic culture was responsible for many great intellectual and scientific discoveries, some of which were later borrowed by the Western world. Arabic numerals, geometry and algebra were all introduced to western Europe through contact with the Islamic traders of Spain and north Africa. In the field of medicine, meanwhile, many important advances were made by philosopher-scientists such as the 11th-century Avicenna.

Allah is One
'"The great stumbling block to Moslems," said Father Chantry-Pigg, "is the Blessed Trinity. To a people who hear the One God proclaimed so many times a day, and so loudly, the Triune God raises all kinds of difficulties in the mind."'
Rose Macaulay, 1956

61

A lavishly illustrated copy of the Koran, the sacred book of Islam

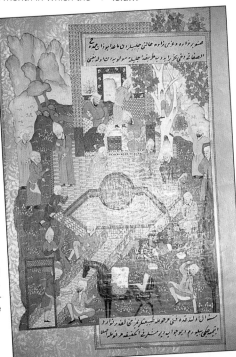

Istanbul sights

▶▶▶ **Arkeoloji Müzesi**   *46C2*
(Archaeological Museum)

Gülhane Parkı, Eminönü
Open: daily except Mon 9.30–5.

This exemplary museum, which won the 'Council of Europe Award' in 1993, was built to house the sarcophagi of the ancient Phoenician kings discovered by the archaeologist Osman Hamdi Bey in 1887. The star attraction is the magnificent Alexander sarcophagus, carved in the 4th century BC with hunting and battle scenes of startling savagery and intensity. The tomb in fact belongs to an unknown Phoenician or Seleucid ruler, not Alexander the Great as was originally thought.

The museum also boasts a superb collection of classical sculptures, including some astonishingly lifelike busts of the Roman emperors, funerary stelai with moving valedictory scenes, and a number of remarkably well-preserved statues – for example, a recumbent Oceanus, sculpted in Ephesus in the 2nd century. The new wing hosts a fascinating exhibition on the history of Istanbul and the neighbouring regions. Here you will find fragments of artwork preserved from lost Byzantine churches, a section of the defensive chain that hung across the Golden Horn in the 15th century, the original bell from the Galata Tower and silver coins dating back to the 5th century BC.

A pair of ancient Hittite lions from the 14th century BC guards the entrance to the **Museum of the Ancient Orient**, which houses a fabulous collection of art and artefacts from the ancient world. One of the most significant is a tablet containing the world's oldest peace accord, the Treaty of Kadesh, made in 1269 BC between Pharaoh Rameses II and the Hittite King Muvatellish. You can also see the world's oldest law code, dictated by the Assyrian King Hammurabi in 1740 BC, and the earliest known standard weight (*c* 2000 BC), a basalt duck weighing 30kg. But it is the reliefs that take the breath away: there are sections from the glazed tile walls that once formed the glorious Processional Way into Babylon and some vivid narrative friezes – look on in awe as the charioteers of Assyria rumble inexorably into battle.

Çinili Köşk
The Çinili Köşk, in the courtyard of the Archaeological Museum, was built for Mehmet II in 1472 and is the oldest secular Islamic building in Istanbul. From here the sultan could watch games of *cirit* and other entertainments. The façade is brilliantly decorated with faience and today the pavilion is, appropriately enough, the Museum of Turkish Ceramics (*Open* with the Archaeological Museum).

The stunning Alexander sarcophagus in the Archaeological Museum

FOCUS ON *Tiles*

■ **The development of tile and ceramic art began in Turkey in the 11th century, when the Seljuks moved westwards from their newly established capital in Persia. When, in 1097, they made Konya their western capital, the town soon became one of the leading tile and ceramic production centres.** ■

Konya ware The Seljuk polychrome technique brought from Persia was known as *minai* (from *mina,* meaning 'enamel' in Persian). The ceramic slabs were first painted in pale blues, greens or turquoise, covered in a transparent glaze and fired. Then they were decorated in black and vitrifiable colours such as red, yellow, blue and brown and fired again. The tiles were generally star-shaped and the motifs used were a blend of Persian styles and images such as hunting dogs and horses, inspired by the steppes of central Asia.

İznik ware In the 15th century, under the Ottomans, the centre of tile production moved to İznik, a traditional centre of Byzantine earthenware, in response to a sudden and unprecedented need for fine tiles and ceramics to decorate the palaces and mosques springing up in the new capital, Istanbul. During the 16th century, styles gradually became more refined, with delicate 'blue and white' decoration used to imitate Chinese motifs such as wave scrolls and lotus flowers. Turquoise, green and red (produced from a thick clay rich in iron, found only near Erzurum in eastern Turkey and especially characteristic of the period 1560–1600) were subsequently added to the range of colours, and flower motifs became popular. İznik production remained highly successful until the 17th century.

The use of tiles to embellish religious and secular buildings was elevated to an art form under the Ottomans. Although most of the faience was manufactured in the workshops of İznik, the intricate and imaginative designs were created by artists in the Topkapı palace in Istanbul.

Kütahya ware With the decline of the İznik workshops in the early 17th century, Kütahya became the main centre of production. High quality tiles, as well as a range of other ceramics, are still being produced here today.

The exquisite tiled mausoleum of Eyüp Ensari

Stirring music
The *Mehter* (musical band) of the Janissaries, the sultans' imperial guard, marched at the front of the army and accompanied the soldiers into battle. The kettledrums, which played no small part in arousing their aggressive instincts, eventually found their way into the Western orchestra via Glück's 18th-century opera, *Iphigénie en Tauride*. Mozart also found inspiration in Turkish sonorities in his opera *Il Seraglio*, while the brother of another famous composer, Donizetti Paşa, served as *Mehter* bandmaster under Mahmut II and Abdül Mecit I and composed a number of stirring military marches.

Opulent ballroom in the 19th-century imperial palace of Dolmabahçe

Undying respect
Each year on the anniversary of Atatürk's death, at 9.05am on 10 November 1938, a minute's silence is observed and all traffic comes to a standstill. Even the Bosphorus ferries switch off their engines to drift on the current, blowing their horns mournfully.

▶▶　　**Dolmabahçe Sarayı**　　　　47D3
　　　　(Dolmabahçe Palace)

Dolmabahçe Caddesi, Beşiktaş
Open: Tue, Wed, Fri–Sun 9–6. Group admission with tour guide.

By far the most sumptuous of the sultans' palaces, Dolmabahçe stands on the site of a reclaimed harbour – the Turkish word means 'filled-in garden'. It was commissioned by Sultan Abdül Mecit I from the architects Karabet Balyan and his son, Nikoğos, in 1843. The royal entourage occupied the palace in 1856, just in time for a magnificent banquet celebrating the victory of Turkey and her allies, Britain and France, in the Crimean War. So much of the state's revenues were thrown at this *folie de grandeur* (roughly £50 million in today's money) that it contributed in part to the bankrupting of the Ottoman treasury in 1881. The first President of the Republic, Mustafa Kemal Atatürk, chose to stay at Dolmabahçe in 1927, rechristening it 'the Palace of the Nation', and he died here on 10 November 1938.

The layout of the palace preserves the traditional division between *selamlık* (state rooms) and harem (private apartments). Separating the two is the largest throne room in the world, its *trompe l'oeil* ceiling supported by 56 Corinthian columns. It was here that the first Ottoman parliament was convened in 1877. Other highlights of the palace include the magnificent formal staircase with a balustrade of Baccarat crystal, the Hünkâr Hamamı (Sultan's bathroom), with walls of alabaster specially imported from Egypt, and the dazzling Mavi Salon. The décor is almost exclusively Western, after a style which the French novelist Théophile Gautier described ironically as 'Louis XIV orientalisé'.

▶　　　　**Galata Kulesi (Galata Tower)**　　46C3

Büyükhendek Sokak, Karaköy
Open: daily 8am–9pm. (Restaurant 12–3, 8–midnight.)
One of the most conspicuous landmarks of Istanbul, the Galata Tower was built by the Genoese community in 1348 and was later used by the Ottomans as a watchtower. Now very much a tourist attraction, with a lively restaurant and nightclub, it rises 140m above the Golden Horn and has commanding views of the Bosphorus. Visit around dusk to watch spectacular sunsets.

▶▶▶ Kariye Camii (St Saviour in Chora)   *46B3*

Kariye Camii Sokak, Edirnekapı
Open: daily except Tue 9.30–4.30.

This lovely church contains one of the world's most precious and best-preserved collections of Byzantine mosaics and frescoes. The dramatic rendering of the Resurrection in the apse speaks directly to us across the gulf of nearly seven centuries.

The Church of St Saviour in Chora (now the Kariye Museum) was built in 1316–21 and incorporates the shell of an earlier 12th-century church. Chora means 'in the country', an allusion to an even older foundation which stood outside the city walls. There is an additional, symbolic meaning: Christ as the 'country' or sphere of the living. The church's patron was Metochites, a distinguished Byzantine scholar and statesman who served Emperor Andronicus II Palaelogus as prime minister and treasurer. When the emperor was overthrown in 1328, Metochites was sent into exile. Two years later he was allowed to return as a monk to live out his days in the confines of the church he had founded.

Fortunately the glory of the church, its mosaics and frescoes, were not destroyed when the building was converted into a mosque in 1511. They represent the late flowering of Byzantine art and are almost certainly the work of a single unknown artist, who left his signature in the hooked tails of the drapery and the peculiar 'shadows' around the feet. The mosaics depict the lives of Christ and of the Virgin Mary. Above the door into the nave is a representation of Metochites presenting his church to Christ, wearing the typical Byzantine sun hat known as a *skiadon*. The frescoes are confined to the parekklesion and depict the Last Judgement, the Mother of God as mediator between God and Man and the Harrowing of Hell.

The Harrowing of Hell, *one of the superb 14th-century frescoes in the Kariye Camii*

Mosaic masterpieces
The remarkable 14th-century mosaics and frescoes of the Kariye Camii were preserved for posterity when the Ottomans painted the walls with whitewash and plaster during the period when the building was used as a mosque.

Gold

Surprisingly, the Spice Bazaar is also home to a number of reputable jewellers. Gold, especially, is a good buy in Turkey because, while the workmanship is excellent, labour costs are much lower than in Europe or the United States. Make sure that any purchases are stamped and carry a label of warranty from the Turkish Standards Institute.

►► Misir Çarşısı (Spice Bazaar)   46C2

Yeni Cami Caddesi, Eminönü
Open: daily except Sun 9–7.

Completed in 1660 for Hatice Turhan Sultan, mother of Mehmet IV, the Spice Bazaar was intended to provide income for the charitable foundations of the nearby Yeni Mosque. The source of this income was the import duty levied on the spices as they passed through Egypt (then part of the Ottoman Empire), which is why the Turks still call this the Egyptian Bazaar. After leaving Egypt, the 'Cairo caravan', continued with its precious cargo to Istanbul, escorted on the last stage of its journey from the island of Chios by Barbary pirates.

The entrance to the bazaar is through one of six double-arched gates. Of the 88 shops here today, fewer than half specialise exclusively in herbs and spices, but even so the aroma is unmistakable, a heady mix of saffron, coriander, ginger, cinnamon, mint, paprika, sage and tamarind. The second overwhelming impression is of riotous colour. Knots of aubergines, paprika and salami hang from the ceiling, trays are filled with sweets, nuts, dried figs and apricots, and counters are stacked with red, yellow, blue and green pots of caviar from Russia, Iran and Azerbaijan. Few can resist the Turkish Delight with hazelnut and pistachio fillings; or the tea, blended with apples, oranges, lemons, cherries, cinnamon and rose-hip. If you are in the mood for an aphrodisiac, head for the dried fruit shop, Malatya Pazarı, or try perfumes at Fuar Pazarı with such erotically suggestive names as 'Sultan's Harem' and 'Istanbul Nights'. And there can be no better way to round off a visit than to have lunch at the famous Pandelli restaurant – ask for one of the window seats overlooking the bazaar.

Exotic wares on sale in the Spice Bazaar

The tram is the only form of transport on İstiklâl Caddesi

► Taksim and İstiklâl Caddesi   46C3–47D3
(Independence Avenue)

Independence Avenue is Istanbul's most famous shopping street and the focus of nighttime entertainment with its cabarets and nightclubs, cinemas, cafés and bars. Known in the 19th century as the Grand Rue de Pera, this was the heart of the city's European quarter, and where most of the foreign embassies were located (many are still here today). A restored 19th-century tram runs from Tünel to Taksim Square, the commercial hub of the city, hectic with traffic and crammed with modern hotels and fast-food chains.

▶▶▶ **Türk ve İslam Eserleri Müzesi** *46C1*
(Museum of Turkish and Islamic Art)

İbrahim Paşa Sarayı, At Meydanı 46, Sultanahmet
Open: daily except Mon 10–5.

This entertaining museum is housed in the former palace of Süleyman the Magnificent's Grand Vizier, İbrahim Paşa, who received it as a gift from the Sultan in 1520. Sixteen years later, when İbrahim fell foul of his master, Süleyman's scheming wife Roxelana conspired to have him murdered, and the palace, by far the largest private residence in Istanbul, reverted to the crown.

The museum has an outstanding collection of arts and crafts representing most of the great Islamic civilisations. You can see items as diverse as carved window shutters, tiles painted with animal motifs, wooden chests and gilded boxes, ceramic bowls, a 13th-century brass astrolabe, hat plumes, stained glass, lacquer-on-leather bookbindings, calligraphic rolls and miniature paintings.

Hanging in the former audience hall of the palace are carpets from as far afield as Hungary, Persia and the Arab provinces of Spain. The earliest fragments of carpet date back to the 13th century and are of the kind that Marco Polo might have seen on his travels across Central Asia. Over time the paired birds, animals and tree motifs favoured by the Seljuks gave way to more stylised geometrical patterns. This transition is recorded in Western art of the period, so it is appropriate that the designs themselves are named after the artists in whose paintings the carpets appear: Bellini, Van Eyck, Holbein, and others.

The ethnography exhibition focuses on carpet weaving as a domestic handicraft originating with the nomadic peoples of Anatolia. Besides learning about the plants and insects used to produce natural dyes, you can 'visit' a *yurt*, a goatskin black tent, and other traditional dwellings.

Luxurious hotel
Istanbul's most celebrated hotel, the Pera Palace, opened in 1895 specifically to cater for passengers arriving in Constantinople by train after their 68-hour journey on the Orient Express. The last word in old-fashioned luxury, the hotel acquired an aura of mystery and suspense after Agatha Christie stayed here while writing her novel *Murder on the Orient Express*. Other famous guests at the Pera Palace include the spy Mata Hari, the actress Sarah Bernhardt and the film star Greta Garbo.

67

Precious carpets hanging in the main hall of the Museum of Turkish and Islamic Art

Turkish carpets
Within the precincts of the Sultan Ahmet Camii, a remarkable collection of ancient kilims and carpets is housed in the Hünkâr Kasri, a mansion belonging to the sultans – the stables and storerooms were in the basement (*Open* Tue–Sat 9–4).

Map labels:

Beyazıt Kulesi

SURURİ

ÇAKMAKÇILAR YOKUŞU

ÇARKCILAR SOKAĞI

MAHMUT PAŞA YOKUŞU

TARAKÇI CAFER SOKAĞI

MERCAN CADDESİ

FUA PAŞA CADDESİ

3

İstanbul Üniversitesi Merkez

TAYA HATUN

TİĞCİLAR SOKAĞI

TARAKÇILAR CADDESİ

SULTAN MEKTEBİ SOKAĞI

Yolgeçen Han

Astarcı Han

Pastırmacı Han

Mahmut Paşa Hamamı

BEZCİLER SOKAĞI

Sarnıçlı Han

İç Cebeci Han

Çukur Han

İnameli Han

Kalcılar Han

MAHMUT PAŞA SOKAĞI

BAKIRCILAR CADDESİ

YAĞLIKÇILAR CADDESİ

Zincirli Han

AYNACILAR

Çıhacılar Hanı

2

CADİROCULAR CADDESİ

Havuzlu

HALICILAR ÇARŞISI CADDESİ

KUYUMCULAR CADDESİ

Nuru Osmaniye Camii

VEZİRHANI CADDESİ

★

BEYAZIT MEYDANI

YORGANCILAR CADDESİ

Ali Paşa Hanı

PTT

İç Bedesten

Sandal Bedesten

NURU OSMANİYE SOKAĞI

Beyazıt Camii

Sahaflar Çarşısı

Bodrum Han

FERACECILE SOKAĞI

KESECİLER CADDESİ

C CADDESİ

Rabia Hanı

Yağcı Hanı

Nuru Osmaniye

Vezir Hanı

BEYAZIT

FESCILER CADDESİ

KALPAKÇILAR CADDESİ

OKCULARBAŞI CADDESİ

BALMUMCULAR SOKAĞI

ÇARŞIKAPI SOKAĞI

BİLEYCİLER SOKAĞI

TAVUK PAZARI SOKAĞI

Cemberlitaş

YENİÇERİLER CADDESİ

1

TİYATRO CADDESİ

YENİÇERİLER CADDESİ

Atik Ali Paşa Camii

Çemberlitaş Hamamı

0   100 m

A   B   C

Walk **The Grand Bazaar**

This walk will help you explore the world's largest bazaar, a labyrinth of seemingly endless vaulted arcades and passageways – a city within a city. It will take you about two hours, allowing a few minutes in which to get lost! The Bazaar is open Mon–Sat and public holidays 8.30–7.

Gold, carpets and embroidered slippers are among myriad items on sale in the Grand Bazaar

Start by taking a taxi to **Beyazıt Meydanı** and walk through the attractive marble-paved courtyard of the **Beyazıt Camii** (see page 50). Descend the steps at the back and follow the alleyway to the right into the Sahaflar Çarşısı, Istanbul's premier used book market.

Leave by the far end and cross the busy Çadırcılar Caddesi, Street of the Tent Makers, to enter the Grand Bazaar at the Fesciler Caddesi, Fez Makers' Street, which, with the demise of the Fez, now sells denim and canvas bags. (In oriental tradition, each trade is assigned its own street to maximise competition.)

Bear left for refreshment at Havuzlu restaurant, considered the best in the Bazaar. From here, head right into Halıcılar Çarşısı Caddesi, the Carpet Sellers Street, until you reach the little fork right into the İç Bedesten, the heart of the Bazaar. Dating from the Ottoman conquest (1456–61), this enormous warehouse was the most secure part of the market where items of the greatest value were stored in iron safes and guarded by soldiers at night.

Leave by the opposite exit and walk straight down to Kalpakçılar Caddesi, Fur Cap Makers' Street. Turn left and, after a short detour into Sandal Bedesten, a 16th-century hall where carpet auctions used to be held, leave the Bazaar by the attractive Nuru Osmaniye Gate. Turn right along Tavukpazarı Sokağı to the Column of Constantine (AD 330), whose dark porphyry drums are reinforced with metal bands. Beside this is Vezir Hanı once Istanbul's principal slave market, next door is the Çemberlitaş Bath, a fitting reward for dusty travellers.

The Middle Gate, the main entrance to the imperial palace at Topkapı

Harem etiquette
The harem system had its origins in a practice adopted by soldiers who were to be away from home for long periods, who had their women locked up and guarded by eunuchs. From this beginning, a whole complex hierarchy evolved, governed by strict rules. Each night, for example, the lucky lady selected by the sultan as his companion in the imperial bedchamber was expected to kiss the imperial bedclothes at the foot of the bed, before wriggling her way under them to encounter the waiting sultan. No Turkish woman is ever thought to have been thus favoured – only thousands of foreigners.

▶▶▶ **Topkapı Sarayı (Topkapı Palace)**   47D2

Sultanahmet
Palace and grounds Open: daily except Tue 9.30–5.
The Harem (separate ticket; guided tour only) Open: daily except Tue 10–4.

From 1461, when Mehmet II ordered the construction of the palace, until 1853, when Abdül Hamid left for Dolmabahçe (see page 64), Topkapı was both the private residence of the sultans and their families and the administrative centre of the Ottoman Empire. The main entrance of the museum is through the turreted Middle Gate of the Second Courtyard. The most important building here is the Divan, or Imperial Council, where the sultans' advisors met to discuss matters of state four days a week. Restored to its 16th-century appearance, the council chamber still contains the divan or couch where the Grand Vizier presided over meetings while the Sultan kept a watchful eye through the grille in the wall above. The Sultan's Audience Hall, a graceful pavilion with a large overhanging eave, supported by 20 marble columns, is approached through the magnificent Gate of the White Eunuchs (Third Courtyard). From the canopied throne the Sultan would receive foreign ambassadors and other dignitaries with elaborate protocol and ceremony.

The Harem The Harem, the private quarters of the Sultan and his family, was a palace within a palace, with its own baths, hospital and kitchens and at least 300 rooms lost in a labyrinth of corridors and courtyards. There were two separate domains: the Valide Sultan (Queen Mother) presided over the wives and concubines, while the *selamlık* (mens' quarters) was the preserve of the sultan himself. Visitors are shown the Imperial Hall where dancers and musicians entertained the sultan and his concubines; the suite of marble-clad bathrooms; Murat

III's bedroom, complete with fountain and stained-glass windows; and the dining room of Ahmet III, gorgeously decorated with fruit and floral motifs

Topkapı Palace Museums In the Second Courtyard, the palace kitchens with their distinctive domes and tall chimneys now house one of the world's finest collections of Chinese porcelain, celadon and silverware – some of the pieces date back to the 10th century. (You may wonder why there is so much celadon here – the answer lies in the rumour, current in the 16th century, that its properties would expose poisoned food!) You can also see distinguished examples of Turkish, Japanese and European porcelain. Some of the original kitchen equipment, including giant *kazans* (cauldrons), ladles, platters and copper dishes are on display at the far end of the building. Across the courtyard in the old Treasury is the superb collection of arms and armour, including many items belonging to the sultans themselves.

A dazzling array of costumes belonging to the sultans and crown princes, including kaftans of satin, silk and velvet brocade, embroidered jackets, quilted turbans, scarfs and slippers is on show in the Pages Quarters in the Third Courtyard, while in the Treasury you can see jewellery belonging to the imperial family and the spoils of war from various military campaigns. The prize exhibits here include the famous Topkapı dagger, studded with emeralds, the 85-carat Spoonmaker's diamond (the fifth largest in the world) and the throne of Murat IV, inlaid with ivory and mother-of-pearl. There is also an exquisite collection of Turkish and Persian miniatures, some dating from the 16th century, and more than 100 of the palace's jewelled clocks. Muslim clerics keep vigil in the Pavilion of the Holy Mantle, where the sacred relics of the Prophet Mohammed are on view.

Don't miss the terraces, pavilions and rose gardens of the Fourth Courtyard, from where there are unmatchable views of the Sea of Marmara and the Bosphorus. The 19th-century Mecidiye Köşkü is now Konyalı Restaurant.

The original palace Begun in the reign of Constantine the Great (AD 324–337), the first imperial palace stretched all the way from the Hippodrome to the sea walls where there was a small private harbour known as the Bukoleon (Bull and Lion). By the time the palace was ransacked by the Crusaders at the beginning of the 13th century, it had fallen into disuse; even so, the soldiers were agog at its magnificence – besides a polo ground, several swimming pools and an indoor riding school, they counted more than 500 halls covered in gold mosaic and 30 chapels.

71

The dining room of Ahmed III in the Harem

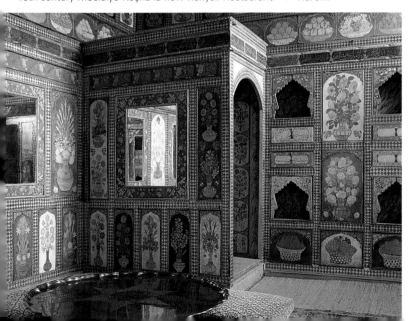

■ **No visit to Turkey is complete without experiencing a Turkish bath. Set aside all notions of prudery and take the plunge, and you will remember this as one of the highpoints of your visit, savouring a feeling of supreme cleanliness and relaxation that is so very different from the typical Western bath or shower.** ■

Ever popular
There are still over 100 functioning *hamams* in Istanbul. These baths were founded by the Ottomans as a public utility with their revenues used to support other foundations, such as schools and hospitals. Because of water shortages, the *hamams* remain as popular with Istanbul's poor as they were in Ottoman times.

The bath is a daily ritual for many Turks

The best time to visit a Turkish bath is at the end of a long and dusty day's sightseeing or shopping. In most large cities and resorts you will find a number of baths where English or German is spoken (see panel on page 73).

The layout The interior design of a Turkish bath is roughly similar to that of an ancient Roman bath, with three distinct areas. The *camekan* (Roman *apoditarium*) is the reception and changing room, where you undress and leave your clothes and where you sip tea afterwards. The *soğukluk* (Roman *tepidarium*) is a passageway between the *camekan* and the steam room, and is where the lavatories are generally situated. The *hararet* (Roman *calidarium*) is the hot steam room, where the massaging and washing take place. The *hararet* is usually the most elaborate and beautiful chamber of all, with marble-clad walls and basins with brass taps round the sides. In the centre is a large marble slab, heated by a wood fire in the furnace room below.

This is the so-called belly-stone, where you lie to sweat, relax and be massaged, all the while gazing up at the shafts of patterned light that pour through the domed ceiling.

Prices for a *kese* massage (during which visitors are rubbed with a camel-hair glove), face massage and foot massage are displayed in the *camekan*. If you are going to make only one visit have the lot, as the total cost still amounts to very little.

The ritual Mixed bathing is not permitted except in the *hamams* of tourist hotels; indeed, the penalty for a man discovered entering the women's baths used to be death. On undressing, both sexes are given wooden clogs in which to enter the *hararet*, and a towel for drying off later. In men's baths, where modesty is strictly observed, a cotton sarong called a *peştamal* is issued for wrapping tightly round the waist, an impediment which makes thorough washing a bit tricky.

Women's baths are altogether more relaxed, with nakedness or knickers adopted according to choice, and children scampering about too. The masseuses are homely and jolly, singing and gossiping as they scrape off the layers of grime, and lather their charges into a soapy bubbling mass. You will emerge feeling you have shed ten years' worth of ingrained dirt. Allow at least an hour for the whole experience.

Best for foreigners
The best *hamams* for foreign visitors in Istanbul are the Cağaloğlu and the Çemberlitaş, both near the Grand Bazaar, or the smaller Çinili Hamam, near the Aqueduct of Valens. They offer separate facilities for men and women and are open between 8am and 8pm daily. Internally, all three are of architectural interest and retain their original marble basins. Prices, though very low by Western standards, are too high for most Turks.

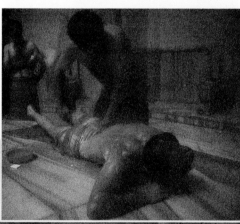

The grim fortress of Yedikule

►► Yedikule Hisarı (Yedikule Castle and the Theodosian Land Walls)

Did you know?
• the Land Walls stretch for a total distance of 6.5km
• the inner walls are 5m thick, 12m high, have 96 towers spaced at 50m–70m intervals
• the outer walls are 9m thick, 8.5m high and also have 96 towers
• there are 7 main gates.

UNESCO protection
There were ten gates in the original 5th-century walls; nearly all are still in use. UNESCO has designated the Land Walls and the area they enclose a cultural World Heritage Site.

Yedikule Meydanı Sokak
Open: daily except Mon 10–5.

It is possible to spend a whole day exploring the old Byzantine fortifications with their watchtowers, gateways, parapets and superb views of the city and the Sea of Marmara. Constantinople's land walls were built in AD 412–22 during the reign of Theodosius II and survived almost intact until they were finally breached in 1453 by Sultan Mehmet the Conqueror.

The 'Fortress of the Seven Towers' (Yedikule) assumed its present appearance around 1460 when Mehmet added five towers to the Porta Aurea (Golden Gate). This was originally a free-standing triumphal arch used exclusively by Roman emperors to enter the city. The gate survives, although the gold-plated doors and statues have long since disappeared. First used as a treasury, the castle became a place of imprisonment as notorious as the Bastille in Paris. Among its victims were foreign ambassadors held as hostages, Ottoman politicians and members of the ruling dynasty. In one of the towers is the cell where, in 1622, the deposed Sultan Osman II, was murdered by the traditional method of strangulation by bowstring – his testicles were crushed simultaneously to add to the torment. You can also see the Well of Blood into which severed heads were unceremoniously tossed.

▶▶ Yerebatan Sarayı (Basilica Cistern) 46C2

Yerebatan Caddesi, Sultanahmet
Open: daily 9–5.30.

This fascinating underground cistern dates from AD 532 and was built in the reign of Emperor Justinian, primarily to supply water to the Grand Palace. Aqueducts carried the water from its source in the Belgrade Forest, about 19km away. After the Ottoman conquest the cistern fell into disuse although attempts were made to repair it in the 18th and 19th centuries. It was only in 1987, however, after a great deal of patient restoration, that this magnificent building was finally reopened to the public in its present condition.

Water still drips from the ceiling of the imposing, brick-vaulted chamber, although the strategically placed spotlights and specially constructed gangways make exploration easy. The main attraction, apart from the fish that continue to thrive in the several centimetres of water remaining, is the forest of pillars that support the magnificent arched roof. Close inspection reveals that these columns are by no means uniform; only about a third of the capitals are Corinthian, for example, while the patterning on the pillars resembles now teardrops, now peacock feathers. These inconsistencies suggest to archaeologists that they were removed from other sites, such as Chalcedon, and reused here – presumably the builders reckoned on no one noticing what went on in the 'underground palace'! This would also account for the recent discovery of two Medusa heads (another suggestion is that they were brought here to ward off evil spirits).

▶▶ Yıldız Sarayı ve Parkı *arrowed from 47E4*
(Yıldız Palace and Park)

Barbaros Bulvarı, Beşiktaş
Open: Wed–Sun 9.30–4.30.

Sultan Abdül Hamid II commissioned this hilltop palace in 1876 because it was more secure from attack than Dolmabahçe (see page 64). There are currently two museums open to the public, the Marangozhane (Palace Museum) and, next door, the Belediye Şehir Müzesi (Municipal Museum), where exhibits range from hand-painted Yıldız porcelain and elegant 19th-century furniture (including items made by Sultan Abdül Hamid himself) to copper incense burners, glass walking sticks, calligraphic paintings and an ornamental halter for a sacrificial ram! Ask at the desk to be shown inside the exquisite theatre in the courtyard behind the Harem Gate.

Behind Yıldız Palace is a magnificent 500,000sq m park, where the air is heavy with the scent of orange blossom (the entrance is on the coast road between Beşiktaş and Ortaköy). The star attraction here is the Şale Köskü; a miniature palace built for the state visit of Kaiser Wilhelm II of Germany in 1889. (*Open* Tue, Wed, Fri–Sun 9.30–4). Otherwise, there are several elegant mansions, now tearooms, and the red-brick Yıldız Porcelain Factory.

The Basilica Cistern:
- is 140m long, 70m wide
- has an additional section approximately 40mx30m, hidden from view
- has an area of 9,800sq m
- has a capacity of 80,000cu m
- has 336 columns, each 12m high and 4.80m apart
- has outer walls 4m thick
- is the only cistern in Istanbul with its own café.

Fishermen's secret
In 1545 Pierre Gilles, a French scholar looking without much success for traces of the 'lost' city of Byzantium, noticed some locals selling fresh fish in inland Sultanahmet. It turned out that they had sunk wells into the floors of their houses and even lowered boats into the pitch-black cavern below, where they had been fishing happily for decades. Gilles had discovered the long-neglected Basilica Cistern.

In the Şale Pavilion of Yıldız Palace even the washbasins are opulent

ISTANBUL

A

6

ALTIN KUM

RUMELI KAVAĞI

Anadolu Kavağı Kalesi

Belgrat Ormanı

Bahçeköy Kısırmandıra

KEMERBUGAZ

SARIYER

ANADOLU KAVAĞI

Sadberk Hanım Müzesi

BÜYÜKDERE

ORTAÇEŞME

5

Seyban

KIREÇBURNU

Boğaziçi

YALIKÖY

BEYKOZ

Fatih Ormanı

TARABYA

See page 77
See page 80

YENIKÖY

PAŞABAHÇE

İSTINYE

Çubuklu Deresi

4

Maslak Kasırları

Emirgân Parkı

Hadiv Kasri Sarayı

AYAZAĞA

EMIRGAN

ÇUBUKLU

MASLAK

KANLICA

BALTA LIMANI

FATIH SULTAN MEHMET KÖPRÜSÜ

FATIH SULTAN MEHMET KÖPRÜSÜ ÇEVRE YOLU

Rumeli Hisarı

Anadolu Hisarı

Kağıthane Deresi

SEYRANTEPE

Boğaziçi Üniversitesi

Aşiyan Müzesi

Göksu Deresi

BEBEK

Küçüksu Kasri

3

KAĞITHANE

KÜÇÜKSU

KANDILLI

Küçüksu Deresi

ARNAVUTKÖY

Kırmızı Yalı

KURUÇEŞME

VANIKÖY

BOĞAZIÇI KÖPRÜSÜ ÇEVRE YOLU

SIŞLI

KURUÇEŞME

KULELI

ÇENGELKÖY

Yıldız Sarayı Şale Köşkü

ORTAKÖY

BOĞAZIÇI KÖPRÜSÜ

Yıldız Parkı

BEYLERBEYI

Ihlamur Kasrı

Ortaköy Camii

Beylerbeyi Sarayı

2

Barbaros Hayreddin Vapur İskelesi

BEŞIKTAŞ

Beşiktaş Vapur İskelesi

Büyük Çamlıca Tepesi

TAKSIM

Dolmabahçe Sarayı

KUZGUNCUK

UMRANIYE

Kabataş Vapur İskelesi

Mihrimah Camii

ANADOLU OTO YOLU

BEYOĞLU

Halıç

BOĞAZIÇI KÖPRÜSÜ ÇEVRE YOLU

GALATA KÖPRÜSÜ

Kız Kulesi

ÜSKÜDAR

Karaca Ahmet Mezarlığı

EMINÖNÜ

HAREM

1

İSTANBUL

Topkapı Sarayı

Selimiye Kışlası

HAYDARPAŞA

Kurbağalı Dere

Marmara Denizi

0   1   2   3 km

KADIKÖY

Kadıköy Vapur İskelesi

A   **B**   **C**

Drive and boat trip — The Asian Bosphorus

This 5–6 hour, 65km excursion begins with a drive along the Asian shore of the Bosphorus to the northernmost point at Anadolu Kavağı but be warned that the taxi fare will be high. The return journey is by ferry, stopping to explore the Asian district of Üsküdar. Take a pair of binoculars, the better to appreciate the magnificent buildings lining either shore.

Take a taxi out through Beyoğlu on the Ankara road, then across the elegant old Bosphorus suspension bridge. The first stop is the **Beylerbeyi Palace**, built in 1865 by Sultan Abdülaziz and used mainly as a summer lodge for visiting royalty (among the guests were Empress Eugénie of France, Emperor Franz Josef of Austria and King Edward VIII of Britain with Mrs Simpson). (Palace *Open* daily except Mon and Thu 9.30–4, by guided tour only. You can take tea in the gardens.)

Continue north through Çengelköy. The next stop is at **Kırmızı Yalı**, the best-preserved of all the Ottoman seaside mansions, built of wood and painted the traditional ox blood colour. The interior is not open to the public.

Carry on north to **Küçüksu Kasrı** (*Open* daily except Mon and Thu 9–4), another charming imperial pleasure palace. Above it stands the ruined castle of **Anadolu Hisarı**. From here boats can be hired (with owner) to explore the Bosphorus at your leisure.

The drive north leads on through Kanlıca, famous for its yogurt, before reaching **Anadolu Kavağı**, an attractive town with typical wooden balconied houses lining the shore and a huge selection of fish restaurants. To build up your appetite, climb up to the Genoese castle for views of the *Clashing Rocks* that Jason and the Argonauts had to navigate in their quest for the Golden Fleece.

After lunch, catch a ferry back down the Bosphorus, disembarking at Üsküdar (formerly Scutari). On the harbourfront visit the **Mihrimah**

İskele Camii, built by Sinan in 1547, then take a taxi to the **Selimiye Barracks**, a colossal building which was once Florence Nightingale's hospital, and is now a school. Continue by taxi to the **Karaca Ahmet Mezarlığı**, the largest Muslim cemetery in the world and a wonderfully wild, overgrown place. From here, you could take the taxi up to the pleasant café and tea house on **Büyük Çamlıca**, the highest point in the area, from where there are unforgettable views over the Stamboul skyline.

Finally, catch the ferry back from Üsküdar to Eminönü, passing close to **Kız Kulesi**, the Maiden's Tower, a 12th-century custom house overlooking the harbour.

Fish restaurants line the waterfront at Anadolu Kavagı

Istanbul environs

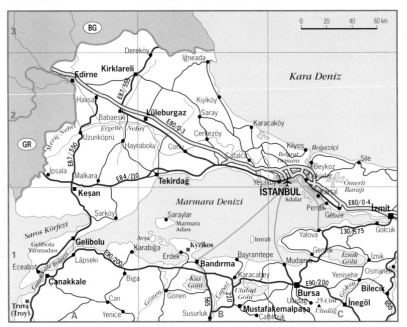

Island ferries

The Princes' Islands lie about 25km from Eminönü waterfront. Ferries leave regularly from Adalar İskelesi year-round and Kabataş İskelesi in summer and take about an hour. In summer, air-conditioned sea buses cut the journey time by half. Most ferry boats call at the four main islands: Kınalı, Burgaz, Heybeli and Büyükada.

Original kebabs

In 1867 a Bursa chef, İskender Usta, designed a vertical grill so that he could baste his lamb kebabs as they turned slowly on a spit – he used his own sword. As the meat cooked, İskender would cut off thin slices and serve them on flat bread with a tomato sauce and brown butter. Does the process sound familiar? It should do – döner kebap, as it is now called, has become Turkey's national dish.

▶▶ **Adalar (The Princes' Islands)** /8C1

The Princes' Islands form an archipelago off the Asian coast of the Sea of Marmara and have been inhabited since classical times – one of Alexander the Great's generals built a fort here in the 3rd century BC. In the Byzantine era the many monasteries served as prisons for exiled members of the imperial family. Sparsely populated until modern times, the islands are now Istanbul's most fashionable holiday resort. Motor traffic is outlawed, but you can hire a pony-and-trap or bicycle to get around. There are sandy coves for swimming, water sport facilities and wonderful walks across the cliff tops and through the pine forests. Some visitors, however, never make it past the fish restaurants that line every seafront.

Büyükada, the largest and most developed of the islands, is hilly and heavily forested. Its old-fashioned charm is enhanced by the extraordinary variety of wooden *yalıs* (holiday homes), each more elaborate than the last. From 1929 to 1933 the mansion of İzzet Paşa on Çankaya Caddesi (no. 55) was the home of the exiled Russian revolutionary Leon Trotsky.

One of the main attractions on the island is St George's Monastery. Take a pony-and-trap from the village as far as the ancient pilgrims' pathway that winds to the top of Yüce Tepe, the highest point on the island. From the grounds of the tiny 10th-century monastic church, there are dramatic views of the archipelago and of Istanbul.

▶▶ **Bursa** 78C1

In 1326 Orhan, son of Osman Gazi, captured this spa town and made it the capital of the new Ottoman state. Recently Bursa has become a significant centre for the manufacture of silk and cotton but, despite modern developments, many delightful Ottoman monuments remain.

If you want to take the waters you should stay in the suburb of Çekirge, where the spas are concentrated. All the largest hotels here have private thermal baths and there are two public baths, dating from the 14th and 16th centuries, which are open to male visitors.

Bursa's covered bazaar is a maze of little streets beside the squat brick minarets of the Ulu Cami (Great Mosque). Don't miss the **Koza Hanı**, the silk cocoon caravanserai, with its cobbled courtyard, plane trees, tea houses and shops selling beautiful silks and brocades. The tourist information office is on the corner of Koza Parkı, where you will find a variety of cafés and restaurants offering the local speciality, İskender Kebap (see panel opposite).

There are good views across the city from the citadel gardens, which also contain the *türbes* of Osman and Orhan Gazi; near by, in Ressamlar Sokak, local artists set up their easels in the small art market.

Across the stream to the west of the castle hill, picturesque Ottoman houses cluster around the Muradiye mosque complex. Worth exploring here is the royal cemetery, where the elaborately decorated tomb of Sehzade Mustafa, son of Süleyman the Magnificent, contrasts with the starkly austere *türbe* of the mystic warrior-sultan Murat II, who commissioned the mosque in 1424.

On a hillside to the east of the city stands the **Yeşil Cami**, considered to be one of the finest examples of early Ottoman architecture. Designed by Hacı Ivaz, it is known as the Green Mosque because of the stunning green and blue tiles that line its walls. Opposite is Bursa's loveliest building, the 15th-century tomb of Sultan Mehmet I, known as the Yeşil Türbe. Like the mosque, the interior is covered with spectacular tilework from the workshops of Tabriz.

The exquisite tiles in the Yeşil Cami have earned it the soubriquet 'Green Mosque'

Karagöz
According to legend, Turkish shadow-puppet theatre (see page 103) originated in Bursa with two medieval builders, Karagöz and Hacıvat, who were employed on the construction of the Uli Cami. Their antics and bawdy humour entertained their fellow workers, but infuriated Sultan Orhan who had them put to death for holding up work on his mosque.

Drive The Belgrade Forest and the European Bosphorus

See map on page 76.

This 5-hour, 70km drive starts by heading straight out to the Belgrade Forest, 20km to the north of Istanbul. It then returns slowly along the European shore of the Bosphorus, stopping to take in the splendid fortress of Rumeli Hisarı, and ends up with tea at the Yıldız Park.

Take the road from Beşiktaş north towards Büyükdere. At Kireçburnu take the road to Bahçeköy, on the eastern edge of the Belgrade Forest. Originally the hunting ground of the Ottomans, this is the largest area of woodland close to Istanbul and is very popular, especially at weekends. Its name derives from the prisoners-of-war from Belgrade settled here by Süleyman after his conquest of the city in 1521. Their job was to look after the reservoirs that supplied the city – the remains of dams, water towers and aqueducts can still be seen here. The finest surviving aqueduct, past Pirgöz on the way to Kısırmandıra, is the Uzun or Long Aqueduct, built by

Rumeli Hisarı, an Ottoman fortress built by Mehmet II

Sinan in 1564 and 716m long.

Return through the forest to **Sarıyer**, a pretty town with a charming waterfront, a lively fish market and a row of fish restaurants. A little further south is the **Sadberk Hanım Müzesi** (*Open* daily except Wed 10–5), a 19th-century *yalı*, or summer house, with exceptional archaeological and ethnographic displays.

Follow the coast road south through **Tarabya**, a wealthy district famous for its fish restaurants and for the Büyük Tarabya, one of the best hotels on the Bosphorus. Many of the mansions that line the shore here are summer residences for foreign embassies.

The highlight of the European shoreline is the fabulous fortress of **Rumeli Hisarı** (*Open* daily except Mon 9.30–5), which dominates the narrowest part of the Bosphorus, here just 500m wide. Built by Mehmet II in preparation for the siege of Constantinople, it was completed within an astonishing four months in 1452. From here there is a good view of the Fatih Sultan Mehmet bridge, built in 1988 and the third longest suspension bridge in the world.

Continuing south, the road enters the sweeping bay of Bebek. Once a pretty village, this is now a wealthy suburb of Istanbul with many splendid mansions on the shore. On a hilltop above is the superb Bosphorus University, the most prestigious in Turkey.

The road continues through Arnavutköy and Ortaköy, suburbs on either side of the old Bosphorus

View from Rumeli Hisarı towards the Sultan Mehmet suspension bridge that links Europe and Asia

bridge (1973) with lively street markets that have now become fashionable.

A fitting climax to this tour of the European shore would be a stroll round **Yıldız Park** (see page 75) (*Open* 8.30–sunset), Istanbul's largest and loveliest park, with a stop for tea at one of the beautifully restored kiosks or conservatories.

*Traditional wooden summer houses (*yalıs*) line the waterfront at Sarıyer*

▶▶ **Çanakkale Strait (Dardanelles)** 78A1

The strategic importance of this strait, connecting the Sea of Marmara to the Aegean, has been recognised since classical times, when it was known as the Hellespont (see panel opposite). In 1451 Mehmet II built fortresses on either shore to secure the approaches to Constantinople – they survive today as ruins. To visit the World War I battlegrounds of the Gallipoli peninsula (see below), take the frequent car ferry service across the strait to Eceabat on the European side. Çanakkale itself has a sprinkling of restaurants and hotels near the harbour, from where boats depart for Gökçeada, one of only two Aegean islands still in Turkish hands (see page 99). The Archaeological Museum displays some exquisite gold and jewellery recovered from tumuli in the area (*Open* Tue–Sun 8.30–12.30 and 1.30–5.30).

Fishing and tourism are the two main industries in Çanakkale

▶▶ **Gelibolu (Gallipoli)** 79A1

This narrow peninsula has been designated a national park to honour the 500,000 Turkish and Allied soldiers who died on the battlefields here during World War I. In 1915 British and French warships attempted to force their way through the Dardanelles with the aim of opening a supply line to Russia via the Black Sea. However, the operation was badly planned and ultimately disastrous as

Victory Beach Memorial Cemetery, Gallipoli

ANZAC Memorial
'Those heroes that shed their blood
And lost their lives...
You are now lying in the soil of a friendly country,
Therefore rest in peace.
There is no difference between the Johnnies And the Mehmets to us as they lie side by side,
Here in this country of ours.
You, the mothers,
Who sent your sons from faraway countries,
Wipe away your tears.
Your sons are now lying in our bosom
And are in peace.
After losing their lives on this land they have
Become our sons as well.'
Kemal Atatürk, 1934

Allied troops succumbed to fierce Turkish resistance under the leadership of Mustafa Kemal Atatürk, founder of the Turkish Republic. Some of the fiercest fighting took place on the west coast in the area now known as Anzac Cove where Australia and New Zealand Army Corps (ANZAC) casualties were especially high. There is a club for veterans and their families in Çanakkale at Cumhuriyet Meydanı 61 (ANZAC House).

The various war memorials are a stark reminder of the fierce battles that took place in this attractive landscape of green hills, pine forests and sandy beaches. Unless you have your own transport, it is best to take an organised tour from Çanakkale, Gelibolu or Eceabat – most last about four hours. The information centre at Kabatepe has a small museum of artefacts found on the sites as well as maps of the area.

Swimming the Hellespont
After emulating Leander and swimming the Hellespont in 1810, Lord Byron observed: '...the immediate distance is not above a mile but the current renders it hazardous, so much so, that I doubt whether Leander's conjugal powers must not have been exhausted in his passage to Paradise.'

▶ **Marmara Denizi (Sea of Marmara)**   78B1
Popular with residents of Istanbul, but relatively undiscovered by tourists, the Sea of Marmara has an attractive coastline backed by rolling hills and fertile valleys.

The main resorts of Thrace (the wine-growing area on the northern shore) are **Şarköy** and **Tekirdağ**. Both have good beaches, hotels, restaurants and other facilities. From here ferries make the crossing to the Marmara Islands and the **Kapıdağı** peninsula (see below).

To reach the southern shore, take the sea bus or ferry from Istanbul to Yalova. Set in wooded hills 12km to the west of the town are the famous hot springs of **Termal**: a fashionable spa in Roman and Byzantine times, it regained popularity at the beginning of the 20th century. The hotels here are on the expensive side, but there are plenty of cheaper *pansiyons* in nearby villages. There are two large indoor baths, the Valide Banyo and the Sultan Banyo; the Kurşunlu Banyo also has an open-air pool.

Unfortunately this part of the coast is badly polluted and further scarred by ugly housing developments. The situation improves around the **Kapıdağı peninsula.** The main town, **Erdek**, one of the oldest resorts in the region, has seen better times but is a convenient stopover on the way to the small group of islands in the Sea of Marmara. The largest of these,

also called Marmara (Prokonessos in Greek) supplied the famous blue-streaked marble used extensively by the Romans. The open-air museum in Saray village reconstructs the marble quarry. Avşa Island with its excellent beaches and clear sea water (not to mention the local wine – ask for Kavalleros) is much more appealing than its neighbour. The main resort here, **Türkeli**, has a good selection of hotels and *pansiyons*.

Cobbled streets and traditional painted houses are attractive features of Erdek, a small town on the Kapıdağı peninsula

Accommodation

In the past, the majority of comfortable hotels in Istanbul were situated in the Beyoğlu district, so that sightseeing involved a taxi ride across the Galata Bridge to the old city of Stamboul. The recent policy of renovating old Ottoman houses and converting them into hotels means that you now have the attractive option of staying in Stamboul itself, within walking distance of the major sights. If you are keen to stay in a particular hotel always book a few weeks ahead, as popular ones fill up quickly. Prices are displayed by law in the reception area, often in US dollars.

Deluxe and 5-star These uniformly large hotels (260–500 rooms), mostly operated by chains such as Hilton and Sheraton, tend to be located in the business and commercial parts of Istanbul. Many boast panoramic rooftop restaurants, and all have beauty salons, health clubs, shopping arcades, swimming pools and bars.

Middle range hotels Usually rated 3- and 4-star, these hotels tend to be in unprepossessing modern buildings in unexciting parts of town. The best known are the Pullman Etap Istanbul, the President and the Kalyon, which enjoys an unusually good location on the Sea of Marmara waterfront, below Sultanahmet. The Pierre Loti Hotel is attractive and centrally located on Divan Yolu, within easy walking distance of the Grand Bazaar and Aya Sofya. Prices range from £70 to £130 per double room.

Height of luxury
The Ciragan-Palace Hotel Kempinski is probably Istanbul's most luxurious, with prices to match. Gutted by fire in 1910, the palace remained a ruin until its recent conversion by the Forte group. The restored palace now houses a conference centre and restaurants, while most of the accommodation is in a new building. The location, on the Bosphorus between Beşiktaş and Ortaköy and below Yıldız Park, is hard to equal.

84

More and more old Ottoman houses are being converted into hotels

Special licence and Touring Club hotels These smaller hotels (14–58 rooms) are housed in historic buildings, almost invariably restored by the Turkish Automobile and Touring Club. They offer comfortable if rather small rooms furnished in Ottoman style. Some, such as the Kariye and the Yeşil Ev, have also acquired a good reputation for traditional yet imaginative Turkish cuisine. A few have Turkish baths, and most have mini-bars and TV in the

rooms. Prices range from £100 per double room (for instance Yeşil Ev) to £55 per double in simpler *pansiyons*, such as the Turkoman Hotel and the Sümengen.

Cheaper hotels Most of the pleasantest cheap hotels and *pansiyons* are located in Sultanahmet, the tourist heart of Istanbul, especially around the Hippodrome. Other reasonable hotels are to be found in the Taksim commercial area, which provides a good base both for nightlife and access to the Bosphorus. The Büyük Londra, a 19th-century Italianate building close to the Pera Palace with a good restaurant and well-furnished rooms, is probably the best of the lot at around £40 per double room.

Campsites Istanbul's campsites – serviceable but rather noisy because of the proximity of the coast road and airport – are all positioned along the Sea of Marmara, beside Kennedy Caddesi, which runs from Atatürk International Airport to the city centre. All have restaurants and most have swimming pools.

The 'Atatürk Room' in Istanbul's Pera Palace Hotel

Famous Pera Palace
The Pera Palace was built at the end of the 19th century as the terminus hotel for passengers from the Orient Express. The rooms are expensive, around £120 for a double, but large and stylish with 19th-century furnishings. If you just want a peek, the bar and café are open to the public.

Taking morning coffee in the sun

Food and drink

Istanbul is the culinary highpoint of any visit to Turkey. Residents take their food very seriously, as can be seen from the colossal range and variety of restaurants. Ranked with French and Chinese as one of the three great cuisines of the world, Turkish cooking prides itself on the quality and freshness of its ingredients, all of which are traditionally home-produced.

Kebabs come in mouthwatering variety

Turkish specialities To the average Westerner, the most novel aspect of Turkish meals is the *meze*, an apparently endless succession of delicious appetisers. Some are cold, such as aubergine purée or yogurt and cucumber; others, for example vine leaves stuffed with meat, and *börek* (fine pastry cases filled with cheese, spinach or meat), are hot. By the time the meat or fish course arrives, usually grilled and accompanied by rice and salad, the uninitiated have often eaten themselves to a standstill. Where the food is on show, always choose from the display rather than the menu; in the simpler *lokantas* (see below), where there may well be no menu anyway, it is the accepted custom to go to the kitchen and choose.

Istanbul is a fast-food paradise

Turkish cooking makes generous use of olive oil: an excellent antidote to this is the Turkish national drink, rakı,

FOOD AND DRINK

Grilled fish is a tasty snack available on many waterfronts

Ortaköy waterfront
One of İstanbul's liveliest and most colourful districts, Ortaköy boasts a waterfront lined with cafés and terrace restaurants with superb views of the Bosphorus and of the exquisite 19th-century mosque. You can choose from Turkish, Italian, Mexican and international menus, although the local fish is the speciality. A street market draws the crowds on Sundays and there are craft and junk shops to explore.

an aniseed-flavoured spirit drunk with ice and water. Turkish wine is surprisingly good and always cheap, the best reds being Yakut and Buzbağ, the best whites, Çankaya and Kavak. The non-alcoholic national drink is *ayran*, a thin rather sour yogurt drink, served chilled and hence very refreshing. Turkish puddings and sweetmeats are described in detail on page 24.

Eating places These range from the *kahve*, serving only Turkish coffee and tea, to the *restoran*, a formal establishment offering Turkish and international food with alcoholic drinks. Somewhere in between are: the *lokanta* with home-cooked Turkish meals and no alcohol; the *içkili lokanta*, licensed for alcohol; the *gazino*, which offers (often sleazy) entertainment; the *kebapçi*, serving grilled meats and kebabs; and the *pideci*, a Turkish pizza parlour.

Where to eat For the best and cheapest fish, head for the Kumkapı district, just inland from the Sea of Marmara, where scores of fish restaurants compete in lively narrow streets. The more expensive fish restaurants are on the shores of the Bosphorus (at Ortaköy for example), and include the Ali Baba in Kireçburnu and Abdullah Effendi at Emirgan. At the Sarnıç, a converted Roman underground cistern in the Sultanahmet district, you can eat interesting if expensive Turkish dishes of all kinds; likewise at the Yeşil Ev, situated in a pretty courtyard between the Sultan Ahmet Camii and the Aya Sofya. Also excellent value is the Sultanahmet Köftecisi, on a corner close to the Yerebatan Sarayı, invariably full of locals eating tasty *köfte* meatballs, which can also be taken away. In the Grand Bazaar, the best *lokanta* is the Havuzlu; at the Egyptian Spice Bazaar, climb the stairs to Pandeli, an excellent lunchtime stop. In the north of the city, Asitane, the restaurant of the Kariye Hotel set in a pretty courtyard garden beside the Kariye Mosque, provides good traditional Ottoman cuisine. Within the Süleymaniye Mosque complex, Darüzziyafe serves authentic Ottoman dishes.

Tasty Turkish dishes:
Arnavut ciğeri – spicy liver with onions
Çerkes tavuğu – chicken in walnut puree
Döner kebap – lamb grilled on a spit
İç pilav – rice with nuts, currants and onions
İmam bayıldı – aubergines with tomatoes and onions
Manti – ravioli with yogurt
Piyaz – haricot bean salad
Sigara böreği – fried filo pastry filled with cheese
Şiş köfte – grilled meatballs
Su böreği – baked pastry filled with meat or cheese
Tas kebab – not kebab! but a meat and vegetable stew
Yaprak dolmaı – stuffed vine leaves.

Shopping

In Istanbul absolutely everything is for sale, as long as you know where to look. Prices vary enormously: bargaining is the norm except in boutiques and bookstores, and you should aim to get at least a third taken off the initial asking price. Normal shopping hours are Mon–Sat 9–1 and 2–7. The Grand Bazaar is open Mon–Sat 8.30–7.

Carpets, kilims and souvenirs Carpet shops abound all over the city, but the biggest concentrations are to be found on Takkeciler Caddesi (Grand Bazaar), and in the secondhand shops off İstiklâl Caddesi around Altıpatler Sokak. You will find a good selection of carpets and souvenirs at the Arasta Bazaar, the renovated Ottoman street market behind the Sultan Ahmet Camii. Prices here are a little higher than in the Grand Bazaar, but the quality is good and the pace gentler.

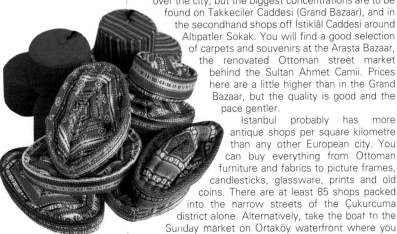

Istanbul probably has more antique shops per square kilometre than any other European city. You can buy everything from Ottoman furniture and fabrics to picture frames, candlesticks, glassware, prints and old coins. There are at least 85 shops packed into the narrow streets of the Çukurcuma district alone. Alternatively, take the boat to the Sunday market on Ortaköy waterfront where you will find local artists selling handicrafts and paintings.

In the Grand Bazaar look out particularly for antique jewellery and copperware. Less expensive, but just as suitable as gifts or souvenirs, are Turkish ceramics, brass pepper mills, onyx candle holders, meerschaum pipes and hand-painted camel-bone boxes. More unusual are the multicoloured woollen socks and gloves knitted by nomads from Erzurum and sold, along with Turkish woollen hats, in the shops on Yağlıkçılar Caddesi (also in the Bazaar).

Embroidered hats make a colourful souvenir

Clothes and leather Turkish *haute-couture*, as represented by top designers such as Rifat Özbek and Arif İlhan, is very much part of the European mainstream, but the use of homegrown fabrics like silk, leather and Angora wool, gives it a certain extra chic. To see local fashions at their best, head for the boutiques of Nişantaşı and Teşvikiye on the European side and Bağdat Caddesi in Asia. You may be able to pick up a bargain if you are here for the sales (*indirim*) in January and July.

Leatherware for sale on Keseciler Caddesi in the Grand Bazaar

The most convenient place for clothes shopping is probably the Galleria complex, a shopping centre at Ataköy, near the airport, where shops are grouped by genre in Turkish bazaar style. Bursa towels, considered among the best in the world, can be bought here at the Özdilek shop. The complex also has fast-food cafés, and even an ice rink.

The Grand Bazaar is an Aladdin's Cave for visitors to Istanbul

Buying carpets
There are no more accomplished practitioners of the 'hard sell' than the carpet merchants of Istanbul. A favourite technique is to waylay unsuspecting carousers returning late at night from the restaurant or nightclub and invite them into the shop for a nightcap (usually no stronger than apple tea). Two or three hours later, the weary 'guest' emerges as a customer laden with carpets and kilims.

Food Turkish delight, sweetmeats and fresh spices all make good presents and the easiest place to buy them is the Egyptian Spice Market, just beside Yeni Camii in Eminönü Square. This crowded, covered pedestrian street is lined with shops bursting with Turkish sweetmeats, which they will package in any combination or quantity you desire. It is easy to get carried away, so remember they are heavy, and that just a few packets will weigh your suitcase down unmercifully. The aroma of spices, on the other hand, may penetrate everything in your case, but at least they weigh almost nothing.

Books The Sahaflar Çarşısı, beside the Grand Bazaar at the Beyazıt Camii end, is an excellent place to browse for new and old books in both English and Turkish. Also to be found here are a few places offering Turkish miniatures and old prints at fairly reasonable prices. The best bookshops for English guides and art books are Haşet Kitabevi and Robinson Crusoe on İstiklâl Caddesi.

Porcelain
Taking a lead from Sèvres and Dresden, Yıldız porcelain made its first appearance in 1895 in the grounds of Sultan Abdül Hamid's palace (see page 75). The Sultan called in experts from France and Germany to advise the local craftsmen on production techniques. The finest collection of antique Yıldız porcelain is on show in Topkapı Palace.

Musical Instruments Lovers of traditional Turkish music, seduced perhaps by the musicians who perform nightly in the Çiçek Pasajı, make a beeline for Galip Dede Caddesi, a street near the Galata Tower full of shops selling authentic instruments. You can choose from the *saz*, a kind of mandolin, dating back to the 12th century, the *ney*, a flute favoured by the Dervishes or the *davul* (drum), which originated in the Janissary regimental bands.

■ **Turkish carpets are famous throughout the world, and their patterns and designs are so complex that it takes years of knowledge and experience to identify their origin at a glance.** ■

Geometrical motifs are a common feature of the kilim

Kilims Most Turkish carpets are of the 'kilim' variety; kilim means 'flat-woven', and these rug-sized carpets are characterised by their lack of pile. Kilims were traditionally made by women for use in their own homes; the patterns

and colours were therefore never dictated by commercial motives, but instead reflected the weaver's character and origins. The craft of weaving these intricately patterned carpets was introduced to Turkey in the 11th century by the nomadic Seljuk people, for whom carpets were an essential piece of tent furniture. The material used is normally sheep's wool, but they are sometimes made of cotton and goat hair. In the Hakkari and Malatya regions of eastern Turkey, silver and even gold lurex thread are sometimes incorporated, as these are thought to ward off the devil or the evil eye. Useful not only as floor coverings, the kilims also served as wall hangings, door curtains, tent dividers and prayer rugs. They were even made into large bags to be used as cushions and saddlebags, or to hold salt, bread, grain and clothes.

Prayer rugs
All prayer rugs have a solid, arch-shaped block of colour to represent the *mihrab*, or prayer niche, of a mosque wall. These rugs are used exclusively for prayer, and the symbols commonly found on them include praying hands, the mosque lamp, the tree of life, the water jug, the jewel of Mohammed and the star of Abraham.

Natural and chemical dyes Traditionally, natural dyes were used to colour the wool, cotton or silk used in both kilims and knotted carpets. These were derived, often by lengthy and laborious processes, from roots, bark, berries, vegetables and minerals. In the second half of the 19th century aniline chemical dyes became available, and these have gradually replaced most of the old vegetable dyes. Watch out for pink and orange in rugs claiming to be older than this, as these are colours that could never be produced from natural dyes. The quality of chemical dyes has now improved considerably, and they can be quite deceptive: if you want to be convinced that colours are natural, look out for mid-weave colour changes, because with natural dyes there are always slight variations of colour between batches.

Buying a carpet Always be prepared to spend time talking with carpet dealers, asking over a cup of tea or coffee about the symbols used and their meanings. This will not only give you a feel for the expertise of the dealer, but will also add to your own knowledge and increase the carpet's interest and sentimental value should you decide to buy it and take it home.

As older carpets have become rarer and more valuable, dealers have not been slow to develop techniques for

A craftsman repairs a kilim in the Arasta Bazaar, Istanbul

Bargaining technique
The best way to get a real bargain is to convince the dealer that you do not like the rug in question. If there are two of you, you can stage-manage this quite well by pretending that one likes it while the other does not. Ask lots of questions about a number rugs so that he cannot tell which is your favourite.

fading newly woven rugs. Leaving them out in sunlight is the most common method – it can often produce quite effective and pleasing results with mellower colours, but it adds nothing to the rug's value. To detect a sun-faded rug, part the surface and compare the colours at the bottom of the weave with those at the top. Comparison with the colours on the underside can also be indicative. Some rugs are artificially aged by washing in bleach, a process which rots the fibres and reduces their life; a quick sniff usually reveals whether or not bleach has been used. Dirt and deliberate scorch marks are other common ageing tricks.

Smaller kilims sell more quickly than larger ones, and sometimes the latter are cut into pieces and sold as original; watch out for the new ends added to make them complete. If colours have been touched up to hide repairs or fading, the felt-tip colouring or shoe polish used may be disclosed by rubbing a damp handkerchief, or sometimes just your hand, over the surface. Look too at the composition of the weave: the closer the weave and, on a pile rug, the smaller the knots, the better the quality and durability of the carpet.

Where to buy
İstanbul's Grand Bazaar offers the greatest selection of carpets and kilims anywhere, as its dealers scour the country in search of rugs to bring back and sell. But you'll also find carpets all around the Turkish coast, especially in resorts like Bodrum and Kuşadası, where you may be able to pick up a bargain.

A carpet salesman proudly displays his wares in Marmaris

Nightlife

For most Istanbullers, nightlife tends to mean listening to a live group or jazz pianist in a bar. Pulsating belly dancers are nowadays found only in expensive cabaret nightclubs visited almost exclusively by tourists – for example Kervansaray and Orient House. More intellectual entertainment, including concerts, ballets and exhibitions, is available at the Atatürk Cultural Centre, especially during the Istanbul Arts and Cultural Festival in June and July.

Clubs You will find nightclubs and discotheques all over the city, with the greatest concentration in Taksim/Harbiye. For disco music and dancing, try Club 29 (see panel), one of Istanbul's most exciting venues. Another well-known disco is Andromeda, where the young clientele (up to 2,000 people in the summer months) arrive around midnight and dance into the small hours. Its futuristic laser show and 'video wall' are added attractions. Hayal Kahvesi welcomes foreign visitors and it's a great night out, but to make sure of getting a table, arrive early, especially if you want to eat – it's sandwiches only after 9pm. Music is disco for most of the evening, but there are also live Turkish rock bands at weekends.

It is common practice for nightclubs in Istanbul to open second venues in the summer. Most of them move out to

Belly-dancing is still a popular entertainment with visitors to Turkey

Galata Tower
The nightclub on the top floor of the famous 14th-century Genoese tower enjoys fabulous views over Istanbul. The after-dinner floor show begins with belly dancing. The club is open 10am–6pm, and from 8pm onwards.

Dining alfresco in Çeşme

There are numerous cinemas on Istanbul's main street, İstiklâl Caddesi

seaside locations on the Bosphorus – Çubuklu on the Asian shore and Yeniköy on the European side, for example. There is a great outdoor atmosphere as the local crowd converges on the waterfront, dancing, promenading or sipping cocktails beneath beach umbrellas.

For 'alternative' cabaret, try Yeşil in Taksim where you will find a Turkish clientele, often from the media and film worlds, and where the floor show offers such delights as 1920s cabaret scripts or spoofs of Ottoman life, with all parts performed by men. The action starts at midnight.

Bars Istanbul's bar scene resembles that of most international cities around the world. If you want a drink with a view, head for one of the downtown hotels or take a taxi to Ortaköy or another waterfront location. Taksim probably has the greatest concentration and variety of bars. Avoid the backstreets and especially *gazinos* – sleazy bars with Turkish floor shows and hostesses – where foreigners are regularly cheated, robbed and even assaulted.

Cinemas Movies are very popular in Istanbul and you will find cinemas all over town, but especially on İstiklâl Caddesi, around Şişli and, on the Asian side, on Bahariye Caddesi in Kadiköy. All films, including the latest American releases are shown with Turkish subtitles. Prices are very reasonable, particularly matinees. In April, look out for the annual Istanbul Film Festival when contemporary Turkish and foreign films are screened at venues all round the city, including the Atatürk Cultural Centre. Turkish films are shown with English subtitles. (For more on Turkish films, see pages 118–19)

Opera and ballet The Istanbul State Opera and Ballet starts its season in October and presents a varied programme, from classics such as Mozart's *Don Giovanni* to experimental ballet, including works by modern Turkish choreographers. Ticket office tel: 251 5600.

Practicalities

To drive in Istanbul is to be faced with the constant headache of navigation and parking problems. By far the best way to get around the city is to walk, or for longer distances to take taxis or ferries. Buses are cheaper but slower, less flexible and impossibly crowded.

From the airport Between 6am and 11pm Turkish Airlines (THY) runs a half-hourly bus service from Atatürk International Airport to the terminal at Taksim Square. If your hotel is centrally located this is ideal; otherwise, most people take a taxi straight from the airport for the sake of speed and convenience: the journey to the centre takes about 30–40 minutes.

Taxis Conspicuous by their yellow colour and black roof signs, Istanbul taxis are prolific and very reasonably priced. They all have meters, and it is always worth checking that you are being clocked up at the appropriate rate: after midnight and before 6am the charge is double the

Taxis are the fastest and most reliable means of getting around

Time-saving funicular
The Tünel, which opened in 1875, is the world's shortest funicular railway, running from Karaköy to the beginning of İstiklâl Caddesi. The ride takes just two minutes, saving an exhausting half-hour climb on foot.

daytime rate. No tip is expected, but the fare is normally rounded up. Taxi drivers usually speak a little English and are glad of a chat.

A *dolmuş* (literally 'stuffed') is a shared taxi, taking up to eight people and running along set routes. The main *dolmuş* stations are at Eminönü, Taksim, Sirkeci, Beşiktaş, Aksaray, Üsküdar and Kadiköy. Most *dolmuşes* are either minibuses or smart new yellow vehicles seating nine passengers.

Buses Istanbul buses are cheap, slow, erratic, perpetually packed and not generally recommended. Tickets, or *Akbil* tokens for multiple journeys, are bought in advance from designated kiosks at the *otogar* (bus station) or from newspaper and cigarette booths. On the European side the main bus stations are at Taksim Square, Eminönü and Beyazıt. On the Asian side they are at Üsküdar and Kadiköy.

Ferries Passenger-only boats run constantly up and down the Golden Horn and across the Bosphorus. The three main landing stages (*iskeles*) are at Eminönü, near the Galata Bridge, and are clearly labelled with the various destinations. To board, you need a brass *jeton* (token) bought at the appropriate *iskele* or an *Akbil* – don't buy from the touts outside the ticket windows, they overcharge. The boats are very crowded with commuters

8–9am and 5.30–8pm, so aim to use them outside these times. The boats are shabby and dilapidated, but have their own faded charm. Tea is brought round on a tray.

Trains The railway is of little use within the confines of the city. The European railway station is at Sirkeci (near the Galata Bridge), from where trains leave for the suburbs of Ataköy and Florya (the campsite). The Asian terminus is at Haydarpaşa, serving Ankara and routes east.

Opening hours Banks are open Monday to Friday 9–12 or 12.30 and 1 or 1.30–5, except at the airport, where they are open 24 hours. If you are changing money, you will get a better rate at one of the numerous exchange offices that are open evenings and weekends. Always make a point of checking the official daily rate first.

Typical restaurant hours are 12–3 and 6.30–11, though most smaller informal restaurants are open all day. Shops open 9–1 and 2–7 and close on Sundays, and the Grand Bazaar is open 8.30–7 daily except Sundays.

Note that most museums close on Mondays, and palaces on Mondays and Thursdays, so plan accordingly. The notable exception is Topkapı, which shuts Tuesdays.

Tour boats of all shapes and sizes ply the Bosphorus

Renovated trams
The tramway which runs the length of İstiklâl Caddesi was re-established in 1990; the old trams have been renovated and brought back into use, and the road is now closed to traffic. Horse-drawn trams came to Istanbul in 1868, and were replaced by electrified vehicles in 1914. There is also a new metro tramway running from Eminönü waterfront to the suburbs, with stops along Divan Yolu and at Gülhane Park (handy for Topkapı). Tickets are sold from kiosks at the stops.

Nowadays trams are little more than a tourist attraction

NORTH AEGEAN

97

NORTH AEGEAN

Pages 96–7: the tranquil North Aegean coast

The North Aegean coast This coast attracts fewer visitors than the shoreline further south on account of the lower sea temperatures (average 20°C in summer), and the relative remoteness of the nearest international airport, İzmir. The main advantage, for the time being at least, is less commercialisation. Another novelty is that you are likely to encounter more Turkish sunseekers here than foreign tourists. The main seaside resort, Ayvalık, has managed to preserve much of the colour and atmosphere of a traditional Turkish fishing village: from here there are regular boat trips to the tiny islands of the Gulf of Edremit, with plenty of opportunities for swimming and sightseeing. The rival resort of Akçay, further north, is livelier (and noisier) in summer. South of the 'Olive Riviera' good beaches are harder to come by and not very accessible without a car. Çandarlı is popular with İzmir residents but the attractive fishing ports of the Çeşme peninsula, where you can canoe and windsurf, are probably more appealing to visitors. As for classical sites, Troy (Truva), though by far the most famous, is likely to disappoint. More impressive is the ancient city of Pergamum (Bergama) and its magnificent mountainside setting.

▶ Aegean Islands 98A2–98A3

The only Aegean islands still in Turkish hands are **Bozcaada** and **Gökçeada**. Both are jealously guarded and have only recently opened up to visitors. The more attractive is Bozcaada (Tenedos), reached by ferry from Odunluk Yeni Yük Yeri İskelesi, 60km south-west of Çanakkale. The hilly slopes around the ruins of Bozcaada's ancient castle are covered in vineyards and there are excellent beaches, although the water here only warms up in September. The best beaches at Ayazma, Sulubahçe and Habbeli are all within a few kilometres of the attractive harbour. The island can comfortably be seen in a day, although it is possible to stay the night in one of the many *pansiyons*.

Gökçeada (Imros) has been heavily garrisoned since the Cyprus conflict in 1964. *Dolmuşes* leave from the harbour at Kuzu Limanı for Çınarlıı, where there are hotels, restaurants and abandoned Greek churches. A better stop for lunch is Kale which offers a ruined castle, beach and cheap fish restaurants. There are daily sailings to Gökçeada from Çanakkale and daily car ferries from Eceabat.

▶ Akçay 98B2

This lively resort, especially popular with Turks, is well served with hotels, restaurants and discothèques. There is a fine 5km beach with sulphur springs and an attractive waterfront. The information office is on Edremit Caddesi.

▶▶ Ayvalık 98B2

The major resort of the North Aegean, Ayvalık boasts a picturesque marina, an attractive traditional town centre, a colourful bazaar and good sandy beaches. While you are here, try the yogurt cheese and *kepekli* bread, available in super-abundance on market day (Thursday). Ayvalık was founded by Ottoman Greeks in the 16th century and quickly became one of the most wealthy towns on the coast. Unfortunately, many of the old buildings suffered serious damage as the result of two earthquakes. The few

The view towards Ayvalık and the Alibey peninsula

Coastal secrets
Turkey's Aegean coastline is tortuously indented with bays and inlets, the result of earth movements over the millennia. Although a few pockets are now heavily developed, you need never travel far along the coast to find empty beaches and unspoilt fishing villages.

Suggested Itinerary
One week, northern Aegean:
İzmir
Pergamum
Ayvalık (good base)
Behramkale
Troy
Behramkale
İzmir.

Above: the stunning view of the Greek island of Lesbos from the site of ancient Assos (Behramkale). The sheltered harbour (opposite page) lies below the ruins

surviving Greek Orthodox churches, notably **Taksiyarhis Kilesesi**, now serve as mosques (most of the Greek inhabitants were expelled following the War of Independence). Five kilometres from the centre is the island/peninsula of Alibey, famous for its fish restaurants and Aegean white wines. The frescoes in the **Church of St Nicholas** are also worth a visit. The little islands in the gulf of Edremit also bear the remains of monasteries and six-hour boat trips leave from the harbour to explore the islands, as well as calling at Alibey for swimming. The best beaches are to be found 6km south of Ayvalık at Sarmısaklı (Garlic Beach), where the tourist hotels are clustered. A popular excursion is Şeytan Sofrası (The Devil's Dining Table), a rocky hill top south of the town where Satan is said to have left his footprint. From here, there are wonderful views of the surrounding countryside. In summer there are daily departures from Ayvalık to the Greek island of Lesbos (2 hours by car ferry) while **Pergamum (Bergama)** (see page 104) is less than an hour's drive away.

Residents of Assos
The Greek philosopher Aristotle lived at Assos from 347 to 344 BC, studying zoology, botany and biology under the patronage of the eunuch ruler Hermeias. St Paul also stayed here in AD 56 during his third apostolic voyage.

► **Behramkale (Assos)** 98A2

Considered by many to be the prettiest of the small harbours in the northern Aegean, Behramkale offers the ruins of a Greek city set on a cliff top and an attractive little fishing port, lined with small hotels, restaurants and cafés. You should book if you want to stay here in season.

As you approach Assos from Ayvacık, passing a 14th-century Ottoman bridge on the way, there are fine views of the headland site with the village clinging to the ridge beside it. The Hellenistic and Byzantine fortifications are still impressive and at the summit stands the Temple of Athena (530 BC), the oldest Doric temple to have survived in Asia Minor. The view from here towards Lesbos and the Gulf of Edremit is quite spectacular.

■ **Visitors will soon come to appreciate that Turks are a humorous as well as friendly people. They appreciate political satire and have a finely developed sense of the absurd, particularly reflected in the continuing popularity of the medieval story teller Nasreddin Hoca.** ■

Nasreddin Hoca   Innumerable tales covering most aspects of everyday life are attributed to this great legendary sage, said to have lived in Akşehir in the 13th century. Here are a few of them.

A neighbour comes to borrow Hoca's rope. 'I'm sorry,' says Nasreddin, 'I can't lend you my rope, my wife's spreading flour on it.' 'What do you mean?' asks the baffled neighbour, 'That doesn't make sense.' 'I'm perfectly serious,' says Hoca. 'If I don't want to lend somebody my rope, flour can very easily be spread on it.' Spreading flour on a rope has passed into idiomatic Turkish as a metaphor for avoiding something you don't want to do.

A young man comes to Hoca in despair, having lost all his money. 'What will become of me,' he wails, 'without my money and my friends?' 'Don't worry,' says Hoca, 'you'll soon be all right.' The young man perks up. 'You mean I'll get rich again and get back my friends?' 'No,' says Hoca, 'but you'll get used to being poor and friendless.'

Hoca has lost his donkey. While looking for it, he prays and thanks God. 'Why are you so grateful, when you have lost your precious donkey?' he is asked. 'I'm happy because I was not riding the animal at the time. Otherwise I would have been lost too!'

Arriving at a banquet in scruffy clothes, Hoca is ignored and not shown to a table. He goes home, changes into his fur coat and comes back again. This time he is shown to the best table. On sitting down he dips his fur coat into the soup, saying, 'Eat, eat, my fur coat, for it is you to whom this meal was proffered, not me.'

102

Political acumen?
'A horse, an ox and a donkey lived up in the hills. One day the devil whispered to them: 'Why not go to town and see what the humans are like?' So they did. A few years later they met to compare stories.

The horse and the ox both related how they were forced to carry heavy loads and pull carts. The donkey laughed and told how he had arrived in town at election time and joined in the shouting. After shouting louder than everyone else, he was elected to rule. 'But didn't they notice you were a donkey?' asked the incredulous horse and ox. 'They did in the end but by that time four years had gone by and it was time for the next election.'
From a left-wing satirical paper.

A Kurdish couple enjoy the joke

Proverbs Turkish proverbs (as opposed to Arabic or Persian) are highly revealing of the national character. Here is a selection:

The thicker the veil, the less it is worth lifting.

Hard work means a long life but short days.

Even if a woman's candlestick is cast in gold, it is the man who must supply the candle.

On a winter's day, the fireside is a bed of tulips.

Where the Turk rides grass will not grow.

Success depends on a man's reputation, not on his soul.

Political jokes Yıldırım Akbulut, figurehead prime minister from 1989 to 1993 under President Türgüt Özal, and notorious for his ineptitude, was the butt of many jokes. In a typical example a taxi driver asks his passenger: 'Have you heard the latest Akbulut joke?' 'I am Akbulut!' cries the outraged passenger. 'Don't worry,' replies the taxi driver, 'I'll tell it very slowly.'

Turkey has a long tradition of satirical newspapers, with cartoons playing a prominent role. Some examples can be seen at the Karikatür Müzesi (Caricature and Humour Museum) in Fatih, Istanbul (Atatürk Bulvarı Kovacılar Sok 12).

Karagöz For centuries shadow-puppet plays were a popular form of entertainment, now alas superseded by press, radio and cinema. The two main characters were Karagöz, the 'common' man, and Hadjivat, the pompous intellectual – many of the skits ended with Hadjivat being kicked off stage. In the decadent twilight of the Ottoman Empire, these shadow plays became a potent vehicle for political satire. A young man would ask Karagöz, for example: 'What should I do to further myself in my job?' And Karagöz would reply: 'As you are completely ignorant, I advise you to become Chief Admiral.' At that time the sultan's son-in-law was Chief Admiral and a notorious incompetent.

Crying shame
Many stories involve the folk hero Nasreddin Hoca and the Mongol conqueror Tamerlane. In one, Tamerlane weeps for two hours because he has glimpsed his face in a mirror and is appalled by his ugliness. Nasreddin carries on weeping and when Tamerlane asks why; 'If His Majesty weeps for two hours after only catching a glimpse of his face, then surely I, who see him all the time, should weep much longer.'

Above: a sense of humour helps break the ice when bartering

Left: the popular shadow puppet character Karagöz

▶▶▶ Bergama (Pergamum) 98B2

So extensive are the remains of this spectacularly sited ancient Greek city, about 30km from the coast, that just to walk between the three main areas would take all day, and even with transport a visit takes a good three hours.

After Athens lost its political importance in the 2nd century BC Pergamum and Alexandria became the two main – and competing – centres of ancient civilisation. Pergamum's famous library, which boasted more than 200,000 manuscripts, and the Altar of Zeus were constructed at this time, along with the vast artificial terraces on the hillside that allowed the city to spread downwards. All its rulers were devoted patrons of the arts and sciences, with the exception of the last king, Attalus III, who in an act of extraordinary eccentricity

The Temple of Trajan dominates the acropolis of Pergamum (Bergama)

bequeathed his entire kingdom to Rome. Pergamum thenceforth became the capital of the Roman province of Asia, which stretched as far south as Caunus.

Beginning with Karl Humann in 1878, German excavators have reconstructed enough of the acropolis area to give an impression of how the upper city would have looked in its heyday during the reign of Eumenes II (179–59 BC). The most spectacular structure remains the theatre; with 80 rows of seats carved out of an exceptionally steep hillside, it is a remarkable piece of engineering. Unfortunately the striking reliefs on the Altar of Zeus, depicting the struggle between the gods and the Titans were removed by Humann to Berlin.

The lower terraces are best explored from the car park at the foot of the acropolis. Here is a vast gymnasium, the Temple of Demeter, and Hellenistic houses and shops on streets rutted by chariot wheels. The lowest part of the city is now largely covered by the bustling town of Bergama, which has an attractive old quarter and a small, but interesting, archaeological museum that exhibits some of the finds (*Open* daily except Mon 8.30–5.30). At the foot of the acropolis hill stands the colossal red brick shell of a Roman basilica, originally a temple to the Egyptian god Serapis, built in the reign of the emperor Hadrian (AD 117–38) and converted to a church by the Byzantines.

At the opposite end of the town is the Asklepeion, the foremost medical centre of the ancient world, founded primarily on the fame and reputation of Galen, the greatest physician and medical writer of late antiquity, born in Pergamum in AD 129. Treatments here included dieting, massages, mud baths, exercise and sleep therapy (doctors hypnotised their patients in preparation for a long untroubled rest in the Temple of Telesphorus.)

There are plenty of *pansiyons*, hotels and restaurants in Bergama, making an overnight stay an attractive possibility. You will then be able to enjoy unforgettable views of the setting sun from the Acropolis.

The sprawling ruins of the upper agora at Pergamum

▶ **Çandarlı** 98B2

This delightful little resort lies about 18km south of Dikili, close enough for the inhabitants of İzmir to visit on summer weekends. There are few reminders of its ancient history, when it was known as Pitane – today the dominant landmark, towering above the neat white houses, is a handsome restored castle, built originally by the Genoese in the 14th century. Çandarlı is an ideal place for strolling and relaxing: near the fishing harbour you'll find a variety of welcoming *lokantas*, bars and cafés, as well as a beach of coarse sand. The best *pansiyons* and hotels are also located on the waterfront, but note that many close between October and April. The commercial quarter is to the east of the castle. The main attraction here, apart from the even cheaper eateries, is the Friday market; there is also a bank and a Post Office (PTT).

105

Origin of books
Jealous of Pergamum's challenge to his cultural supremacy, Ptolemy, creator of the mighty library at Alexandria, banned the export of papyrus from Egypt. In response, the King of Pergamum ordered that animal skins should be used instead. The results came to be known as 'Pergamum books', from which the English word 'parchment' is derived. As the skins were too thick and heavy to be scrolled like papyrus, they were cut into pages which were laid on top of one another.

Old han and court-yard in the bazaar at İzmir

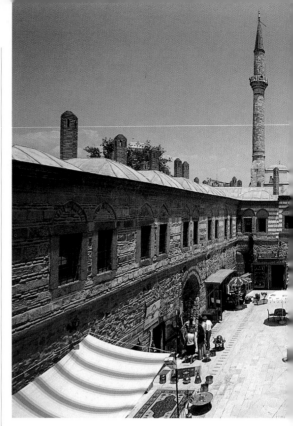

Hard to swallow
The famous Pramnian wine, described by Homer as the drink of heroes, is said to have come from his home town of Smyrna. Mixed with sea water or honey, chalk and powdered marble (thought to make it sweet), it must have been truly revolting in its original, undiluted state in order to have warranted such adulteration.

Cultural capital
İzmir has built quite a reputation for itself as Turkey's second cultural capital after Istanbul. The cultural centre hosts opera, theatre, ballet and concert performances, the high points of the season being the international arts festival in June and July and the international fair in August and September. Many of the events are staged in the beautiful Kültür Park in the city centre.

▶ **Çeşme Peninsula**   98A1

The biggest and most famous of the beach resorts around İzmir, Çeşme is an essentially Turkish resort and thermal spa (Çeşme means 'spring'), dominated by its 14th-century Genoese fortress. Behind is a labyrinth of twisting back streets, while the attractive promenade is lined with restaurants. The best local beaches are at Ilıca, Alaçatı and Altınkum, where you can rent kayaks or windsurf. From Çeşme ferries leave daily (Jul–Sep) for the Greek island of Chíos (Sakız), only 10km away and therefore an easy day trip.

▶▶ **İzmir (Smyrna)**   98B1

İzmir is the modern successor to Miletos and Ephesus as the major port of the Aegean; with a population well in excess of 2 million, it is also Turkey's third largest city after Istanbul and Ankara. The setting is dramatic: overlooking a magnificent bay, the buildings seem to be arranged in tiers ascending the mountain slopes. Overpopulated, lively, dusty and colourful, İzmir is a typically Levantine city; this is especially true of its old quarters, where little houses painted green, yellow, blue or ochre crowd together beneath red-tiled roofs. If you want to get away from the noise and bustle, stay in Foça to the north (see page 107) or Sığacık to the south (see page 110).

Earthquakes and a disastrous fire that swept through the city in 1922 during the War of Independence, have destroyed most of İzmir's buildings of historic interest. Even so, there are enough sights to keep most visitors

İZMİR (SMYRNA)

İzmir practicalities
İzmir's main tourist office is in the same building as the Grand Hotel Efes (Gaziosmanpaşa Bulvarı 1/D. Open daily 8.30–5.30). As the water around İzmir is still not clean enough to swim in, you may like to use the pool in the hotel, but be warned – it's very expensive. The offices of Turkish airlines, as well as a variety of coach tour operators and a PTT (post office) are near the hotel.

There is a good range of medium-price accommodation near the Basmane railway station: rooms vary considerably in size and quality so it's worth asking to see what's available before you commit yourself. İzmir's nightlife is centred on the waterfront bars and cafés on Atatürk Caddesi, popularly known as the Birinci Kordon. There are two or three streets of very tempting fish restaurants in nearby Alsancak, serving specialities such as lobster and sea bass.

occupied for a day or two. The ancient agora or market place (*Open* daily except Mon 8.30–12, 1.30–5.30) was founded by Alexander the Great in the 4th century BC but reconstructed by the Roman emperor Marcus Aurelius after an earthquake in AD 187. You can see artefacts from this site and others in the region in the excellent **Archaeological Museum** (*Open* daily except Mon 8.30–12.30, 1.30–5.30).

Today the ancient acropolis of Smyrna is crowned by a medieval castle known as Kadifekale (Velvet Fortress). From the battlements there are wonderful views of the town and harbour, especially at sunset. (Bus no. 33 from Konak takes about 20 minutes.) However, with its ornate clocktower and attractive mosque, Konak is the seafront area most visitors come to know best. From here you can take a short ferry ride to the opposite shore at Karşıyaka, where it is cooler and where you will find plenty of terrace bars and cafés as well as shops. Konak also has a small information office (look out for the blue signs). See panel for practical information about İzmir.

Very well placed for İzmir airport, the pretty fishing village of **Foça**, with its whitewashed houses and cobbled streets, has retained a Turkish feel. There are excellent seafood restaurants on the harbour front. Club Med has a village near by, but there are few hotels.

Weaving bags for visitors to Kadifekale Castle, İzmir

■ One of the greatest pleasures of taking a holiday in Turkey is the sheer variety of boating trips – anything from a short hop to the nearest beach to a cruise along the coast or even a leisurely outing to one of the Greek islands. ■

Day trips Many resorts on the Aegean and Mediterranean coasts offer boat trips exploring the neighbouring islands and beaches with stops for swimming and snorkelling. Itineraries are usually posted on the harbourfront; departure times are around 10–11am, returning between 5 and 6pm. Prices are very reasonable and usually include lunch on board. From Bodrum, for example, you could sail to Karaada (Black Island) for a mud bath in a grotto filled by warm mineral springs. Typical attractions elsewhere might include a scenic waterfall (Antalya), a ruined Greek church or two (Ayvalık) or the famous Ölüdeniz lagoon (Fethiye).

Island hopping The closest of the Greek Islands to the Turkish mainland are Lesbos (Lésvos) (reached from Ayvalık), Chíos (reached from Çeşme), Sámos (from Kuşadası) and Kos (from Bodrum). There are regular services in season and fares are reasonable. Tickets are usually sold on the harbourfronts.

Perhaps the most popular destination is the historic island of Rhodes (Ródos): there are daily sailings (except

The formalities
If you do intend to visit one of the Greek islands from Turkey, remember to allow for the cost of an additional visa for the return trip. You will need to register your passport with the Turkish authorities before you leave, usually the night before, so plan your journey well ahead.

A traditional gulet *makes a stop in Antalya harbour*

Sundays) from Marmaris, with a journey time of about two and a half hours, and there is enough to see to merit an overnight stay.

Blue cruising The Blue Cruise (in Turkish, Mavi Yolculuk) is the invention of the Turkish writer, Cevat Şakir Kabaağaçlı, who wrote an entertaining account of his adventures sailing around the Carian (southern Aegean) and Lycian (western Mediterranean) coastlines. Ever since, the book's title has been synonymous with cruising in the region. The traditional vessel for this kind of voyage is the *gulet* (from the Italian 'goletta'), a motor schooner built from the red pine wood found in profusion along Turkey's southern shore.

The main charter ports are Marmaris, Bodrum, Fethiye, Kalkan and Kaş. A *gulet* sleeps 8–12 people and children under 12 will be accommodated only if the entire boat has been booked by a single party. Most cabins are equipped with private shower and toilet, while hot water is supplied by an on-board generator. There is usually a cassette player available to while away the hours, so bring your own tapes. There may even be a windsurfing board or two. As space is at a premium, pack sparingly.

The captain will take suggestions on where to drop anchor – there is no shortage of secluded coves, sandy beaches and romantic ruins to hand. The other member of the crew, the cook, will cater for your menu preferences at breakfast and lunch – the evening meal is usually taken in a restaurant at the night's port of call.

Blue Cruise holidays can be booked through specialist tour operators – the local Turkish tourist office will supply you with a list of charter companies. Out of season (May, April and October) you may not have to book in advance, though expect to pay a hefty deposit. In high season (June to September) prices rise steeply.

A cruiseboat off the shore at Kale

Sortie to Turkish Cyprus
If you happen to be in the neighbourhood of Alanya or Taşucu, consider catching a boat to Girne (Kyrenia) on the northern coast of Cyprus: journey time from Alanya is 5 hours and from Taşucu 2 hours. Fares are cheap and no visa is required for US or EU citizens. The currency here is the Turkish *lira* and the cost of living is lower than on the mainland with car hire rates only a third of those in Turkey. The sights include the usual mix of Crusader castles, classical sites and Greek monasteries.

A Genoese fortress guards the harbour at Sığacık

Excavating a dream
The discovery of the site of ancient Troy became a romantic obsession for a 19th-century German businessman, Heinrich Schliemann. In 1870 he obtained permission to excavate here, using money he had amassed in the Californian goldrush. Schliemann devoted the next 20 years of his life to the excavations and was rewarded with the discovery of no fewer than four Troys, built one on top of the other. He also claimed to have uncovered the fabulous 'jewels of Helen', which he kept for his wife's use, eventually bequeathing them to the Berlin museum (they disappeared after the Russians entered the city in 1945 and were recently exhibited in Moscow). Despite his success, Schliemann never gained the acceptance he craved from the academic world, which scorned him as an amateur who had destroyed much valuable evidence.

► **Sığacık** 98B1

This little resort, 75 minutes' drive south of İzmir, sits on a headland on either side of which lies a small sheltered bay where there are hotels and camping. Sığacık has a ruined Genoese fortress rising above its little fishing harbour and yachting marina. Near by is the ancient site of Teos, picturesquely lost among the olive groves. For swimming, the clean white sands of Akkum are a short walk (1.5km) away.

► **Troy (Truva)** 98A2

Open: daily from 8.30 to sunset
According to Homer's famous epic poem the *Iliad*, Odysseus, having unsuccessfully laid siege to Ilium (Troy) for ten years, resorted to the stratagem of a wooden horse filled with soldiers. Tricked into believing that the horse was a gift from the gods, the Trojans opened the gates of the city; the Greeks emerged under cover of darkness and set upon them.

Troy is a city that lives in the imagination through Homer's tales in the *Iliad* and the *Odyssey*. To find that it is a real place may come as a surprise although, sadly, the once mighty capital of Helen and King Priam is today little more than a series of shapeless mounds and ditches with occasional outcrops of wall and foundation. The excavations that followed Schliemann's pioneering work (see panel) have uncovered nine major layers of habitation, although a total of 46 have been documented. The earliest, Troy I dates from the Bronze Age (3000–2500 BC) while the latest, Troy IX, is thought to be the Roman town Novum Ilium. The favoured contenders for Homer's city are Troy VI (1800–1275 BC) and Troy VIIa (1275–1240 BC). All the layers are clearly labelled and the recommended circuit is signposted. To help the imagination and to make up for the lack of exciting remains, the authorities have constructed an enormous wooden horse at the site entrance.

■ Turks love music, and you will be struck by the number of audio cassette shops offering a bewildering variety of styles. 'Arabesque' or taverna music is frequently to be heard in shops, teahouses and even on coaches, and live music is often played in restaurants, especially in the evenings. ■

Turkish folk music Apart from the special folkloric evenings held for tourists in cities, Turkish folk music is also still performed in its natural setting at village weddings or festivals, as an accompaniment to dancing mainly by segregated groups of men and women. A specialised style is *ozan*, the music of the folk poets or *aşık* ('those in love') of Anatolia, who accompany themselves on the *saz*, a kind of lute with three sets of strings. *Aşık* still wander the towns and villages of central Anatolia, and many of them – notably the blind *Aşık* Veysel, who died in 1973 – have recorded their music on cassette.

Kurdish folk music differs markedly from Turkish folk music: its *dengbeis* (bards), the best-known of whom are Sivan, Perwer and Temo, sing of Kurdish myths and legends and the Kurdish struggle for freedom, to the accompaniment of haunting wind instruments. In the cities you may hear *özgün*, the protest music of Turkey, sophisticated and quite addictive. The most impressive of *özgün* musicians is Livaneli, whose cassettes – some of them recorded with the famous Greek musician Theodorakis – are widely available.

Jazz renaissance
Istanbul has recently become a flourishing jazz centre, featuring performers of international stature as well as home-grown talent. An interesting new dimension is provided by Süleyman Erguner, who plays the *ney*, the traditional Ottoman reed flute, as part of his jazz set.

111

'Erotic whine'
Turkish music on the radio was described by Rose Macaulay as 'the eternal Turkish erotic whine'. 'The Tukish radio seems to love and cuddle and yearn without a break,' she continued, 'Turks being an excessively loving people...'

Traditional music still flourishes in Turkey

Turkish Ottoman and religious music The music of the Ottoman court can be heard on the radio or in concert, performed on traditional instruments such as the *ney* (a reed flute), the *tambur* (a lute) and the *kemençe* (a three-stringed fiddle held vertically). The dominant religious music of Turkey is that composed by the Mevlevi order of Whirling Dervishes. This mystical music performed on the *ney* and the *kudum* (small kettledrums) can be heard at the *semahane* ('dance room') in Galatasaray in Istanbul or at the annual Mevlana Festival in **Konya** (December).

SOUTH AEGEAN

REGION HIGHLIGHTS ◄ ◄ ◄ ◄

EXCURSION HIGHLIGHTS ◄ ◄ ◄ ◄

The South Aegean coast Resorts such as Bodrum, Marmaris and Kuşadası are now growing at an impressive, some would say alarming, rate. You can therefore expect fairly intensive development, especially near the shoreline, with high-rise hotels, holiday flats, yachting marinas, restaurants, discos and nightclubs – which is why the region is so popular with the young. Most of the best beaches lie outside the resorts themselves but are readily accessible by boat. Coaches link the main towns and introduce visitors to a countryside of gently rolling hills and fertile valleys with olive groves, vineyards, cypresses and pine trees, although the mountains are never far away. The most popular excursion is to Pamukkale, famous for its thermal springs and calcified rock formations, but Lake Bafa, beautifully situated near the foot of Mount Latmos, and the old Ottoman town of Muğla are also worth exploring. The South Aegean is rich in ancient sites: Ephesus, one of the largest and best-preserved in the world, should not be missed, and can easily be reached from Selçuk or Kuşadası.

Pages 112–13: cruising off the South Aegean coast
Below: the majestic Roman library of Celsus in Ephesus

The harbour at Marmaris in the early morning sunlight

The Crusader castle at Bodrum presides over the harbour

▶▶▶ **Bodrum (Halicarnassus)** 114B2

Reputedly the most upmarket and bohemian of Turkish resorts, Bodrum, with its pretty whitewashed houses and abundant flowers, has always attracted a discerning crowd. Despite the arrival of mass tourism in recent years (the population increases from 25,000 to around 400,000 in the summer), the town retains the atmosphere of a Turkish fishing village. The wonderful harbour and marina, crammed with sleek yachts and elegant wooden Turkish caiques, available for charter or daily hire, is also the yachting centre of the Aegean. While swimming at the small town beach is not recommended, *dolmuşes* (shared taxis) run regularly to the nearby beaches on the peninsula (see page 121). If you are touring, two nights are enough to sample the nightlife and restaurants and visit the castle. The tourist information office on İskele Meydanı has details of local ferry schedules – there are daily sailings to the Greek island of Kos, the secluded Datça Peninsula and Didyma (Altınkum beach). Bodrum is not a suitable base for visiting inland, however, as each outing involves an hour-long, winding drive across the peninsula to join the main coast road.

The castle Overlooking the harbour is the splendid Castle of St Peter, built by the Knights Hospitallers of St John in 1402, and one of the last and finest examples of Crusader architecture in the region. The knights occupied the fortress until 1523, when the capture of nearby Rhodes by Süleyman the Magnificent forced them to withdraw to Malta. The castle now houses the Museum of Underwater Archaeology (*Open* daily except Mon 9–7; 8–5 in winter). About 90 per cent of the exhibits, mostly amphorae, coins and jewellery, have been recovered from the sea by international teams of divers and the quest is continuing. Visitors can see the reconstructed stern of a 7th-century Byzantine ship, complete with galley and cargo of wine and, in the Glass Wreck Hall, the

Boat trips
There are plenty of opportunities for swimming around Bodrum if you take one of the boats that leave the west harbour every day at around 10am. (Lunch on board is included.) The itinerary usually takes in Akvaryum, which with its shoals of small fish is popular with snorkellers; Meteor, where you can dive from the cliff top into a deep crater; and Karaada (Black Island), famous for its hot springs and mud baths. See page 120 for diving outings.

actual remains of a trading vessel that sank in 1025 while on a voyage to the Black Sea (*Open* Tue–Fri 10–11, 2–4; separate entry charge). The cargo of glassware and some of the crew's personal effects, including combs, tools and games, have been preserved.

The Mausoleum *Bodrum* in Turkish means dungeon or subterranean vault, thought to be a reference to the magnificent tomb built for King Mausolus by his wife Artemisia in the 4th century BC, and renowned as one of the Seven Wonders of the World. Originally 39m long, 33m wide and 55m high, the world's first mausoleum survived until the 15th century when it was broken up by crusaders taking stone for Bodrum Castle – you can still see some of the marble fragments set into the walls. The foundations of the Mausoleum have been preserved (*Open* daily 8–5). Artists' models and drawings give visitors a good idea of what the monument would once have looked like.

Shopping and nightlife The main bazaar area, where you can shop until late at night, lies in the pedestrian precinct at the foot of the castle. Local specialities, sold in the bazaar and in the narrow streets around it, include natural sponges, soft cotton clothes and lapis lazuli beads to ward off the evil eye, along with an endless selection of carpets, jewellery, copper, ceramics, leather and embroidery.

Bodrum is justly renowned for its nightlife, with scores of bars, restaurants and nightclubs – most notably the Halikarnas on Cumhuriyet Caddesi, which puts on a laser show focused on the castle. Another enjoyable way to spend the evening is to dine out in one of the waterfront restaurants on Dr Alim Bey Caddesi, where the tables overlook the sea and the castle.

Suggested itinerary
One week, southern Aegean:
Dalaman
Dalyan, Bodrum,
Milas, Lake Bafa, Altınkum (good base)
Didyma, Miletos, Priene, Kuşadası (good base)
Ephesus, Kuşadası
Pamukkale
Muğla, Dalaman

Building ban
A five-year building ban has now been imposed to halt further development in Bodrum and to ensure the preservation of its unique townscape of low-rise whitewashed buildings, with their blue shutters and tumbling bougainvillaea.

117

Dining out with views of the sea is an experience not to be missed in Bodrum

Cinema

■ **Turkish cinema audiences have traditionally enjoyed cloyingly romantic tales and adventure stories featuring crudely drawn heroes and villains. In the 1970s, however, a new generation of directors appeared on the scene, committed to exploring subjects of greater social relevance, such as the impact of the rural population drift to the cities and the breakdown of traditional values and lifestyles.** ■

Yılmaz Güney By far the best-known of these directors, and possibly the only one to have established an international reputation, is Yılmaz Güney. He produced his first major film in 1970: called *Umut* (*Hope*), it is the tale of a desperate and gullible taxi driver who loses his house, his horse, and finally his mind. The final scene, in which the blindfolded hero circles a hole in the ground to the accompaniment of haunting music played on the reed flute, makes an unforgettable impression.

The following year Güney made two more films, *Ağıt* (*The Elegy*), about a man driven by abject poverty to smuggling, and *Acık* (*Sorrow*) on the subject of lost love and revenge. In 1974 Güney was arrested on the charge of murdering a judge and it was during his imprisonment that he managed to produce his best work, writing scripts in his cell and passing them out secretly to friends, along with exact instructions on how to film each scene. These scripts tended to revolve around Güney's abiding interest, the problems of the rural poor.

Turkey's most controversial and best-known film director, Yılmaz Güney

1979 saw the release of *Sürü* (*The Herd*), directed in Güney's absence by Zeki Ökten, which follows a Kurdish family taking their sheep to market in Ankara and revealing their total bewilderment at the world in which they find themselves.

Şerif Gören directed Güney's most famous film, *Yol* (*The Road*), which was finally released in 1982. It follows the fortunes of five prisoners allowed out on parole for one week, each of whom encounters a changed and alien world and finally meets with tragedy. These reflections on life outside prison seemed to have inspired Güney who escaped from jail and was able to edit the film himself while in exile in France. He died of cancer aged 46.

New developments Political turbulence and censorship imposed severe restrictions on Turkish cinema in the late

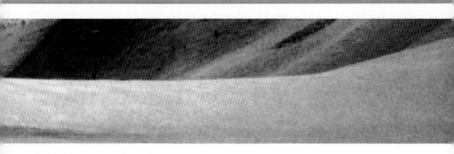

1970s and 1980s, but a few notable films did nevertheless emerge. One of these, *A Season in Hakkari* by Erden Kıral, was a West German co-production and follows the experiences of a young schoolteacher sent to work in a remote Kurdish village.

Other subjects treated for the first time during this period include the situation of women in Turkish society, social hypocrisy, and the problems faced by migrant workers in Germany. Of these the best is *Forty Square Metres of Germany*, directed by Tevfik Başar and released in 1986.

Recently, leading Turkish directors have become still more daring in testing the confines of censorship. Reis Çelik's *The Lights Must Not Go Out*, released in 1996, tackles that most contentious of all contemporary subjects, the secret wars against the Kurds.

Censorship
Censorship is fairly strict in Turkey and many films are banned for being too sexually, or politically, explicit. Turkish filmmakers face the same constraints, with the result that they are often obliged to deal with their subjects obliquely, using allegorical characters and plots.

119

Sürü (The Herd) follows the fortunes of a Kurdish family taking its sheep to market in Ankara

Modest beginnings
Turkish cinema began in 1897 in the Beyoğlu district of Istanbul when Sigmund Weinberg, a Romanian café owner, put on a film show for the benefit of his customers. Until World War I there were no cinemas catering for Muslims in Turkey, so most of the early audiences were made up of foreigners. The first independent film company was set up in 1922 to make mainly patriotic films.

Diving outings
Diving has recently become a popular way of exploring the reefs near Bodrum, with their caves and unusual rock formations. Day outings, with transport and a picnic, can be arranged through Era Turizm or Crystal Diving Center. A popular spot is the Akvaryum in the Ada Boğazı (Island Strait), where the water is unusually clear and fish are abundant.

Two in one
Bardakçi, on the Bodrum peninsula, claims to be the site of the ancient fountain where, according to the Roman poet Ovid, Hermaphroditus, son of Hermes and Aphrodite, became so enamoured of his own reflection in the clear pool that he rejected the advances of the water nymph Salmacis. The gods then answered her prayer that their bodies be joined in one for ever, making the Hermaphrodite.

Soaking up the sun on Karaincir (Black Fig) beach

►► **Bodrum peninsula**   *114B2*

Water sports, including swimming, water skiing, diving, windsurfing and canoeing are well catered for in the attractive resorts of this charming peninsula. Despite the modern encroachment of hotels and holiday villages, the area remains defiantly unspoilt with white stone houses, dilapidated churches, Ottoman defences and even camel caravans. The landscape is rugged and hilly with stretches of pine forest and numerous sheltered bays.

On the southern coast, Karaincir (Black Fig) has more than 600m of sandy beach, where canoeing and windsurfing are the main attractions. Just a stone's throw away is the picturesque fishing village of Akyarlar, where there are some excellent, reasonably priced restaurants. Closer to Bodrum, Bitez is favoured by yachtsmen and windsurfers. For swimmers there are better beaches near Ortakent and around Bağla, Yahşi Yalı and Kargı, where you can ride a camel along the sand. Turgutreis, the main resort on the west side of the peninsula has little character and not much of a beach, although there are some good waterfront restaurants. Just a few kilometres to the north, Kadıkalesi offers excellent white sands overlooked by a deserted Greek church. Cars are banned from the beautiful and quite unspoilt village of Gümüşlük, site of ancient Myndos. Some of the ruins are underwater and you can explore them or climb over the headland before returning for an evening meal on the harbourfront (the last *dolmuş* to Bodrum leaves at midnight). The drive from Bodrum to the north coast offers some of the most spectacular scenery on the peninsula although the main resort, the fishing port of Yalıkavak, is gradually being overwhelmed by tourism. Swimming is possible at Gündoğan, Türkbükü, Torba and several other points, but decent beaches are few and far between. The most appealing resort is Gölköy, where traditional village life goes on largely impervious to the changes around it.

▶▶ Dalyan (Kaunos) 114C2

Charmingly situated on the banks of the Dalyan Çayı, near the mouth of the freshwater Lake Köyceğiz, Dalyan has escaped the worst excesses of tourist development, and offers a small but growing selection of hotels, bars and restaurants. Most of the best *pansiyons* are located just south of the town centre along Maraş (İskele) Caddesi, where you will also find the tourist information office.

River *dolmuşes* depart every day from about 9 for İstuzu beach, returning at approximately half-hourly intervals during the afternoon. Alternatively, you can take a day cruise, stopping off at İztuzu beach, the ancient ruins of Kaunos and the thermal springs (see below). If you are with a group of more than eight people, it's even possible to hire your own boat. More energetic travellers may prefer to rent a mountain bike from one of the main hotels and take the land route.

Dalyan environs

İstuzu beach▶▶ is famous throughout Turkey as the main nesting ground of the loggerhead turtle (see panel). The 5km-long stretch of sandy beach also has excellent swimming. It is particularly suitable for children although there's little shade – bring hats and plenty of sunscreen with you. There's also not much in the way of food here, so a picnic may also be a good idea.

The ancient city of **Kaunos▶** flourished in the 4th century BC under the Hellenising influence of King Mausolus. Malaria claimed the lives of many of its citizens, and mosquitoes are still a nuisance today so bring repellent. You can see the remains of the defensive walls, a well-preserved theatre (2nd century BC), an enormous Roman baths and a Byzantine basilica. You may also come across storks, herons, flamingoes, tortoises, lizards – and snakes.

The **thermal springs** at Ilıca will allow you to wallow in mud that reaches a temperature of about 40°C. The baths at Sultaniye are less accessible but also less crowded.

Lycian rock tombs at Kaunos

Turtle sanctuary
Dalyan is famous for its loggerhead turtles (*Caretta caretta*), which hatch on İstuzu beach between May and October. The beach is now protected by wardens and all building projects have been banned; it is thought that the lights of restaurants and hotels confuse the young, luring them to the shore rather than the safety of the sea.

Enjoying the hot mud springs near Dalyan

The Curetes Way, one of the main thoroughfares of ancient Ephesus

▶▶▶ Efes (Ephesus) 114B3

One of the best-preserved ancient cities in the Mediterranean region, Ephesus ranks as Turkey's most popular tourist destination outside Istanbul. The extensive archaeological site is within walking distance (3km) of **Selçuk**, where you will find plenty of restaurants and reasonably priced accommodation. There are cafés and souvenir stalls at the site (*Open* daily 8.00–6.30; 5.30 in winter) but precious little shade – bring a bottle of water and arrive as early in the day as possible.

In Roman times, Ephesus was the capital of Asia Minor and one of the leading cities of the empire, with a population of 250,000. From the middle of the 1st century AD it was also an important centre of Christianity: St John the Evangelist visited, and then St Paul, whose preaching against the cult of Artemis provoked a riot. At that time the harbour was clearly visible from the theatre, but continual silting destroyed the port and, with it, the city's commercial viability.

The site The road from Selçuk passes the rather forlorn ruins of the Temple of Artemis, once one of the Seven Wonders of the World. From around 1000 BC the Artemision was the centre of the cult of the Anatolian mother-goddess also known as Cybele.

Beyond the ticket office are the remains of the Harbour Baths, whose hypocaust (heating system) is still visible. Follow the path to the right for the curiously elongated, 2nd-century AD Church of the Virgin Mary.

The road from the harbour to the theatre, known as the Arcadian Way, was lined with shops and illuminated by oil lamps at night. Cleopatra took this route when she entered Ephesus in triumph to visit her lover, Mark Antony. Built into the hillside, the theatre, with seating for 24,000 spectators, was completed early in the 2nd century AD in the

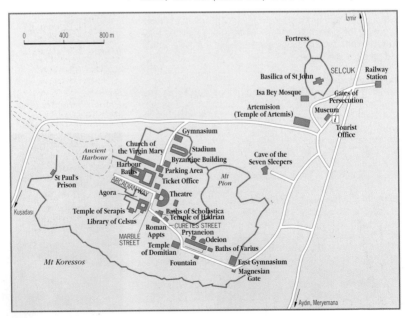

EFES (EPHESUS)

Mary's House
In the hills some 8km from Ephesus lies the little chapel known as Meryemana, where the Virgin Mary is said to have lived her last days. The house was 'discovered' early in the 19th century by a German invalid, Catherine Emmerich, who saw it in a vision (she had never actually set foot in Turkey). A priest from İzmir read her description of the location and it subsequently became a place of pilgrimage. In 1967 Pope Paul VI visited the site and solemnly authenticated the site.

A statue of Arethe (Goodness) in a niche on the façade of the Library of Celsus. The library has recently been restored with the assistance of the Austrian Archaeological Institute

reign of the Emperor Trajan. Explore the ruined stage area and the cavernous entrances before climbing the tiers of seats for a commanding view of the entire site.

Running at right angles to the Arcadian Way is Marble Street, where you will see a large footprint with a heart and a woman's head, pointing the way to the city brothel. Beyond the agora (market place) is the stupendous, two-storey façade of the Library of Celsus, the best-preserved structure of its kind in the world. The greatest philosophers of the age gave lectures in the auditorium here.

From the library, Curetes (Priests') Street snakes over the hill towards the Magnesian Gate. On the opposite corner, the main hall of the brothel is decorated with mosaic fragments depicting the four seasons; while near by are the public latrines where today's visitors still queue up to try out the stone seats! A Medusa's head wards off evil spirits over an arch in the Temple of Hadrian – the remarkable mosaic in front of the temple dates from the 5th century AD when the neighbouring baths were restored. The most impressive monument on the upper reaches of Curetes Street is the Odeion or council chamber. You can gain an insight into daily life in Ephesus by visiting the Museum of Inscriptions (*Open* daily 8–5. *Admission* free). Many of the original statues and friezes from the site are now displayed in the Selçuk Museum.

A modern red-brick structure protects the well-preserved remains of several Ephesian villas from the elements. To see the mosaic floors and beautiful wall frescoes you need special permission from the curator at the Selçuk Museum.

The big sleep
Just outside Ephesus is the Cave of the Seven Sleepers where, according to legend, seven local Christians took shelter during the Decian persecution in the 2nd century AD. The cave was walled up by Roman soldiers and the young men fell into a deep sleep. When the entrance was shattered by an earthquake two centuries later, the youths awoke to discover that Ephesus was now a Christian city. After their deaths they were reburied in the grotto and a shrine was built over their graves.

Walk **Alinda**

The impressive hilltop ruins of the ancient Greek city of Alinda, where Alexander the Great once stayed, are an easy day trip from Bodrum, Marmaris, Kuşadası or even İzmir, with a chance to see some beautiful inland scenery.

The remains of Alinda, unquestionably among the finest in the area, are rarely visited as they lie rather off the beaten track. The modern town at the foot of the hill is Karpuzlu, 25km off the main Aydın to Muğla highway. The walk up to the site is quite steep and takes about 90 minutes, but you can drive to the summit if you prefer.

In Karpuzlu, take the busy market street; at the end, a small blue sign marked 'Alinda' points up a winding track. Follow this and park at the side of the road on the edge of town, looking out for a small path to the right that zigzags up past the final group of houses.

After a few minutes' walk you will arrive at the agora (market place) at the end of which is a three-storey trading hall; vast and impressive, it is the best-preserved building of its kind in Asia Minor, evoking the experience of ancient Greek shopping more

vividly than any other structure.

From here a steep and slippery path climbs to a hollow in the hillside where the heavily overgrown theatre looks out over the town. Characteristic vaulted entrance passages added by the Romans have survived intact, as has much of the stage building. There are excellent views of the superb defensive walls.

An energetic half-hour scramble will take you to the Hellenistic tower on the summit. Alternatively, you can return to the car and drive up the track to the well-preserved arches of an aqueduct, a good picnic spot with

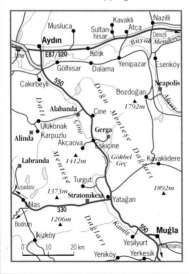

fine views. Beyond, a small path leads to the main acropolis of Alinda. Here are the foundations of what were probably the royal apartments of Queen Ada, exiled to Alinda in a power struggle with her own family. When Alexander the Great swept through Asia Minor in 333 BC, she conspired with him in laying siege to Halicarnassus (modern Bodrum), where her younger brother was ruler. After the success of their campaign, Alexander brought Ada out of exile and proclaimed her Queen of Caria.

Back at the car, it is worth taking time to explore the derelict houses on the outskirts of the town, some whitewashed with blue shutters, others with wooden overhanging balconies and courtyards littered with carved blocks from the ancient ruins.

Only a short drive from the coast, Alinda offers well-preserved ancient ruins as well as superb views across the surrounding countryside

► **Ionian cities** *114B2*

First settled by the Ionian Greeks in the 12th century BC, the Aegean coastline, from the island of Samos in the north to the River Meander in the south, witnessed a great flowering of culture in the 6th and 7th centuries BC. Most of the 12 wealthy ports that formed the Ionian League have long disappeared, but the sites of **Ephesus** (see pages 122–3), **Priene**, **Miletus** and the ancient shrine at **Didyma** hint at the size and importance of these cities. Day tours from Selçuk, Milas and Bodrum usually take in the three sites below as well as a stop at Altınkum beach.

Priene► Best preserved of all the classical Greek cities, with a spectacular setting on the slopes of Mount Mycale, Priene dates from the 4th century BC. Once a flourishing port on the Meander delta, it now languishes a full 15km away from the Aegean. A steepish 10-minute climb leads from the ticket kiosk (*Open* daily 8.30 to sunset) to the ancient city centre. The most impressive sight is the Temple of Athena, where five of the original 30 Ionic columns have recently been re-erected. Designed by Pythius, a builder of the Mausoleum at Halicarnassus, the temple was erected in the third quarter of the 3rd century BC and was regarded as the ideal Ionic temple, a model for other architects. The theatre is also remarkable, with an orchestra that is horseshoe-shaped rather than circular, allowing for a broader stage. The auditorium was also used for assemblies, when civic dignitaries would occupy the five marble seats in the front row.

Milet (Miletos)► Once the most important Greek city in the region, ancient Milet was marooned by the retreating sea. Today, the magnificent theatre rises from the river plain, from where there is a good view of the site and its orderly grid layout, typical of Greek town planning. Among the monuments are a nymphaeum (monumental foun-

Only five columns now stand in the Temple of Athena at Priene

tain) and a 28m-wide processional way with an agora (market place) on one side and a baths and gymnasium on the other. The outline of the two ancient harbours is also clearly visible. Much of this area is marshy or even under water, and a raised dirt track has been constructed to give easier access (bring mosquito repellent). The ticket kiosk (*Open* daily 8.30 to sunset) is in front of the theatre.

Didyma► (*Open* daily 8.30–5.30) The ruins of the oracle temple of Apollo, the third largest edifice in the entire Greek world, are at their most impressive in the late afternoon when the soft rays of the setting sun illuminate the columns and the sheer scale of the building can best be appreciated. Steep steps lead to the main platform, over 109m long and 51m wide. It was originally graced by 120 colossal columns, 103 of which survive, many with decorated bases and capitals. A remarkable survivor from the 1st century BC frieze is the huge cracked head of Medusa. In Hellenistic times the Temple of Apollo was even more celebrated than its namesake at Delphi. Before issuing a prophecy, an oracle priestess was said to fast for three days before inhaling the sulphur fumes from the spring until she swooned in a state of divine inspiration. Her utterances were then translated into hexameter verse by the oracle priests.

There are shops and restaurants by the site entrance.

Beyond the neighbouring town of Yenihisar lies the beautiful but crowded Altınkum (Golden Sand) beach. It is popular with Turks, so accommodation gets booked up.

> **End of an era**
> The spread of Christianity led to the end of the oracle tradition. In AD 385 Emperor Theodosius announced that 'No mortal man shall have the effrontery to encourage vain hopes by the inspection of entrails, or, which is worse, to attempt to learn the future by the detestable consultation of oracles'.

The giant Medusa's head at Didyma is a logo for the site

A view of Bird Island, from which Kuşadası takes its name

►► Kuşadası (Bird Island) 114B2

Kuşadası is arguably the most overdeveloped resort in the Aegean. That said, its location makes it a good base for excursions to Ephesus and other classical sites, while the town itself offers the usual variety of seaside activities, from swimming and water skiing to scuba diving and sailing out of the new, well-equipped yachting marina. Kuşadası takes its name from an island in the bay, now linked to the mainland by a concrete causeway – enterprising local businessmen have converted the Genoese castle into discos and cafés. Another focal point for nightlife and entertainment (Kuşadası's strong suit) is the legendary Barlar Sokak 'Bar Street', where you will find every conceivable kind of bar from the traditional English 'Queen Vic' pub, to Irish, German, Turkish and even 'Extraterrestial' variants. Restaurants cluster around İnönü Bulvarı and along the seafront. Kuşadası has a good selection of shops, but prices are on the steep side – for jewellery and clothing bargains the best bet is the bazaar. The public beach in the main bay is very overcrowded in season and, in any case, the sandy **Kadınlar Plajı** (Ladies' Beach) 3km away is preferable; an alternative is **Pamucak** 15km to the north. In summer there are daily sailings (including day excursions) to the Greek island of **Sámos**, departing from İskele Meydanı.

Kuşadası environs

See pages 122–3 for **Ephesus►►►**, pages 126–7 for the Ionian cities►, and pages 130–1 for **Lake Bafa►**.
Dilek Yarımadası National Park► lies at the southern end of Kuşadası Bay and provides a welcome relief from the noise and commotion of the resort. Parts of the park are closed to protect wildlife, but there are restful forest walks and several beautiful unspoilt beaches. For those who decide to stay here, there are holiday villas and a couple of hotels in the village of **Güzelçamlı** at the edge of the reserve. All the usual water sports are available from the pebbled beach.

►► Marmaris *114B2*

This sprawling resort sits in a vast, almost landlocked bay reminiscent of a fjord and boasts the largest yachting marina in Turkey. The tourist information office situated on İskele Meydanı, below the crumbling Ottoman castle, will help with accommodation.

Unfortunately there is not much in the way of cheap *pansiyons* in Marmaris itself; most of the larger hotel complexes are located in the extensive suburb of İçmeler or on Uzunyalı Street.

In the older part of town (Kaleiçi), the colourful streets of the pedestrianised bazaar are crammed with restaurants, shops and cafés. You will be tempted by the delicious local honey on sale here, as well as the usual range of Turkish crafts. Leading from the bazaar towards the marina is Hacı Mustafa Sokağı, known locally (for obvious reasons) as the Street of Bars. Rather than swim in the polluted waters of the town beach, you may prefer to take a boat trip to the coves at **Kumlubükü** or **Turunç** or go diving. (Ask about diving schools at the tourist information office.)

A daily ferry and hydrofoil serves the Greek island of Rhodes (Ródos) (journey time 2–3 hours).

Marmaris environs

The harbours of the Daraya peninsula south of Marmaris (at **Orhaniye**, **Selimiye** and **Bozburun**) are popular with *gulet* cruisers, who stop for lunch at the tantalising fish restaurants. The main port of the Reşadiye peninsula to the west is **Datça►** (an official port of entry to Turkey). From here minibuses run to Marmaris and Muğla and there are ferry departures to Bodrum. A small town with limited accommodation, bars and restaurants, Datça is generally cheaper than its larger more popular neighbours. Its two beaches can be very crowded but, as elsewhere, there are boat trips to quieter, more secluded spots along the coast. (See **Knidos**, page 133.)

Festivals
There are two red-letter days for yachting enthusiasts in Marmaris. The Marmaris yacht festival, usually held in the second week of May, is a gathering of owners and enthusiasts around the harbour and marina area. The yachting fraternity reappears in all its glory during Race Week, at the end of October, when the harbour is once again a hive of boating activity. For further details contact Marmaris International Yacht Club (252 412 3835).

Enjoying a smoke in the Marmaris Bazaar. Meerschaum clay, found in Turkey, gives its name to all pipes sold in the region.

Drive Kuşadası or Bodrum to Lake Bafa and Heracleia

An exhilarating day trip from either Kuşadası or Bodrum, this drive offers the chance to enjoy the charming lakeside setting of Bafa, sample its fish, swim in its waters, and explore the romantic ruined city of Heracleia ad Latmos.

From Bodrum, Lake Bafa is a 90-minute drive (107km), and from Kuşadası, about one hour (83km). The main highway skirts the southern shore of the lake, passing a cluster of simple restaurants and a campsite/motel. Lunch can be taken here or at a restaurant on the opposite shore, below Heracleia ad Latmos itself; the local fish is excellent.

At the village of Çamiçi a yellow sign points left to Heracleia (9km). The narrow track winds back to the eastern lake shore, where the ancient ruins lie in their dramatic setting beneath Mount Latmos (1500m). The mystery and charm of the lake are enhanced by the remains of Byzantine churches and monasteries on the scattered islets. Over the centuries a number of religious communities sought refuge from persecution here, but the buildings fell into ruin after the Turkish conquest. By the restaurant at the foot of the site it is just possible to swim through the reeds to the nearest island.

In antiquity Heracleia was a coastal town and Lake Bafa, now a freshwater lake, was an inlet of the Aegean, later cut off by the silting up of the Meander river. From 300 BC Heracleia was enclosed by extensive

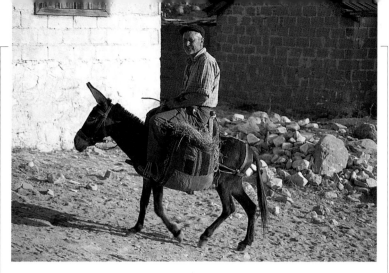

defence walls, which are still its most remarkable feature: they climb 6.5km to a ridge some 500m up the slopes of Mount Latmos. Many of the towers, windows, gates and stairways leading to the parapets are in excellent condition even today.

Below left: the ancient town of Heracleia beside Lake Bafa, where transport (above) is not a problem for the local people

According to legend, this is the spot where the handsome demi-god Endymion was sleeping when the moon goddess, Selene, fell in love with him. Zeus, jealous of a rumoured amour between Endymion and his own wife, Hera, decreed that he should sleep for ever on Mount Latmos; while Endymion dreamed, Selene slept with him and bore him 50 daughters. In Christian times Endymion was adopted as a local mystic saint, and his sanctuary can still be seen to the right of the road as you approach. Walk on beyond it to the ruins of a fortified Byzantine monastery on the headland.

Returning to the centre of ancient Heracleia, you will come across its most prominent monument, the Temple of Athena, a simple edifice with beautifully crafted masonry walls perched on a promontory. Inland from this lies the agora (market place), where the school of the adjacent village of Kapıkırı now stands. On the south side of the agora is a well-preserved market building, divided into shops. A little further inland is the romantically dilapidated bouleuterion, or council chamber, set in trees on the edge of the village. About 300m away is a Roman theatre, and there are other ruins from the same period, including a baths, dotted over the hillside.

▶ **Milas (Mylasa)** *114B2*

You are most likely to encounter this busy market town *en route* to Bodrum. Its modern appearance is misleading as this was an important centre of the ancient Carian civilisation. On the western outskirts of town is the large Roman mausoleum known as Gümüşkesen, thought to be a scaled-down replica of the famous **Mausoleum of Halicarnassus** (see page 117). Carpets are traditionally sold in the market on Hisarbaşı Hill, where you can also see an 18th-century caravanserai (inn), one of the few still functioning in western Turkey. The Firuz Bey mosque at the foot of the hill was built in 1394 using pinkish marble blocks from neighbouring Greek ruins. Milas's splendid castle, Peçin Kale, is Byzantine in origin but was adapted by the 14th-century Menteşe emirs (*Open* daily 8 to sunset). Within the small walled citadel are some old houses, a *medrese* (theological school) and a mosque.

Milas environs

For **Lake Bafa**▶ see pages 130–1.
Excursions go from Milas through the pine hills to the 'carpet villages' of Mumcular, Bozalan, Mezget, Etrim and Çömlekçi, where you can watch weavers making the traditional Milas carpets, recognisable for their muted colours and geometric patterns. You may even buy one.

▶ **Muğla** *114C2*

This large town, capital of Muğla province, still retains an attractive Ottoman quarter with picturesque winding streets and a flourishing bazaar where the old Yağcılar Hanı has been converted into a smart shopping centre and the Konakaltı Hanı serves as an art gallery. If you want accommodation, ask at the tourist information office, opposite Atatürk's statue on Cumhuriyet Meydanı.

Muğla environs

For **Alinda**▶▶ see pages 124–5.
The sandy beaches and clear waters of **Akyaka**▶, a small resort in Gökova Bay are a magnet for the more discerning tourist. There are a few restaurants, *pansiyons* and campsites set against a backdrop of thick pine forests. There are regular *dolmuş* services from here to Muğla.

Labranda
Set high in the hills above Milas is Labranda, the site of a sanctuary to Zeus, originally joined to ancient Mylasa by a paved sacred way. Athletics competitions and other festivals were once held here and the remains of a stadium have recently been located. The ruins of the sanctuary are impressive, with gateways, monumental tombs and baths. One of the buildings is thought to have contained a sacred pool where the fish were adorned with necklaces and gold earrings. They were consulted in the manner of an oracle – if the fish ate the morsels of food thrown to them, the answer was 'yes'.

Men playing dominoes in a bar in Muğla

Drive & boat trip
Marmaris to Knidos

This excursion follows a scenic route from Marmaris to the tip of the Reşadiye peninsula, where you can lunch at one of Palamutbükü's charming fish restaurants, explore the atmospheric ruins of Knidos and swim in the sheltered headland bay.

The drive to **Datça** takes about an hour. Leaving Marmaris, the road winds over densely wooded hills with spectacular hairpin bends and perpendicular precipices, then descends through lush, fertile meadows, planted with almond and olive groves, to the small resort of **Datça** (see page 129). The road to **Knidos** becomes little more than a rough track at this point so it is advisable to complete the journey by sea. You can charter a boat direct to Knidos or join an excursion from Datça harbourfront, departing between 9 and 9.30 and

Knidos' romantic, windswept ruins

returning 5–5.30 and including a stop for lunch at Palamut Bükü. Either way, you can enjoy a swim in one of the many coves *en route*.

The boat anchors in one of Knidos' windswept twin harbours. Founded in 400 BC, this ancient city was one of the most prosperous in antiquity. Its great claim to fame was the statue of the goddess Aphrodite, thought to be the first free-standing image of a naked woman in Greece.

The ruins are scattered over a large area, from the necropolis on the hillside to the harbour, where part of the lighthouse has survived. There are wonderful views of the Aegean from the theatre. The round base stones of the Temple of Aphrodite were discovered in 1969 by the aptly named American archaeologist, Dr Iris Love.

Pamukkale's unique calcified water basins

▶▶▶ **Pamukkale** *114C3*

A unique natural phenomenon, the thermal spa at Pamukkale – the name means 'cotton castle' – has left an unforgettable impression on visitors since Roman times. For more than 14,000 years, hot spring water has been flowing over the edge of a plateau, 150m above the Lycos valley. It leaves behind solid deposits of calcium carbonate (travertines), creating fantastic rock formations: stalactites, cataracts and basins, which take on different hues according to the light; sunsets, in particular, can be spectacular.

The remaining hotels on the terraces and those at nearby Karahayit Köyü tend to fill with group bookings in summer, but there is plenty of alternative accommodation in Pamukkale Köyü, the town at the foot of the cliffs, where you will also find a rather tacky assortment of restaurants, carpet shops, souvenir stalls and discos. There is a regular *dolmuş* service from Pamukkale Köyü to the springs. The tourist information office is near the

Fury of the dead
Many of the tombs in the necropolis at Hierapolis bear inscriptions in the form of curses, including this particularly all-embracing example: 'May he who commits transgression, and he who incites thereto, have no joy of life or children; may he find no land to tread nor sea to sail, but, childless and destitute, crippled by every form of affliction, let him perish, and after death may he meet the wrath and the vengeance of the gods below. And the same curses on those who fail to prosecute him.'

The wonderfully preserved Roman theatre at Hierapolis

coach park (*Open* daily 8–noon, 1.30–7; 1.30–5 in winter).

Because of potential damage to the travertines, visitors are now forbidden to bathe in the rock pools themselves. The most popular alternative is the Pamukkale Motel where the floor of the swimming pool is strewn with broken marble columns, a reminder that this was once a sacred Roman site. If you are unable to get in here, there are one or two other hotel pools near by, also fed by the springs, and several thermal pools at the new Karahayit hotels. The health-giving waters are said to be particularly beneficial for those with heart and circulation complaints, as well as digestive, rheumatic and kidney disorders.

From the earliest times, Pamukkale's hot springs were credited with religious and mystical qualities, which is why the city of Hierapolis (Holy City) grew up here in antiquity. The major monument, in terms of size, is the large Roman theatre with its well-preserved stage building. Beyond this, the road leads through the monumental northern gateway to the vast necropolis, one of the most extensive in all Asia Minor, with over 1,200 sarcophagi.

►► Selçuk   114B3

This unassuming agricultural town, where tractors outnumber cars on the country lanes leading to the cotton and tobacco fields, owes its recent growth as a tourist centre to the proximity of ancient **Ephesus** (see pages 122–3). Selçuk is well provided with reasonably priced *pansiyons* and the helpful tourist information office on Atatürk Caddesi, near the bus station, has lists of accommodation in all categories. The centre of town is Cengiz Topel Caddesi, a pedestrianised street where you will find a PTT (Post Office), carpet and souvenir shops, and any number of welcoming terrace restaurants. Storks nest in the ruined Byzantine aqueduct at one end, while the other leads to Selçuk's ancient heart, Ayasoluk Hill, first settled around 2000 BC. The impressive citadel was reconstructed in the Middle Ages by the Seljuk rulers who gave the town its name. Just below are the remains of St John's Basilica (*Open* daily 8–6), commissioned in the 6th century by the Byzantine Emperor Justinian and built over the tomb of St John the Evangelist. Crowned with six cupolas, each 29m high, this was once the seventh largest church in Christendom. Lying in the river valley to the west is the **Artemision** (see page 122) and the pre-Ottoman İsa Bey mosque, currently closed to the public.

No one should leave Selçuk without visiting the excellent **Ephesus Museum** (*Open* Tue–Sun 8.30–noon, 1–7). The numerous artefacts recovered from the site offer a vivid insight into everyday life in this sophisticated Roman port city. The finds range from exquisite bronze statuettes to early Christian amulets and toys. The most remarkable exhibit, however, is the statue of the great Artemis, dating from the 1st century AD.

Noxious grotto
The infamous Plutonium Grotto lies in a chamber below the Temple of Apollo. The noxious fumes here were said by ancient historians, such as Strabo, to kill anyone who breathed them. The exception to the rule, according to another historian Dio Cassius, were eunuchs who were able to enter the grotto unscathed as they were particularly good at holding their breath! When the grotto was rediscovered by Italian archaeologists in 1957, the foul fumes seriously impeded their excavations, although no deaths were reported.

Akhan
Just 1km after the turn-off to Pamukkale on the road east towards Dinar an impressive Seljuk caravanserai, faced in pinkish marble, offers traditional overnight accommodation for travelling merchants. There are at least 50 of these handsome Seljuk *hans* on the main trade routes of central Anatolia, all built in the 13th century when the Seljuk Turks were the dominant power in the region.

The marble statue of the fertility goddess Artemis Ephesia, in the museum at Selçuk. The egg-like protrusions on her breasts represent bulls' testes

WEST MEDITERRANEAN

REGION HIGHLIGHTS ◄◄◄◄◄

EXCURSION HIGHLIGHTS ◄◄◄◄◄

WEST MEDITERRANEAN

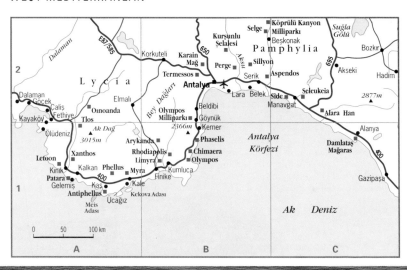

The West Mediterranean coast Served by the airports at Antalya and Adana, the western Mediterranean is popularly known from the colour of the sea as the Turquoise Coast. It is, indisputably, one of the most beautiful stretches of coastline anywhere in Turkey, with dramatic mountain scenery and glorious beaches, including the enchanting Ölüdeniz (Dead Lagoon), near Fethiye.

Apart from Fethiye, the main resorts are Kemer, Kalkan, Kaş, Antalya, Side and Alanya. Fortunately, tourist development is still relatively small-scale with the emphasis on family-run *pansiyons* and modest-sized hotels. The tarmac coast road was not completed until 1981, so the region's charms have only fairly recently become accessible to all comers. To cater for the increasing number of visitors choosing to arrive by sea, there are yachting marinas in almost every town.

Antalya, the premier resort on the south coast is Turkey's fastest growing city, with a permanent population of 500,000 that almost doubles in summer with the annual influx of tourists.

Pages 136–7: a beach on the west Mediterranean coast

Kaputaş beach, near Kalkan, is easily accessible by boat

WEST MEDITERRANEAN

The famous Red Tower at Alanya has stood guard over the promontory for more than 700 years

Suggested Itinerary:
Two weeks, western
Mediterranean:
Antalya
Side
Alanya
Antalya (Termessos)
Kemer
Finike
Kaş
Kalkan (Xanthos)
Ölüdeniz
Fethiye
Dalaman

The Origins of Lycia
According to Greek legend, Leto was beloved by Zeus. When she became pregnant with the twins Artemis and Apollo, she was forced to flee by Hera, Zeus's jealous wife. Spurned by many cities, she finally arrived at Letoon and gave birth. Wolves guided her to the River Xanthos where she washed her children and drank. In gratitude to the wolves she called the land Lycia, Lykos being Greek for wolf.

▶▶ Alanya 138C1

The approach to Alanya is unmistakable: crowning the headland, at one end of the great rocky promontory on which the town sits, is its magnificent crenellated citadel, built by the Seljuks in the 13th century. This booming resort has outgrown itself in the last decade but fortunately most of the campsites, holiday homes and new hotel developments are spread out along the coast road, leaving the picturesque harbour area unspoilt.

Reaching the citadel involves a long uphill climb of about an hour, but there are cafés and drink stalls *en route*. Alternatively you can drive or catch a bus from near the tourist information office at Damlataş Caddesi 1. There are superb views from the platform on the cliff edge; condemned prisoners (including women convicted of adultery) were hurled to their deaths from here. Down on the harbourfront you can see the aptly named Red Tower (Kızıl Kule) and the old shipyards.

Most visitors come to Alanya for the climate (the sun shines on average for 300 days a year) and for the clean beaches, which extend more than 20km on either side of the castle. To the west is the stalactite grotto of Damlataş, thought to be beneficial to asthma and bronchial sufferers. From here, there are boat excursions, lasting 1–2½ hours, to the various caverns, including Phosphorous Cave where the water shimmers green.

▶▶ Antalya 138B2

The self-designated capital of the 'Turkish Riviera' is a fast-expanding city with an attractive old town and a prize-winning yachting marina. For most of the 500,000 tourists who make their way here annually, Antalya is not so much a beach resort as an excellent base for exploring the numerous attractions of the coastline and its mountainous hinterland.

The main tourist area is Kaleiçi, the old quarter situated near the harbour. Many of the Ottoman houses here have been converted into pleasant and comfortable *pansiyons*, and there are enough of them to encourage healthy competition. You will find craft and souvenir shops, as well as restaurants, crammed into the narrow streets between the marina and Antalya's best-known historical landmark, the Yivli Minare (fluted minaret).

The Roman Emperor Hadrian visited Antalya in AD 130 and the triple-arched gateway in the city walls, named in his honour, has survived. Near the entrance to the delightful Karaalıoğlu Park, where the air is filled with the scents of exotic flowers, is the Hıdırlık Kulesi, which may be a 2nd-century lighthouse. People converge on this lovely area around sunset for views across the sea to the snow-capped Beydağları beyond. The excellent archaeological museum has exhibits stretching back to palaeolithic times (*Open* Tue–Sun 9–6).

Hadrian's Gate, built to mark a visit to Antalya by the Roman emperor in AD *130*

The closest beach to Antalya, Konyaaltı, lacks shade and its proximity to the port makes it doubly unappealing. Boats leave daily from the marina for the surrounding coast and islands; some visit the superior, paying, beach at Lara, as well as the Lower Düden waterfalls. There is also a minibus service to Lara from the old bus station (Doğu Garajı) on Ali Çetinkaya Caddesi. The nearest blue flag beaches are an hour or so west of Alanya, at Beldibi, Göynük and Kızıltepe, on the way to **Kemer** (see page 149).

Antalya environs

The tourist information offices on Mermelı Sokak in Kaleiçi and Cumhuriyet Caddesi, in the same building as Turkish Airlines, have information on excursions. These include the Kurşunlu Waterfalls, **Olympos National Park** (see page 149), **Termessos** (see page 154) and the Pamphylian cities including **Side** (see page 152). There is an 18-hole golf course and holiday centre (with beach) at Belek, 40km east of Antalya.

The Archaeological Museum at Antalya is one of Turkey's best

The Lycian rock tombs form a magnificently striking backdrop to Fethiye

Who were the Lycians?
Fethiye lies on the western edge of the ancient kingdom of Lycia. Until 1981 the tarmac road stopped here, leaving the region beyond inaccessible except to four-wheel drive vehicles and horses. Now all this has changed: a new road links the small towns round the coastline to Antalya, and Lycia has become one of Turkey's most popular tourist destinations, offering magnificent mountain scenery, secluded beaches and romantic ancient ruins.

The origins of the Lycians remain mysterious. Most scholars now agree that they came from Crete around 1400 BC under the leadership of Sarpedon, brother of King Minos. They were a fiercely independent people with their own language, which bears some resemblance to Hittite but even now is not fully understood. Lycia was the last region in Asia Minor to be incorporated into the Roman Empire.

▶▶▶ **Fethiye** 138A2

A busy market town set in a serene, island-studded bay with a turquoise sea and a mountainous backdrop, Fethiye is one of the most attractive resorts on the Mediterranean coast. Much of the town was destroyed in an earthquake in 1957, so its appearance is unashamedly modern. Hotels, restaurants, bars and discos are conveniently located on the harbourfront or just inland, where you will also find a good selection of shops and an open-air food market. The tourist information office, opposite the quay on İskele Meydanı, will help with accommodation – the *pansiyons* to the west of the marina are quieter and offer superb views of the bay.

In ancient times, Fethiye (or Termessos) was the chief port of Lycia (see panel) and the rock tombs, carved into the hillside to commemorate its leading citizens, are the main tourist sight (*Open* daily 8.30–sunset). A Roman amphitheatre has been uncovered near the tourist office, and local children hoping for a tip will point the way to the ruins of a Crusader castle, built by the Knights of St John.

There is no beach in Fethiye itself but Ölüdeniz, one of Turkey's best-known beauty spots (see opposite), is only a *dolmuş* ride away, as is Çalış, a small resort on the other side of the bay. There are hotels and *pansiyons* here, as well as a beach, but the sand is coarse and the sea isn't always clean. Boat excursions leave daily from the harbour at around 10, returning at about 6. Prices are reasonable and lunch on board is included. The most popular trip explores the 12 islands in the bay, allowing plenty of time to swim out to the Step Cave, Cleopatra's baths and a ruined Ottoman dockyard. Other options include Ölüdeniz and Butterfly Valley, St Nicholas' Island (Lycian ruins and a ruined Byzantine monastery) and a shopping expedition to the Sunday market at Göçek.

Fethiye environs
Kaya Köyü▶ This eerie ghost town 7km south of Fethiye, reached on foot or, less directly, by *dolmuş*, was abandoned when its Greek inhabitants were expelled in 1923 after the War of Independence. You can wander freely.

Ölüdeniz►► Images of this tranquil lagoon occur in virtually every Turkish tourist brochure. Sadly this has led to a great deal of commercial exploitation near by – although the lagoon itself is a conservation area – and hotels, *pansiyons*, restaurants and holiday homes abound in the surrounding villages, notably Ovacık and Hisarönü, which are noted for their boisterous nightlife. If you are not into partying and loud disco music, give this area a wide berth. The warm and placid waters of the lagoon are ideal for young children, but beware of mosquitoes and midges. There is a stretch of beach at the bottom of the main road, but it is stony and crowded. Twenty minutes' walk along the shoreline, Kudrak Paradise beach is still relatively unpopulated. Other attractions include paragliding, parasailing, scuba diving and jeep safaris.

The beautiful lagoon at Ölüdeniz, sheltered from the open sea by steeply forested hills, has recently been designated a conservation area

Walk Selge Canyon

This inland trip, unquestionably one of the most exciting on Turkey's Mediterranean coast, explores the magnificent scenery of the Köprülü Kanyon National Park and culminates in a majestic ascent to the ancient town of Selge. There is a *meyhane* at the bottom of the canyon, but if you plan to venture all the way to Selge, take your own provisions.

Turn off the main Antalya to Side road and drive inland 37km to Beşkonak, also signposted as Köprülü Kanyon Milli Parkı. From Side the drive takes about one and a quarter hours, winding through forest with glimpses of the expansive Eurymedon river. From Beşkonak the road is untarmacked but continues as a passable dirt track

Above: preparing yufka, *a flat bread not unlike the Indian chapati*

for 6km to reach the stone Roman bridge that spans the canyon over the river. On the river's edge is the attractive Kanyon Restaurant.

Follow the signs to Altınkaya (Golden Rock), a new name for the cluster of small settlements 14km away on the plateau, near the modern village of Zerk.

Cross the Roman bridge. If you wish to limit your walk to the canyon and river area, take the left fork for a kilometre or so to reach a second Roman bridge beside a picnic area.

The right fork to Altınkaya is quite rough in places, but recent improve-

Right: stunning views can be expected in the Köprülü Kanyon National Park

ments have made it accessible to most cars. The distance from the bridge to Selge is 13km, so you can stop the car at any point and walk if you prefer. The scenery along the way is dramatic, with weird rock formations known as 'fairy chimneys' on the upper reaches. On every side are the deep gullies and precipices that successfully shielded ancient Selge against successive conquering armies.

The plateau at the end of the road is 900m high, and the temperature here is noticeably cooler than on the coast. The cultivated fields outside Zerk soon give way to the first sight of Selge's ancient theatre which stands in the middle of the village, against the backdrop of the impressive snow-covered peaks of the Kuyucük range (2,500m).

Park the car in the designated area and children will doubtless appear and escort you round for a small tip. Walk up through the village past the remains of a stoa (colonnade of shops) on your right and a barely recognisable hippodrome (for horse races) on your left, and you will emerge at the back of the well-preserved theatre.

From here a small path leads off to the hill where the ruined Temples of Artemis and Zeus have been identified. Following the course of the main street, where traces of the drainage system are still visible, the path eventually leads to the fine paved courtyard of what was once the agora (market place), littered with fragments of carved marble blocks including a lovely white marble bull's head. A scramble down the hillside affords good views of the extensive walls that encircled the city in its heyday, when 20,000 fiercely independent citizens lived here. Rejoin the track beside the old Roman spring, from where a small amount of drinkable water still trickles.

Rock tomb terraces at Myra imitate the façades of Lycian houses. The largest is decorated with beautiful reliefs depicting a funeral banquet, while others portray warriors and battle scenes

Legacy of tombs
Lycia's most striking legacy is its tombs, scattered over the hillsides, cut into cliff faces and even submerged in the sea. The building of imposing funerary monuments was a notable feature of the ancient world. Great care was taken to protect the bodies and Lycian tombs frequently carry inscriptions threatening to bring down curses upon anyone violating them.

Kale
138A1

A sprawling, dusty town, Kale (formerly known as Demre), is not somewhere you would choose to linger, were it not for the splendid and unusual necropolis in nearby ancient **Myra** (see below). The only attraction in Kale itself is the Byzantine Church of St Nicholas, which contains the tomb of the famous 4th-century Bishop of Myra, the original Noel Baba or Santa Claus, who earned his reputation for generosity by providing dowries for poor girls in the area. Pilgrims still visit the church for a celebratory mass on 6 December, his feast day.

Kale environs
Kale's small harbour, **Çayağzı►**, lies some 3km from the town centre. The road ends at an attractive beach with camping facilities and good bathing in the icy estuary waters; a footbridge over the river leads to a welcoming fish restaurant. South of the road are the remains of an impressive Roman warehouse, dating from the reign of Emperor Hadrian (AD 117–138). You can see busts of the emperor and his wife Sabina, above the central gate.

The ruins of the ancient town of **Myra►** nestle at the foot of the cliff behind Kale (*Open* daily 8.30–7). Apart from the theatre, where the vaulted entrance passages below the seats have survived more or less intact, the highlight must be the cluster of tombs hewn out of the cliff face. Most of them were designed to imitate the façades of Lycian houses. Follow the path beyond the main site to the river necropolis, where you will find the 'painted tomb' with its striking relief of a bearded man and ten other life-sized figures, perhaps his family. Traces of the original red and blue paint are still visible.

▶▶ Kalkan   138A1

This attractive town clings to the hillsides that encircle its fishing harbour. Many of the traditional whitewashed houses in the Yalıboyu district have been converted to *pansiyons* offering splendid views across the bay from their roof terraces. (The modern hotel development is to the west of the town.) You will find a good selection of souvenir shops and restaurants lining Kalkan's narrow cobbled streets – the more upmarket establishments are concentrated near the yachting marina. Swimming is not possible in the town itself but there are daily boat trips to the nearby beaches, including Kaputaş, a small cove barely accessible by road.

Kalkan environs

See page 154 for the beautiful beach at **Patara**, only 13km from Kalkan.

Tour companies offer excursions from Kalkan to the magical, 18km-long **Saklıkent Gorge▶▶**. A roped catwalk negotiates the river for the first 1.5km, as far as a series of piers crossing the waterfalls. There are souvenir shops here, as well as restaurant stalls selling fresh trout. Enthusiasts can hire plastic shoes to wade and scramble further into the gorge.

Eighteen kilometres inland from Kalkan, **Xanthos▶**, once Lycia's greatest city, is a fascinating mix of Lycian, Roman and Byzantine remains. The site contains a Byzantine monastery and a basilica with mosaic flooring, a Roman temple, a theatre and an extraordinary pair of pillar tombs, 8m high, carved with mythical figures. On the acropolis stand the remains of a Lycian royal palace.

Mass suicides
So fiercely independent were the people of Xanthos, Lycia's principal city, that on two occasions they fought to the death rather than submit to foreign rule. Under threat from the Persians in the 6th century BC, the men of Xanthos set fire to their homes, killing all the women and children, before marching out to fight to the last man. Again during the Roman civil wars in the 1st century BC, when Brutus laid seige to Xanthos, the citizens slaughtered their families, then burnt themselves alive. Even the cold-hearted Brutus is said to have wept at the spectacle.

147

The remarkable pillar tombs at Xanthos: the reliefs depict mythical creatures, half-bird, half-woman, with children in their arms, thought to represent either the Harpies or spirits carrying off the souls of the dead

▶▶ **Kaş** *138A1*

Set in a lovely bay encircled by high mountains, Kaş retains its traditions as a fishing village while warmly welcoming yachting enthusiasts and other visitors. A few fragments of the ancient site of Antiphellus remain, including the small theatre above the town, a number of rock tombs, and various Lycian sarcophagi scattered about the streets and harbourfront. The whitewashed mosque is recognisable as a former Greek church, a relic of the days before 1923, when Kaş had a thriving Greek community. The town offers a good choice of shops and restaurants and a range of hotels and small family *pansiyons*. Much development has taken place on the snake-like Çukurbağ peninsula to the west, but the rocky beaches here are not so good for children. Kaş comes alive at night: the restaurants and bars are boisterous and in season even the shops stay open until the early hours. The helpful staff at the tourist office on Cumhuriyet Meydanı will have information on the hiring of a *gulet* for cruising, on day trips along the coast to Kekova and Üçağız, and about sailings to the Greek island of Castellorizo (see map page 155). Kaş is also a centre for scuba diving and qualified instructors offer interesting beginner and advanced dives a little way off the coast.

Phaselian tricks
Demosthenes described the Phaselians thus: 'They are clever at borrowing money in the market, then as soon as they have it they forget it was a loan, and when called on for repayment think up all sorts of excuses and pretexts, and, if they do repay it they feel they have been cheated of their own property; and in general they are the most scoundrely and unscrupulous of men.'

Wooden verandas in a narrow street of the Kaş bazaar

Kaş environs
For **Kekova Adasi (Kekova Island)▶▶▶** see page 155. Many visitors arrive in **Üçağız** (Teimiussa), the central village of the Kekova region, by boat, but the drive is an interesting one through rural, sparsely populated countryside. Despite the growing number of tourist facilities, Üçağız manages to retain its village atmosphere. One feature of the coastline here is the ancient Lycian sites that stand on the water's edge or even lie half buried in the sea. East of Üçağız is the little fortress of Teimiussa, and the remnants of ancient Lycian tombs, some of which have fine carvings.

► **Kemer** *138B1*

The most easterly of the Lycian resorts, Kemer is probably also the most developed, with a wide range of hotels, holiday villages, campsites, restaurants and shops. Wooded mountain slopes tumble down into the sea forming a magnificent backdrop to the bay, where the immaculately maintained sand and shingle beaches have been awarded a Blue Flag by the European Union. There is a busy yachting marina and opportunities for parasailing, water skiing and windsurfing from the beach. Among the black goat-hair tents in the Yörük (Nomad) Theme Park you can watch carpet weaving and other traditional crafts. The tourist information desk in the Belediye Binası (town hall) has accommodation lists and maps.

►► **Olympos** *138B1*

Set in its own national park, Olympos probably enjoys the loveliest site in all Lycia. Take a picnic and allow plenty of time to enjoy the ancient ruins, the beach with its freshwater stream and the mountainside, shaded by bay, fig and pine trees, and pink flowering oleander bushes. (See the **Chimaera Walk**, page 151.)

► **Phaselis** *138B1*

Just 13km south of Kemer, the ancient port of Phaselis has been extensively excavated and is a popular destination for school outings and picnics. The new buildings near the entrance include a souvenir shop and café. Phaselis has three natural harbours (all suitable for swimming), from where you must be sure to look back at the pine-clad mountains falling away to the sea.

A track leads to a Roman aqueduct among the trees. The paved main street is lined with the foundations of shops and the extensive ruins of the baths, complete with their underground central-heating systems. From here a stairway leads up to the pleasantly overgrown and shady theatre. Across the headland, towards the most distant of the harbours, is a magnificent gateway, erected to honour Emperor Hadrian in about AD 130.

Stunning beaches are a feature of the Olympos National Park

The Lycian League
The Lycians always had an instinct for unity, an unusual trait in an age of constant warfare between city states. To defend their region, they formed themselves into a league of 23 cities in the 2nd century BC. They even introduced a system of proportional representation to their assemblies: delegates from the chief cities had three votes, those from the intermediate ones, two votes, and representatives from the smallest communities, just one vote. Taxes were levied in the same proportions. The resulting peace and good order meant that the country prospered while huge fortunes were amassed by private citizens, many of whom lavished money on public building works.

Walk The Chimaera

This short but dramatic walk climbs through forest, inland from Olympos, to reach the extraordinary flames that burn eternally on the hillside, home of the legendary fire-breathing Chimaera.

The starting point for the walk, which takes about an hour each way, is the beach of Olympos, on the eastern Lycian coast between Kemer and Finike (see page 149). Boat trips run daily from Kemer in season. Bring a picnic if you intend to be here over lunchtime. The pebbly beach offers excellent swimming, against the lovely backdrop of the mountains and constantly flowering oleander bushes, and there is good paddling for children in a river estuary. If you swim round the bay, you can examine the full extent of the castle crenellations up on the cliffs, part of the defences erected by a den of pirates in the 1st century BC.

The ruins of the ancient city of Olympos – partly covered in dense undergrowth, partly submerged – are quite difficult to explore, but persistence will be rewarded by the discovery of the remains of a theatre, baths, a basilica and a fine temple doorway dating to the 2nd century AD.

Return northwards along the beach and take the dirt road through the small village. Beyond the village the track comes to a dead end in a cleft between two hillsides. Red paint on rocks and tree trunks now marks the path, which climbs gently from this point to reach the Chimaera in less than 30 minutes.

Suddenly the character of the hillside undergoes a dramatic change, becoming bare and rocky. Issuing from it in at least a dozen places are flames the size of camp fires. These were the eternal flames that inspired the ancient pirates of Olympos to hold secret rites to Mithras, the Zoroastrian god of light whose cult they must have met in their eastern exploits. Visible far out to sea, the

The Chimaera (eternal flame) burning in the foothills of Tahtalı Dağ

flames also served to guide sailors round the cape, notorious for its violent storms and shipwrecks.

In antiquity this was believed to be the home of the Chimaera, a mythical beast, part lion, part serpent, part goat. Homer relates how the King of Lycia set Bellerophon, the youthful suitor for his daughter's hand, the task of slaying the Chimaera.

Over the ages the flames have fluctuated greatly in their intensity, from a huge fire that the ancients claimed could not be extinguished, to a few feeble flickers, easily put out with handfuls of earth. In the 19th century travellers used to come here to wallow in the waters of a nearby sulphurous pit, supposedly good for

Relaxing on the beach at Olympos

skin diseases, while their servants cooked food on the flames.

Lower down on the bare mountainside stand the remains of the pirates' temple, where the citizens of Olympos later came to worship Hephaistos, god of fire and forging.

Communal latrines
In the western corner of the agora (market place) in Side, against the theatre, are the ancient public latrines, consisting of a semi-circular arched passage, lined with marble and originally containing 24 seats above a water channel. In ancient times one's daily achievements were not, as now, private affairs to be performed in solitary confinement, but rather an excuse for social gatherings and a chat.

Reliefs at Perge
The marble reliefs on the stage building at Perge portray the life of Dionysus, the Greek god of theatre as well as wine and revelry. One relief shows his birth; another his initiation into the cult of Artemis Pergea (the local deity); while a third depicts a Dionysian procession, in which the god is borne on a chariot drawn by two panthers and bedecked with vine leaves and ivy.

► ►   **Pamphylian cities**   _138B2_

The vast plain known as Pamphylia ('Land of the Tribes') was settled by refugees from Troy in 1184 BC. From these humble beginnings, five great cities grew up and the area became renowned as a centre of Hellenistic civilisation. Today, all that is left of Aspendos, Perge and Sillyon are remnants of their former glory; Side and Attaleia (now **Antalya**, see page 140–1), on the other hand, have survived to become flourishing modern cities.

Aspendos►►   Boasting the best-preserved Roman theatre in the world, Aspendos lies 30 minutes' drive east of Antalya on the banks of the Köprü river, where a delightful 13th-century Seljuk bridge is still in use. The main track leads directly to the theatre which dates from the 2nd century AD. This magnificent structure – the stage, auditorium and arcade are all virtually intact – is still in use today. Near by stand the ruins of the basilica, a nymphaeum (monumental fountain) and one of the largest aqueducts in Anatolia.

Don't leave without visiting the workshops of the Aspendos Jewellery Centre, where you can watch the craftsmen at work.

Perge► Situated on the flat plain just 5km north-east of Antalya, the ruined city of Perge has some striking features, notably tall, round Hellenistic gates and an evocative main street complete with chariot ruts. The stadium is one of the best-preserved in Asia Minor.

Sillyon► Many of the ruins of ancient Sillyon disappeared in a severe landslide in 1969, but enough have survived to make a visit worth while. Particularly impressive are the paved ramps leading to the gate of the acropolis, visible from miles around.

Side►►► The most charming resort on Turkey's southern coast, where the ruins of the ancient city mingle with new buildings, Side offers an ever-increasing number of hotels, motels, _pansiyons_ and campsites, mostly lining the excellent, sandy beaches to the west of the town. Boat excursions, lasting six or seven hours, leave daily from the harbour to explore the local coastline and offer plenty of opportunities for swimming. Despite

PAMPHYLIAN CITIES

The ancient theatre at Aspendos, the finest example of its kind in the world

Magnificent views of the Mediterranean beyond the ruins at Side

the modern development, Side has retained its special identity and atmosphere, and it is less than an hour's drive from Antalya airport. You will find the tourist information office outside the city gates near the *otogar* (bus station), on Side Yolu. Cars are not allowed into the narrow streets of the centre and must be left in the car park area next to the museum.

The old town is well served with restaurants and souvenir shops, drawing visitors in increasingly large numbers, but the main attraction is the ancient ruins. The museum (*Open* daily 9–12, 1.30–3) is housed in the 5th-century Roman baths, which retain their original floor plan. Directly opposite is the agora (market place), from where you can climb to the theatre. This dates from the 2nd century and is one of the largest in Asia Minor, with a capacity of 17,000. There are fine views across the Hellenistic defence walls towards the sea.

Pamphylian cities environs

Lunch in the market town of **Manavgat**, which is only 20 minutes' drive away from Side, makes a pleasant excursion. It is also a cheaper place to stay in than Side. River boats run regular trips from the centre of town to the celebrated water-falls, an area of shady parkland with souvenir shops and cafés. Just beyond is an unusual river-side restaurant, where the tables are scattered beneath the trees or perched on individual plat-forms built on the edge of the rushing water. The staple fare is the local trout, helped down by refreshing white Turkish wine – all enjoyed in the cooling breeze that fans the air even in the height of summer.

Cooling down in the shade of the Manavgat Falls

▶▶ **Patara** *138A1*

Most visitors to Patara will relish the 18km-long sandy beach. The beach is also a conservation area, protecting the bird life of the lagoon and the nesting turtles, and no development is allowed around it. You will find *pansiyons* as well as bars and restaurants in the nearby village of Gelemiş.

Ancient Patara served as the port for Xanthos although the connecting river has long since disappeared and an immense sandbank has silted up the harbour. The ruins have never been excavated and the half-buried theatre makes a strangely attractive sight, although the tricky terrain and the distances involved make exploration a challenge. The indefatigable may not be able to resist a trek right across the harbour to Hadrian's Granary, a colossal structure that serves as an evocative reminder of how these outlying parts of the empire once served as bread baskets to feed the citizens of Rome.

Breathtaking mountain scenery surrounds the classical ruins at Termessos

Formidable city
Inhabited in ancient times by people of legendary ferocity known as Solymians, Termessos boasted some of the most formidable natural defences of any ancient city in Turkey. Alexander the Great took one look and decided to waste no more time, moving on to easier prey. Homer tells us that one of the trio of seemingly impossible tasks allotted to the young hero Bellerophon was the slaying of the Solymi.

▶▶ **Termessos** *138A2*

Open: daily 8–7 (5.30 in winter).

One of the most exciting excursions in all Turkey is to the ruins of Termessos, set high in the mountains behind Antalya and popularly known as the Eagle's Nest. Despite being overgrown and never properly excavated, the remains of this ancient city have a grandeur rarely equalled anywhere.

Exploring the site involves some steep climbing, so you will need to bring a sturdy pair of shoes. A well-signed path leads through the city walls to the gymnasium, fashioned from the dark grey stone characteristic of Termessos. From the theatre there are breathtaking views of a ravine on one side and of snow-capped mountains on the other. On the hillside beyond, the cluster of temples surrounding the agora (market place) is an extraordinary necropolis, where literally hundreds of gaping, desecrated sarcophagi, dating from the 1st to 3rd centuries AD, present an almost apocalyptic vision.

Boat trip **Kekova**

An enjoyable day trip combining a swim with a simple lunch at a village restaurant, and calling in at several partly submerged ancient Lycian settlements around the island of **Kekova**.

Tickets can be bought at **Kaş** harbourfront. The boat generally leaves at 9 and returns by 6. Boats also run from the little harbour of **Demre**, called Çayağzı. Bring a mask and flippers, so you can snorkel round the underwater ruins. Skindiving is forbidden, to discourage theft from the antiquities.

After setting off from Kaş and passing the Greek island of Kastellorizo, 90 minutes' cruising brings you to the ruins of **Aperlae**, a Lycian town of the 4th century BC. In the shallow waters of the bay you can discern the outlines of streets and buildings submerged as a result of earthquakes over the centuries.

Another 45 minutes and you reach a pretty cove on Kekova Island, where the ruined apse of a Byzantine church stands on the beach. This is a good swimming spot; look out for the foundations of houses at the far end of the bay. Watch out too for occasional sea urchins.

Continuing the trip, the boat now hugs the shoreline of Kekova Island, where you will see more ruins beneath the turquoise water. The final port of call is the village of Kale (Turkish for castle), named after the Crusader fort whose crenellated walls crown the hilltop, enclosing a tiny ancient theatre with seats cut into the rock. A few simple fish restaurants have grown up on the waterfront, overlooking more submerged ruins.

The return journey to Kaş takes about 2½ hours.

Excursion boats stop at the submerged settlement at Kekova

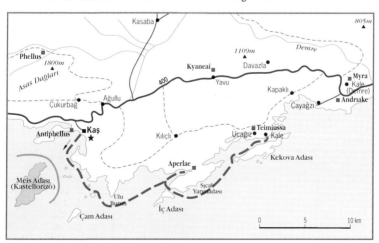

EAST MEDITERRANEAN

REGION HIGHLIGHTS ◄◄◄◄◄◄

The East Mediterranean coast This coastline, from Alanya to the Syrian border, can be divided into three main areas: the first, following the headland round to Silifke, is rugged and sparsely populated; the second, the Cilician Plain, is a monotonous but fertile flatland devoted to rice and cotton crops; while the third, known as the Hatay, a narrow finger of land stretching south towards Syria, is more industrial. The scenery between Alanya and Silifke is magnificent, but in ancient times this was dangerous territory where the secluded bays and steep wooded cliffs made perfect hiding places for the pirates and brigands that plagued the coast of Cilicia.

The main resort is Silifke, a modern town built around ancient Seleucia. For most visitors this is little more than a stopover on the way to the cities of Mersin, İskenderun and Adana, which offer a wider selection of hotels and tourist facilities and are, perhaps, more suitable bases for exploring the region.

Pages 156–7: an exhibit from the Mosaics Museum in Antalya

Right: the crenellated Crusader castle at Anamur stands on the site of a Byzantine fort
Below: street vendors in Adana shelter from the blazing afternoon sun

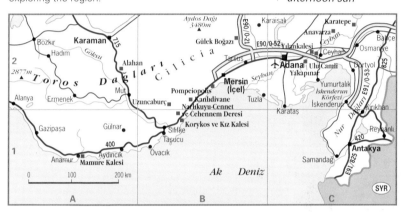

Adana's 16th-century Ulu Cami seen behind the Stone Bridge, built by Emperor Hadrian

Young boys selling simit (bread rings sprinkled with sesame seeds)

Local delicacy
The Castle of the Snakes (Yılankalesi) earned its name from the snakes that still abound in the region. They are eaten with relish by the local pigs, whose flabby snouts protect them from bites.

▶   **Adana**   158C2

Turkey's fourth largest city, with a population of 1.6 million and growing fast, lies in the heart of a rich agricultural plain and is the centre of the prosperous cotton industry. Running through the city is the River Seyhan, which is spanned by the 16-arched Taş Köprü (Stone Bridge) built by the Roman Emperor Hadrian (117–138). Near by is the Ulu Cami (Great Mosque), built in 1507 of black and white marble, with fine tile work and mosaics inside. Adana has many good hotels and is a convenient base from which to explore the area. Tourist information can be found at Atatürk Caddesi 13.

Adana environs

Beyond the small coastal resort of **Karataş**, 50km south of Adana, is **Yumurtalık▶**, which has better facilities than Karataş, including a fishing harbour and an ancient castle built by the Knights of St John in the Middle Ages.

Some 39km east of Adana is **Yılankalesi▶** (Castle of Snakes). This magnificent 12th-century Armenian fortress commands the hill to the right of the road. Inside, visitors can see the well-preserved dungeons and living quarters. (*Admission* free.)

▶▶   **Anamur**   158A1

The modern town of Anamur is a good starting point for exploring the coast, with its long stretches of clean sands as yet undiscovered by tourists. Completely unspoilt, the area is a breeding ground for sea turtles and monk seals. Here the pine-clad mountain slopes plunge unnervingly down to the sea, offering spectacular views of cliff tops, natural inlets and the brilliant turquoise waters of the Mediterranean. (For more information, contact the helpful tourist office at Bulvar Caddesi 42/B.)

Seven kilometres from the town, the medieval castle with its walls and 36 towers intact, is the largest and best-preserved on the southern coast. Known locally as Mamure Kalesi (Marble Castle), it stands on the water's edge with the waves lapping at its outer walls. The castle was the last foothold of the Cypriot Lusignan kings; Cyprus is only 65km away. The Ottomans expanded the castle and continued to use it until the last days of the empire in 1921. The mosque in the west courtyard has been restored and is open for prayers and there is a handful of *lokantas* and motels near by (*Open* daily except Mon 8.30–12.30 and 1.30–5.30).

On a hillside 2km west of the castle are the ruins of ancient Anemurium, a Byzantine city deserted in the 7th century when the wave of Arab incursions began from Damascus. So complete are the remains – many private houses have traces of mosaic and painting – that it has the feel of a ghost town deserted just a few years ago.

▶ ### Antakya (Antioch) 158C1

The site of ancient Antioch, this city is close to the Syrian border and though only a shadow of its former self, is still picturesque enough with narrow lanes leading down to the Orontes river, and segregated districts that in Ottoman times were inhabited by different religious communities. The outline of the ancient city walls, 30km long in total, gives an indication of the extent of the city in its heyday. The only ancient monuments in Antakya today are a Roman bridge and the mosque of Habib Neccar, which was originally built as a church. The Hatay Museum should not be missed for its collection of Roman floor mosaics, the finest in the world, assembled from the villas of ancient Antioch and nearby Daphne, once home to many wealthy Romans.

Licentious Antioch
In Roman times the city of Antioch was a great cultural, artistic and commercial centre which became notorious for depravity and indulgence in life's pleasures. For this reason it was chosen by St Peter for his first mission to the Gentiles, and his converts here were the first to be called Christians. Out of town, on the Aleppo road, is a grotto with a secret escape tunnel where St Peter is said to have founded the first Christian community. The church here was built by Crusaders in the 13th century.

Cave church
On a hillside above Antakya is the famous cave church of Sen Piyer Kilisesi (*Open* daily except Mon 8–12 and 1.30–6). One of the earliest Christian communities was founded here by St Peter himself, some time between AD 47 and 54 and, according to legend, he preached in this church. The 'font' is fed by a spring and there are traces of the original mosaic. Mass is celebrated here every Sunday afternoon at 3.

The cave church of St Peter, carved from a hillside outside Antakya

■ **Turkey is blessed with huge tracts of virgin lands which, in recent years, have been preserved by the creation of numerous national parks throughout the country. Most of these lie in heavily forested areas, often with lakes and rivers, and are rich in flora and fauna.** ■

162

Hunting
As in most Mediterranean countries, hunting has long been a popular pastime in Turkey, with the result that many species, including the brown bear, have been hunted virtually to extinction. Popular game birds include wild duck, wild goose, quail, partridge and pheasant. Foreigners may hunt only in parties organised by Turkish travel agencies, which will provide all relevant information on seasons, authorised zones, permits and weapons. In non-prohibited regions, tourists can fish for sport without obtaining permits.

Egyptian vulture (neophron percnopterus)

National parks In the south Aegean region the Dilek Milli Parkı, on Dilek Burnu south of Ephesus and close to Priene (see page 126), combines a spectacular area of 1,200m-high jagged mountains with flat marshland rich in birdlife. The mountains are home to many birds of prey, as well as to jackals, striped hyenas, wild boar and even the occasional leopard.

Abundant wildlife is also to be found in the Olympos Milli Parkı on the Lycian coast near Antalya (see page 149), its 2,000m-high mountains covered in Calabrian pines. On the coast here you may see shearwaters flying in long formations – Cory's shearwaters are also common. April and May are the loveliest months, with flowering shrubs such as lavender and rock roses attracting hosts of butterflies.

In inland parks, such as the Kovada Milli Parkı between Lake Eğirdir and Antalya, the forests provide shelter for red and roe deer, wild boar, wolves and even a small number of brown bears. In the Yedigöller Milli Parkı (the name means seven lakes), 50km inland from Zonguldak on the Black Sea, the deciduous and coniferous woodland of the national park is home to a similar range of wildlife.

Birdwatching Birdwatching in Turkey can usually be combined with sightseeing or even lazing on the beach: armed with a pair of binoculars and a field guide, you can add a whole new dimension to your holiday. Due to its geographical position on the edge of Europe, Asia and Africa, Turkey has a tremendous range of birdlife. Spring and autumn are the most exciting times because of the great north–south migrations of birds, from sparrowhawks and eagles to black and white storks. They are visible even from Istanbul, especially from the Çamlıca hills on the Asiatic side.

May is probably the best month for birdwatching, when even the inexperienced may spot well over 100 species on a typical touring holiday. No one can fail to notice the tall storks that build enormous nests on minarets, rooftops and telegraph poles, or the vultures and birds of prey that hover overhead. Crested larks fly up from the roadside, while you can usually spot yellow black-headed buntings, colourful bee-eaters and bright blue rollers on the telegraph wires .

Turkey also boasts several bird sanctuaries, notably Kuş Cenneti (Bird Paradise) by the Sea of Marmara, Çamaltı, near İzmir, and Birecik near the Syrian border. Among other species here you can see the monstrously

İstuzu Beach near Dalyan, nesting ground of the loggerhead turtle

ugly and near-extinct bald ibis, the subject of a rescue operation by the Worldwide Fund for Nature.

Turtles The beach at Dalyan, near Dalaman airport on the south Aegean coast (see page 121), is the biggest nesting beach for loggerhead turtles (*Caretta caretta*) in Turkey, and the second most important in the whole Mediterranean after the Greek island of Zakynthos. The turtles are threatened because the sandy beaches where they come to lay their eggs are increasingly being developed for tourism. During their two-month incubation period, the eggs are vulnerable to disturbance from digging and trampling. When they hatch, at night-time, the baby turtles scurry down to the sea, attracted by the natural luminescence of the surface and the reflected light of the moon; bright lights from hotels confuse them, and as they hesitate, they are easily picked off by scavengers. Many others simply die of exhaustion before ever reaching the sea.

Dangers to the explorer
In summer, the most aggravating form of wildlife you are likely to encounter is the mosquito, so travel equipped with repellent, especially if you intend to eat outdoors. Scorpions and snakes are not so common, but it is worth being careful when walking off the beaten track in sandals or with bare legs.

163

Loggerhead turtles are threatened by tourist developments that disrupt their nesting beach

Kanlıdivane

The ancient city of Kanyatelis (Kanlıdivane) was built around a vast gorge into which, according to local tradition, criminals were hurled to their deaths – Kanlıdivane means 'place of blood'. Today visitors prefer to contemplate the ancient ruins clinging to the sides of the chasm, notably the necropolis with its Roman and Byzantine sarcophagi built into the rock.

Commerce in the port of İskenderun

Cennet and Cehennem (Heaven and Hell)

The names of these two caves near Narlıkuyu are a clue to their contrasting characters. Only Heaven can be visited, a huge natural chasm on the edge of a field of Roman and Byzantine ruins. Descent is via a path which becomes more slippery near the entrance to the cave, where a pretty church dedicated to the Virgin has stood since the 5th century. Inside you will hear the roar of an underground river, said to be the Stream of Paradise. Hell, by contrast, is a frightening narrow pit, accessible only to potholers. Superstitious locals tie rags to nearby trees and bushes in order to ward off any evil spirits who might escape from below.

► **İskenderun (Alexandretta)**   *158C2*

Founded by Alexander the Great in 333 BC, İskenderun is a flourishing commercial port and harbour in the Hatay region close to the Syrian border. Here Arab customs and traditions begin to make their presence felt – the food, for example, is decidedly spicier. Tourist information is at Atatürk Bulvarı 49/B, but you may prefer to stay at the nearby beach of Uluçınar (Arsuz) where the hotels and restaurants are popular with Syrian tourists.

► **Mersin**   *158B2*

Situated on the fertile Cilician Plain, Mersin, characterised by shady palm-lined avenues and parks, is a rapidly developing city with a free-trade port. In the town centre, around İstıklâl Caddesi, you will find modern, reasonably priced hotels that can be used as a base for exploring Icel province. The tourist information office is on İsmet İnönü Bulvarı 5/1 near the harbour, where there are also numerous cheap restaurants, water sports facilities and a fish market. A car ferry leaves from here for Famagusta in Turkish Cyprus on Mondays, Wednesdays and Fridays.

Mersin environs

Not far from Mersin is St Paul's birthplace, the market town of Tarsus. Although little remains of the Roman city, visitors can see the 'Cleopatra Gate' through which the famous Egyptian queen is said to have passed with Mark Antony after their first meeting.

►► **Silifke**   *158B1*

This small but attractive town set on the banks of the broad Göksu river is relatively untouched by tourists and the centre has a pleasant, open feel. A large castle on a hill above the town was built originally by the Byzantines in the 7th century as a defence against Arab raiders, and rebuilt by the Crusader knights of Rhodes, complete with 23 towers and bastions. Now it is wild and overgrown so take care if you decide to walk the crumbling battlements. On the hill to the west of Silifke stands the Byzantine church of Haghia Thekla, dedicated to St Paul's first convert, who was also

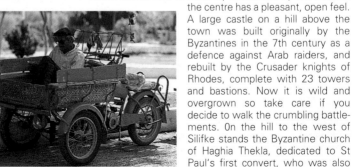

the first female Christian martyr. Thekla lived in hiding in the cave here, teaching and healing the sick. The Byzantines built the church on the site in her honour in the 5th century.

Fortified on land and sea, Kız Kalesi (Maiden's Castle) is a magnet for tourists

Silifke environs
The shoreline around Silifke is characterised by pine-covered slopes, breathtaking stretches of sandy beach and small resorts such as Boğacik, Yeşilovacık, Aydıncık (popular with sailing enthusiasts) and the fishing village of Ovacik, from where divers can explore the delights of Kösrelik Bay and Island. Taşucu, Silifke's nearest beach and harbour, is also the embarkation point for car ferries and hydrofoils to Girne (Kyrenia) in Turkish Cyprus.

The much-photographed castle complex **Kız Kalesi (Maiden's Castle)**►► consists of two buildings: the first, constructed in the 12th century by Armenian kings, stands on the sandy beach, while the other rises from its own island in the sea (see panel). Boats take summer visitors to the island castle. The beaches here are popular with campers but there are also some comfortable *pansiyons* and small hotels.

Narlıkuyu►► is situated in a delightful bay 20km east of Silifke and offers visitors the remains of a Roman bath with a well-preserved mosaic of the Three Graces. The adventurous can explore some of the nearby caves, including the Cave of Heaven (Cennet Deresi, see panel opposite) and the Wishing Cave, where the humid air is said to benefit asthma sufferers.

The ancient site of **Uzuncaburc**►►, 30km north of Silifke, is one of the most impressive along this coast. From the centre of the small village that lies among the ruins, a monumental Roman arch leads to the Temple of Zeus Olbius, where most of the columns still stand. Built by Seleucus I in the 3rd century BC, it is the oldest known temple of the Corinthian order. Other monuments include a theatre, the Temple of Tyche and a powerful Hellenistic tower nearly 25m high.

No escape from Fate
According to legend, Kız Kalesi (Maiden's Castle) was built out to sea by a king who wished to protect his only daughter, after it was predicted that she would die of a snakebite. However, one of her admirers unwittingly sent her a basket of fruit in which a snake was lurking, and so, indeed, she was bitten and died.

BLACK SEA

BLACK SEA

Pages 166-7: beach near Tirebolu on the Black Sea coast

The Black Sea coast There are two main surprises in store for the first-time visitor to the Black Sea coast: the lush green vegetation, and the high concentration of buildings and population. Since the introduction of tea in the 1930s (see panel on page 170) the region has grown in prosperity, attracting large numbers of migrant workers from the interior.

The general absence of ancient ruins around the Black Sea is explained partly by the fact that the Romans penetrated only as far as the western coastline, and partly by the heavy rainfall, which has washed all but the sturdiest

ruins away. Even in the height of summer, visitors can expect regular downpours while the temperature can fluctuate from a pleasant 26°C to a cool 18°C. Perhaps the best time to visit is the late spring, when the cherry and hazel trees blossom – hazelnuts are an important Turkish export.

Several Black Sea resorts lie within striking distance of Istanbul, including Kilyos, Şile and Amasra, although the most attractive part of the coastline begins east of the largest city, Samsun. Trabzon is also worth exploring for its substantial Byzantine remains.

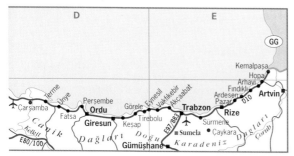

Fishing is still an important part of the local economy in the Black Sea region

169

Perfect for tea
The rain-saturated hillsides east of Trabzon are perfect for the cultivation of tea, and the bushes are planted up the steep hillsides to a height of 600m. Tea was introduced to the Black Sea only in the 1930s, but remarkably quickly it became the mainstay of the local economy. In 1986 the entire crop was condemned because of the nuclear disaster at Chernobyl, but, even so, production levels have increased to the point where some of the crop is now exported. Women dressed in colourful clothes and white headscarves harvest the tea. You will see them carrying the huge baskets on their backs along the road, with only a pair of feet visible from behind.

▶▶ **Amasra**   *168B2*

An attractive resort, beautifully situated on its own wooded peninsula, Amasra has a sleepy, relaxed feel that may induce you to stay overnight in one of the *pansiyons* clustered around the citadel gate. The main landmark is the Genoese castle; also worth seeing are two Byzantine churches, hidden away in the maze of alleyways that characterise the town. Souvenir hunters should look for the wooden knick-knacks which Amasra's craftsmen turn out in abundance. The fish restaurants on the waterfront specialise in Black Sea mackerel, but you will also find turbot and crayfish. Avoid the town beach for swimming – it's badly polluted and there are better beaches further east.

▶ **Giresun**   *169D1*

A bustling town some two hours' drive from Trabzon, Giresun is dominated by its castle, Giresun Kalesi, which crowns the acropolis of the ancient Milesian settlement of Cerasus. From here the Roman general Lucullus brought back the first cherry trees to Europe. (The words 'cherry' and 'cerise' both derive from Cerasus.) Just offshore is Büyük Ada, a small island where according to legend Jason and the Argonauts were attacked while on their quest for the Golden Fleece by birds dropping feathered darts. Today the island is inhabited by fishermen and can easily be visited by boat.

A traditional wooden house near Giresun

Giresun environs
Along the rocky shore towards the charming port of Ünye are caves where seals have made their homes. The resort itself has good-quality motels, camping facilities and *pansiyons* with direct access to its excellent beaches. There are rock tombs in the cliffs above.

▶ **Kilyos**   *168A1*

On the European shores of the Black Sea, Kilyos is just about the closest seaside resort to Istanbul, 12km by bus from Sarıyer. As the road threads across the backs of the surrounding hills there are superb views of the Bosphorus while the Black Sea shimmers in the sunlight ahead. There are long stretches of sand and several hotels in the village; cafés and restaurant facilities are spread thinly at the moment, but there are definite signs of improvement.

▶▶ Şile 168A1

Situated near the Asian shore of the Bosphorus, the resort of Şile has extensive sandy beaches that become very crowded during holiday times. The excellent restaurants and nightlife make it a popular weekend retreat for Istanbul residents.

Fishy staple
The fish available on the Black Sea coast vary with the season. In April there is turbot (*kalkan*), and from May onwards there are red mullet (*barbunya*), tuna (*palamut*) and anchovies (*hamsi*). Anchovies, the most abundant and the cheapest fish, are the staple diet of the fishing villages.

The 13th-century monastery church of St Sophia in Trabzon

▶▶ Trabzon (Trebizond) 169E1

Fabulous Trebizond, source of inspiration for countless writers from Marco Polo to Rose Macaulay, has long since disappeared. Today the only reminders of the town's romantic past are the old walled citadel, its Byzantine churches (which are now mosques) and the royal palace of the exiled Comnene emperors who fled here from Constantinople in 1204.

Aya Sofya (Cathedral of Haghia Sophia), 3km west of the city, is justly the most famous site. Built in the mid-13th century as a monastery church, it was converted to a mosque in 1461, shortly after the Ottoman conquest. Following local custom, the walls were covered with hard plaster and white-washed. This treatment inadvertently preserved for posterity the magnificent frescoes that adorned the walls and ceilings. Among the most beautiful are the *Marriage Feast at Cana*, the *Feeding of the Five Thousand* and *Christ Walking on the Water*, all dating from the late 13th century. On the porch of the northern façade, overlooking the Black Sea, is a poignant representation of Job plagued by boils.

Trabzon is now a trading nexus for Georgians, Armenians and other visitors from the former Soviet republic and visitors will see a Russian market, Cyrillic shop signs and restaurants offering Russian specialities. If you have time, take the short excursion to **Atatürk Köskü**, the summer residence of the former Turkish leader, situated in heavily wooded hills 4km from the city. An attractive white stucco villa set in beautifully manicured gardens, it serves today as a museum of Atatürk memorabilia.

Fabled Trebizond
'Still the Towers of Trebizond, the fabled city, shimmer on a far horizon, gated and walled and held in a luminous enchantment.'
Rose Macaulay, *The Towers of Trebizond*, 1956

The Laz

■ **A seafaring race of obscure Caucasian origin, the Laz inhabit the region between Rize and Hopa. They are remote cousins of the Georgians, but with the important difference that they converted to Islam early and have remained staunch Muslims.** ■

Unlazy Laz
The Laz are a hard-working people with a good deal of business acumen. Much of Turkey's shipping is owned and operated by Laz, who use crews from their own villages, leaving the women to work in the tea plantations. Envied because of their relative prosperity, they have become the butt of Turkish humour, with many jokes referring to their supposed stupidity and slowness.

The Laz were loyal to the Turks in the perennial wars against Russia, while the Christian Georgians and Armenians were viewed as suspect. Their language is related to Georgian and is still spoken in the villages, though not written. There are thought to be about 100,000 Laz still living in and around Pazar, Ardeşen, Fındıklı, Arhani and Hopa, as well as in some inland enclaves.

Laz business enterprises have brought a certain affluence. The people are relatively progressive in outlook and in their dress, which is colourful and fashionable. Often extrovert by nature, they traditionally enjoy dancing and playing the bagpipes. Their well-made houses of timber and stone, always set in gardens, are unlike others in Turkey; never clustered in rows and terraces, they are spread out along the tops of ridges to allow for more breathing space.

The ancient Greeks described the Laz as savage tribesmen, and they do have a reputation for being fiercely aggressive as enemies – but generous as friends. Like most Turks, they are patient and good natured until pushed beyond a certain point: 'The Laz talks with a pistol,' runs a local saying.

The Laz, often distinguished by their red hair, are also renowned for their sense of humour and business acumen

By air
Most international flights arrive at Atatürk Airport in the suburb of Yeşilköy, 20km west of Istanbul city centre. Taxis to the centre take 45 minutes and are reasonably priced. Turkish Airlines run buses (which are cheaper) every hour to Taksim Square in the centre with stops at Bakırköy and Laleli. Onward flights to North Cyprus (Ercan) depart from the international airport, while transit flights to other cities within Turkey depart from the nearby domestic terminal, linked by a shuttle bus.

Other cities International flights also serve: İzmir, Ankara, Antalya, Adana, Trabzon, Bodrum, Dalaman.

Munich, Vienna and Belgrade, with connecting services from Sofia in Bulgaria. Weekly services to Istanbul leave from Moscow, Kiev, Budapest and Bucharest.

By coach
Regular coach services run to Turkey from Austria, France, Germany, Holland, Italy, Switzerland and Greece, and from the other direction, Iraq, Iran, Jordan, Syria, Saudi Arabia and Kuwait.

By private car
No documents are required for visits of less than three months; the car is entered on the driver's passport as

By sea
There are three ways to arrive in Turkey by boat. Turkish Maritime Lines (TML) operate comfortable car ferries from Venice to İzmir, once a week from April to October and fortnightly between November and March. Daily services operate from North Cyprus all year round from Girne (Kyrenia) to Taşucu (near Adana) and Alanya, and from Magosa (Famagusta) to Mersin. There are also ferries from the Greek islands of Lesbos, Chios, Samos, Cos, and Rhodes.

By train
Rail travel via Europe has been severely disrupted by the troubles in former Yugoslavia. The Istanbul Express leaves daily for Istanbul from

Dalaman airport is the gateway to the Turquoise Coast

imported goods. For stays of over three months you must obtain a *carnet de passage* from the Turkish Touring and Automobile Club, Birinci Oto Sanayi Sitesi Yanı, Dördüncü Levent (tel: 0212 280 4449) or from your own national car club.

Customs
Duty-free limits on entry are
• 200 cigarettes
• 50 cigars
• 200g of pipe tobacco
• 1.5kg instant coffee
• five 100cc or seven 70cc bottles of wine and/or spirits
• five bottles of perfume, 120ml maximum each.

Evening ferry across the Çanakkale Strait (Dardanelles)

The import of all narcotics is strictly forbidden and carries stiff prison sentences. On leaving, you need to show proof of purchase for a new carpet, or a certificate from a museum directorate for an old one. Note: It is illegal to buy and export antiquities.

Visas
Visas (valid three months) are required for British, Irish and American nationals and can be bought on entry at the airport. They cost £10 ($20 for US citizens). Change is rarely available. Visas are not required for visitors holding Australian, Canadian or New Zealand passports. Other nationals should enquire at their nearest consulate or embassy.

Foreign currency
There is no limit on the amount of foreign currency that can be taken into Turkey. Keep any exchange slips, as you may be asked to show them when converting Turkish *liras* back into foreign currency, or to prove that souvenirs have been purchased with legally exchanged foreign currency. There is no departure tax, so change all Turkish *liras* back into foreign currency at the airport, where the rate is likely to be better than in your own country.

The image of Atatürk is prominent on Turkish bank notes

When to go

Istanbul, Aegean and Mediterranean coasts The tourist season runs from 1 April to 31 October. May, June and September are the best months; July and August can be too hot for sightseeing in the midday sun.

The swimming season in the Sea of Marmara and the northern Aegean is from June to September, while in the southern Aegean and Mediterranean you can swim from April to November.

Istanbul is at its best from April to June, and in September and October.

Black Sea coast June to September is the swimming season, with summer temperatures rarely exceeding 28°C. Winters are mild with high rainfall.

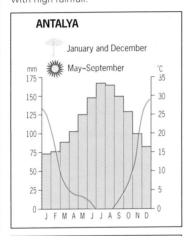

ANTALYA

☂ January and December
☀ May–September

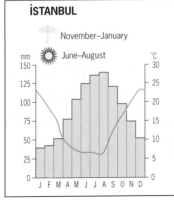

İSTANBUL

☂ November–January
☀ June–August

What to take

Loose light cotton clothing is best, with a pullover for the cooler evenings. In the Black Sea region warmer clothing may be needed, even in the height of summer. Comfortable shoes are essential for scrambling over rocky archaeological sites, and sun hats, sunglasses and high-protection factor sun cream are recommended. A headscarf is useful for women when visiting mosques, and a torch can be handy when visiting castles, caves and tunnels. If you like instant coffee for breakfast, bring your own jar and just ask for hot water. Colour print film is widely available, though expensive; colour transparency (slide) film is virtually unobtainable. Contact lens accessories are also hard to find. Spare toilet rolls and mosquito repellent are always useful. If you are considering long distance bus travel, a personal stereo is the best antidote to Turkish radio music.

National holidays

Government offices and businesses shut on these days, but shops and tourist sites remain open:

• **New Year's Day** 1 January
• **National Independence and Children's Day** 23 April
• **Atatürk Commemoration and Youth and Sports Day** 19 May
• **Victory Day (end of War of Independence)** 30 August
• **Republic Day** 29 October

Religious holidays

The **Feast of Ramadan (Şeker Bayramı)** is a three-day national holiday celebrating the end of the month of fasting. The **Feast of the Sacrifice (Kurban Bayramı)** is a four-day holiday commemorating Abraham's willingness to sacrifice his son Isaac. Shops (except food shops, which are open from the third day), bazaars, offices and banks are shut during these festivals (the dates follow the lunar calendar and therefore move back by 11 days each year). For 1999, the Feast of Ramadan ends in the middle of January and the Feast of the Sacrifice begins in early April. Museums and tourist sites are open as usual.

Time differences
Turkish time is GMT + 2 hours in winter, 3 hours in summer. Australia +8, Canada –7, UK –2, Ireland –2, New Zealand +10, USA –7

Money matters
The monetary unit is the Turkish *lira* (TL). Exchange rates are published daily in the newspapers. Most banks exchange foreign currency, as do most hotels of three or more stars. There are also numerous exchange offices in major cities, offering better rates and staying open later than banks. Visa, Mastercard and Eurocard can be used to obtain local currency from cash dispensers at Iş Bank, Yapı-Kredi Bank and other major banks. Eurocheques and travellers cheques can be cashed at banks and hotels, and credit cards are widely accepted.

Statistics
• Area: 780,000sq km
• Population: 62 million, 37 per cent of whom live in the countryside.
• Major cities: Istanbul 8 million, Ankara 3.5 million, İzmir 3 million, Adana 3 million, Bursa 1.5 million, Antalya 1.5 million.

Opening times
Government offices Mon–Fri 9–12.30, 1.30–5.30

Most banks exchange foreign currency

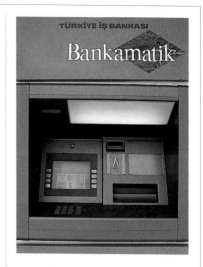

Cash dispensers are becoming quite common

Banks Mon–Fri 9–12 or 12.30, 1 or 1.30–5
Shops Mon–Sat 9.30–7
Grand Bazaar, Istanbul Mon–Sat 8–7
Museums Tue–Sun 9–5 (check individual museums). Closed Mon.
Archaeological sites daily 8.30–dusk

Information on opening times has been provided for guidance only. We have tried to ensure accuracy, but things do change and readers are advised to check locally to avoid any possible disappointment.

Domestic air travel

Turkish Airlines (THY) operates internal flights between Ankara, Istanbul, İzmir, Adana, Antalya, Dalaman, Samsun, Trabzon and other cities. All major towns have THY offices where tickets can be bought. Flights are frequent and fares good value: there is a 90 per cent discount for a child under two travelling on your lap, 50 per cent for children from two to twelve, and 10 per cent for a family or married couple travelling together. THY buses run from all city airports to the THY office in the city centre. The main THY offices are in Istanbul (tel: 0212 225 0556 or 252 1106; reservations: 0212 663 6363) and Ankara (tel: 0312 398 0100 or fax: 0312 398 0336).

Intercity buses

Many private companies offer frequent day and night services between all Turkish cities. The buses – comfortable, air-conditioned, reliable and inexpensive – depart from the bus station (*otogar*), and seats should be booked a day or two in advance, either at the *otogar* or at a travel agent.

Train

Turkish State Railways run between many major cities, offering couchettes, sleeping cars and restaurants, with first- and second-class seating, but trains

The dolmuş is a familiar sight on the streets of every Turkish town

are both more expensive and less efficient than the bus network. On the European side, trains from Edirne and Greece arrive at Sirkeci Station near Eminönü Square in Istanbul, while on the Asian side trains from Ankara and all points east terminate at Haydarpaşa Station (20 minutes across the Bosphorus by ferry). The Mavi Tren (Blue Train) is a fast inter-city service, leaving Haydarpaşa twice daily.

Ferries

Turkish Maritime Lines (TML) operate several coastal services from Istanbul's Karaköy, Sirkeci and Eminönü, as well as a car ferry from Istanbul to İzmir once a week. From

May to September, TML also operate a Black Sea line from Istanbul to Trabzon, departing Mondays and calling at Sinop, Samsun, Ordu and Giresun. TML Central Office is at Karaköy, Rıhtım Caddesi, Istanbul tel: 0212 249 9222 or 244-0207 or fax: 0212 251 9025. Ferries across the Bosphorus are frequent and very cheap. Main departure points are the quays beside the Galata Bridge at Eminönü and Karaköy; Beşiktaş and Kabataş on the European side; Üsküdar and Kadıköy on the Asian shore.

Taxis and *dolmuşes*
Yellow taxis are the best way to get about in Turkish cities. They are metered, with a day tariff (one light on the meter) and a night tariff (two lights on the meter). The night tariff operates between midnight and 6am, and costs 50 per cent extra. Tips are not usual.

The *dolmuş*, recognisable by its yellow band, is a shared taxi which follows specific routes. Passengers pay according to the distance travelled and may alight at any convenient place. Fares, cheaper than a taxi, are fixed by the municipality.

Trams
Within Istanbul, high-speed trams

A municipal bus on the streets of Istanbul

run from Aksaray to Esenler and Bakirköy, and from Bakirköy to Sirkeci. This line will shortly be extended to the airport. An old-fashioned tram has been reinstated along İstikâl Caddesi, between Tünel Square and Taksim.

Student and youth travel
Turkish Airlines, Turkish Maritime Lines and Turkish State Railways offer reductions for most internationally recognised student cards. Gençtur at Yerebatan Caddesi 15/3, Sultanahmet (tel: 0212 520 5274) are agents for IYC, ISIC and IYHF. They organise 'Green Tours' in the Istanbul area as well as help with all reservations. Students can also stay at Turkish Youth Hostels: The main office in Istanbul should be contacted for accommodation arrangements (tel: 0212 528 1201).

Buses
The favourite means of public transport outside the cities in Turkey is the bus – a remarkably efficient, punctual and comfortable way to get around. It is also cheap. If you are travelling light and on a tight budget, you will find the bus suits your needs perfectly.

Car hire

This is expensive, though good deals can frequently be had by booking in advance. Drivers must be over 21 and have a valid driving licence from their own country. Third party insurance is compulsory, and it is advisable to take out additional collision damage waiver (CDW) and personal accident insurance, which gives you comprehensive cover. Cars commonly offered are Murat (a locally made Fiat), Renault and Suzuki Jeeps. Seat belts are compulsory in front seats only, so you must specify if you want them in

The humble horse-and-cart still has a place in modern-day Turkey

The superb view can be a distraction, even on the open road

the back as well. It is also worth asking in advance what the rental firm undertakes to do if the car breaks down.

Car breakdown

If you break down in your own car, call the Turkish Touring and Automobile Club (Istanbul tel: 0212 282 8140). There are also numerous repair garages in towns, usually grouped together, and spare parts are readily available; Turkish mechanics are surprisingly resourceful when it comes to mending foreign makes of car.

Traffic regulations

Traffic drives on the right in Turkey. The speed limit is 50kph in towns, 90kph on state highways and 120kph on motorways. Traffic police frequently carry out spot checks, especially at the entry to towns, where the limit changes from 90kph to 50kph. On-the-spot fines are levied according to the level of speeding. Turkish road signs conform to international protocol and the Turkish highway code is similar to the European one.

The road network is extremely good and generally well maintained. The only really busy road is the Istanbul–Ankara highway, which continues as the E23, the E5 and the E24 transit routes to Iran, Syria and Iraq respectively. These three routes carry heavy goods vehicles and should be avoided if possible. All other roads are pleasantly clear of traffic, and on the whole driving in most parts of Turkey is a positive pleasure.

Petrol

Petrol stations selling super (4-star equivalent), normal (2-star equivalent) and diesel are abundant in all western parts of the country, but become less so in central and eastern regions. Unleaded petrol is found only in the biggest cities. Petrol stations on the main highways often have service stations and restaurants attached, and are open round the clock.

Driving Tips

Night-driving outside the cities can be an unnerving experience in Turkey: oncoming vehicles frequently do not use their lights until the last minute, when they suddenly switch them on, dazzling you completely; while agricultural vehicles often drive on the road with no lights at all.

Police sign: Turkish signs follow international protocol

Cat's eyes are very rare and broken-down vehicles often display no warning triangle, so it is important to make sure that your own lights are strong and properly adjusted to give maximum visibility.

Road signs

- *Dur*: stop
- *Dikkat*: watch out, e.g. because of road works ahead
- *Şehir merkezi*: town centre
- Yellow signs indicate archaeological sites.

Archaeological sites are signposted in yellow

The media

Turks are avid readers of their numerous newspapers. Foreign newspapers and magazines, mainly English, American and German, are available in the big cities and tourist centres one day late. The only English language daily, the *Turkish Daily News*, is bland but informative.

The *Voice of Turkey* radio, to be found on the FM waveband, broadcasts daily in English on general subjects and current events, 7.30–12.45 and 6.30–10 local time, on the following frequencies: 100.6MHz, 97.4MHz, 101.6MHz, 100.5MHz, 101.9MHz and 103MHz.

News is broadcast in English on TRT3, FM 88.2, at 9,10, 2, 5, 7 and 10; English language news on TV follows the Turkish news on TRT2 at 10pm.

PTT is the Turkish postal and telegraph service

Post Offices

The main post offices (PTT) in Ankara and Istanbul are open Monday–Saturday 8–midnight, Sunday 9–7, while the smaller ones throughout the country are open 8.30–12.30 and 1.30–5.30, closed Saturdays and Sundays. Poste restante letters should be addressed 'postrestant' to the central post office (*Merkez Postanesi*) in the relevant town. Proof of identity is required on collection. Most post offices also offer fax and 'valuable despatch' services, and will exchange foreign currency, international postal orders and travellers cheques. An express postal service (*Acele Posta Servisi* or APS) is available for sending letters, documents and small packages abroad.

Telephones

The cheapest way to telephone in Turkey is from a PTT telephone booth, though most hotels of 3-star standard and above have direct-dial national and international lines from their rooms. PTT offices sell phone cards and three sizes of *jeton*, for local, intercity and international calls.

Within Turkey cheap rates apply between 6pm and 8am. The intercity code for Istanbul is 212 for the European side and 216 for the Asian side.

International calls are cheap between midnight and 10am and on Sundays. To call abroad from Turkey, dial 0, then dial 0 again for an international line, followed by the country code and the individual number. UK country code is 44, Ireland 353, USA 1, Australia 61, Canada 1 and New Zealand 64.

Useful telephone numbers

- 110 Fire service
- 112 Emergency ambulance services
- 115 International operator
- 118 Directory enquiries
- 131 Operator
- 135 Wake-up calls
- 155 Intercity police
- 156 Gendarmerie (country areas)
- 528 5369/527 4503 Istanbul Tourism Police

Language guide

Pronunciation

c = j, as in cami (mosque) = jami
ç = ch, as in Foça = Focha
ğ = soft g, unpronounced, but used to extend the preceding vowel, as in dağ (mountain) = daa
ı (dotless i) = the initial 'a' in away, as in Topkapı = Topkapeu
ö = oe, as in Göreme = Goereme
ş = sh, as in Kuşadası = Kushadaseu
ü - as in French tu, e.g.Uerguep

Greetings and polite expressions

hello **merhaba**
goodbye (said by the person staying behind) **güle güle**
goodbye (said by the person leaving) **allaha ısmarladık**
good morning **günaydın**
good evening **iyi akşamlar**
good night **iyi geceler**
please **lütfen**
thank you **mersi** or **teşekkür ederim**

how are you? **nasılsınız?**
I am well, thank you **iyiyim, teşekkür ederim**

Everyday expressions
yes **evet**
no **hayır** or **yok**
there is **var**
there is not **yok**
I want **istiyorum**
I would like coffee please **kahve istiyorum, lütfen**
how much is this? **bu ne kadar?**
expensive **pahalı**
cheap **ucuz**
money **para**
very beautiful **çok güzel**
toilet **tuvalet**
men's (toilet) **baylar**
ladies' (toilet) **bayanlar**

Time
today **bugün**
yesterday **dün**
tomorrow **yarın**
what is the time? **şaat kaç?**

Travel
airport **hava alanı**
port **liman**
is it far? **uzak mı?**
where is...? **nerede...?**
bus station **otogar**
petrol **benzin**
oil (engine) **yağı**
tyre **lastik**
brakes **frenler**
it does not work **çalışmıyor**

The cheapest way to make a call is from a phone booth. Phone cards are available from PTT

Food
bread **ekmek**
water **su**
mineral water **maden suyu**
fruit juice **meyva suyu**
wine **şarap**
sweet wine **tatlı şarap**
dry wine **sek şarap**
red wine **kırmızı şarap**
white wine **beyaz şarap**
beer **bira**
ice **buz**
breakfast **kahvaltı**
tea **çay**
coffee **kahve**
milk **süt**
sugar **şeker**
jam **reçel**
cheese **peynir**
soup **çorba**
salad **salata**
fish **balık**
eggs **yumurta**
chips **patates**
ice cream **dondurma**

Numbers

1	bir	8	sekiz
2	iki	9	dokuz
3	üç	10	on
4	dört	20	yirmi
5	beş	50	elli
6	altı	100	yuz
7	yedi	1000	bin

Crime and police

Rates of petty crimes such as theft have always been low but, with rising unemployment, these crimes are on the increase in the cities. Pickpocketing has also become more common in the bazaar areas, although violent crime such as mugging or rape is rare. In the event of a crime, report the matter to the tourist police (beige uniforms and maroon berets). They have offices in all towns throughout the country (Istanbul tel: 0212 527 4503 or 528 5369; Ankara tel: 0312 212 0437; İzmir tel: 0232 449 0438).

Any traffic accident should be reported to the traffic police (navy uniforms with white caps). Market police (in blue uniforms) patrol the markets and bazaars to check commercial practice. The *Jandarmas* (gendarmerie) are soldiers (with green army uniform with a red armband) whose duties include keeping the peace and preventing smuggling and the like.

Traffic police wear white caps

Embassies and consulates

Australia Ankara: Gaziosmanpaşa, Nenehatun Caddesi no. 83 (tel: 0312 446 1180/87); Istanbul: Etiler, Tepecik Yolu Üzeri no. 58 (tel: 0212 257 7050).
Canada Ankara: Gaziosmanpaşa, Nenehatun Caddesi no. 75 (tel: 0312 436 1275/79); Istanbul: Gayrettepe, Büyükdere Caddesi no. 107 Bengun

Han, Kat 3 (tel: 0212 272 5174).
Republic of Ireland Istanbul (Honorary Consul), Harbiye (tel: 0212 246 6025).
United Kingdom Ankara: Çankaya, Şehit Ersan Caddesi no. 46/A (tel: 0312 468 6230); Istanbul: Beyoğlu/ Tepebaşi, Meşrutiyet Caddesi no. 34 (tel: 0212 252 6436); İzmir: 1442 Sokak no. 49, P.K. 300 (tel: 0232 463 5151); Antalya: Kazım Özalp Caddesi no. 149/A (tel: 0242 247 7000).
United States of America Ankara: Kavaklıdere, Atatürk Bulvarı no. 110 (tel: 0312 468 6110); Istanbul: Tepebaşı, Meşrutiyet Caddesi no. 104/108 (tel: 0212 251 36 02); İzmir: Alsancak, Atatürk Caddesi no. 92 (tel: 0232 421 3643).

Health, vaccinations and pharmacies

There are no mandatory vaccination requirements but immunisations against typhoid, tetanus, polio, and hepatitis A are recommended. There is no risk of malaria in the Mediterranean coastal regions, but east of Ankara anti-malarial tablets are recommended between March and November. Avoid swimming in fresh water near the Syrian border because of bilharzia. AIDS is present in Turkey, as in all parts of the world.

For minor problems go to the pharmacy (*eczane*) and describe your symptoms. Most medicines, including antibiotics, are available over the counter. In cities there is always a 24-hour chemist; normal opening hours are 9–7 except Sundays. If necessary your hotel will call a doctor, but there will be a charge for this.

In Istanbul the three best hospitals are the American Hospital in Nişantaşi (tel: 0212 231 4050), the International Hospital at Yeşilyurt (tel: 0212 663 3000) and the German Hospital in Taksim (tel: 0212 293 2150). All treatment must be paid for, so make sure that your travel insurance includes medical cover.

Dangers

In the sea, watch out for the black sea urchins that lurk on rocks in shallow water: their spines are poisonous and very painful if stepped

185

High-protection sunblock is essential on all Turkish beaches

on. On land poisonous snakes and scorpions are sometimes to be found in remote, little-trodden areas. These can easily be avoided by watching your step, and if you do chance to step on one, sturdy footwear provides sufficient protection.

Emergency telephone numbers
- Ambulance 112
- Police 155
- Gendarmerie 156

Preventative measures
Drink bottled water, as the tap water, though chlorinated, can become contaminated in the water tanks. Eat raw salad only in small quantities, squeezing lots of lemon juice on it. Eat plenty of yogurt and bread to counterbalance the olive oil in meat and vegetable dishes. Use a high-protection sun cream and from June to August stay out of the sun between 11 and 3.

All crimes should be reported to the police

Camping

Most campsites in Turkey have a restaurant, cooking facilities, hot showers and electricity. Some offer simple chalets. Altogether there are currently around 40 campsites in the Istanbul and Marmara region, 35 in the Aegean and 30 in the Mediterranean. East of Adana there are no campsites, and along the Black Sea coast there are none between Zonguldak and Hopa. The Turkish camping organisation is Türkiye Kamp ve Karavan Derneği, Nenehatun Caddesi 96, Gaziosmanpaşa, Ankara (tel: 0312 136 3151); Istanbul tel: 0212 560 6080.

Children

Turkey is an excellent place for children. Turks love them and are very welcoming in their shops, hotels and restaurants.

Pushchairs can be awkward, as there are so many steps to negotiate in cities such as Istanbul, but there always seems to be an obliging Turk willing to help carry them up steps or navigate any apparent impasse.

The best stretches of coast for children, with safe sandy bays, are Alanya, Altınkum, Çeşme, İçmeler, Kemer, Ölüdeniz, Patara and Side. It might be best to avoid Kaş and

Camping is a pleasure in Turkey

Kalkan, where the beaches are generally rocky, and the Black Sea beaches near Istanbul, where there are dangerous undertows.

Pharmacies stock disposable nappies for infants up to 12kg, as well as tins of babies' powdered formula milk and packets of instant baby food that just need mixing with mineral water. Baby products such

Friendly faces are the norm

Don't forget to remove your shoes before entering a mosque

as those manufactured by Johnson's are available in all pharmacies, as are Turkish equivalents of the usual children's medicines.

> ❑ Children love mosques. There is plenty of space in the courtyard, with the ablution fountain for chasing round; there are windows with huge sills for peeping out of and climbing on to; and, perhaps best of all, there is no pressure to be sober and pious. ❑

Travellers with disabilities
There is still little provision for people with disabilities in Turkey. Istanbul International Airport has adapted lifts and toilets, and the arrival hall, baggage collection point and customs are all on the ground floor, so trolleys and wheelchairs can easily be manoeuvred straight to the taxi rank. Ramps have been installed in many museums and in the state theatres, opera and concert halls of the capital.

Turkish State Railways (TCDD) offer a reduction of 70 per cent for disabled travellers, and 30 per cent for those accompanying them. For more information contact: Ortopedik Özürlüler Federasyonu, Gureba Hüseyin Ağa Caddesi, Bostan Sokak, Mermer Iş Hanı, Aksaray, Istanbul (tel: 0212 534 5980).

Electricity
Current is 220 volts throughout the country, 50 cycles, with two-pin European-style plugs.

Etiquette
When visiting a mosque, always remove your shoes before stepping on the carpet, leaving them outside in the rack provided. Women should wear a headscarf to cover their hair. Avoid visiting on Fridays or at prayer times; the larger city mosques close daily to non-Muslims from noon until 1pm for midday prayers in winter, 1–2pm in summer.

During Ramadan, do not walk about in public in the daytime eating, smoking or drinking.

Nudity on beaches is against Turkish law: toplessness, introduced by the Germans, is quite widespread in the Aegean and Mediterranean resorts, but always use your discretion.

It is considered offensive to hug or kiss members of the opposite sex in public, and to blow your nose in public. A too-firm handshake is thought impolite.

Hitch-hiking
Hitch-hiking is not illegal but neither is it widespread – and hitch-hikers are an unusual sight. Because public transport is so cheap, most people simply use the bus.

CONVERSION CHARTS

FROM	TO	MULTIPLY BY
Inches	Centimetres	2.54
Centimetres	Inches	0.3937
Feet	Metres	0.3048
Metres	Feet	3.2810
Yards	Metres	0.9144
Metres	Yards	1.0940
Miles	Kilometres	1.6090
Kilometres	Miles	0.6214
Acres	Hectares	0.4047
Hectares	Acres	2.4710
Gallons	Litres	4.5460
Litres	Gallons	0.2200
Ounces	Grams	28.35
Grams	Ounces	0.0353
Pounds	Grams	453.6
Grams	Pounds	0.0022
Pounds	Kilograms	0.4536
Kilograms	Pounds	2.205
Tons	Tonnes	1.0160
Tonnes	Tons	0.9842

MEN'S SUITS

UK	36	38	40	42	44	46	48
Rest of Europe	46	48	50	52	54	56	58
US	36	38	40	42	44	46	48

DRESS SIZES

UK	8	10	12	14	16	18
France	36	38	40	42	44	46
Italy	38	40	42	44	46	48
Rest of Europe	34	36	38	40	42	44
US	6	8	10	12	14	16

MEN'S SHIRTS

UK	14	14.5	15	15.5	16	16.5	17
Rest of Europe	36	37	38	39/40	41	42	43
US	14	14.5	15	15.5	16	16.5	17

MEN'S SHOES

UK	7	7.5	8.5	9.5	10.5	11
Rest of Europe	41	42	43	44	45	46
US	8	8.5	9.5	10.5	11.5	12

WOMEN'S SHOES

UK	4.5	5	5.5	6	6.5	7
Rest of Europe	38	38	39	39	40	41
US	6	6.5	7	7.5	8	8.5

Maps

Turkish tourist offices provide a free road map, which is adequate for most purposes. If you want a more detailed map, Kummerley and Frey and Roger Lascelles both produce larger-scale maps.

Organised tours

All resorts and tourist centres have travel agencies that operate organised tours and excursions. One of the principal ones in Istanbul is Plan Tours at Cumhuriyet Caddesi no. 131/1, Elmadağ (tel: 0212 230 2272, fax: 0212 231 8965), which collects clients from their hotels.

Photography

Never risk photography where a notice expressly forbids it, as this is an offence that carries a prison sentence. Higher entry charges for cameras and video cameras are often levied at tourist sites.

Places of worship

There are mosques for Muslim worship on most street corners throughout Turkey Istanbul, with its large Christian and Jewish communities, also has the Catholic San Antonio di Padova on İstiklâl Caddesi, Beyoğlu; the Anglican Christ Church (Crimean Memorial), Serdar Ekrem Sokak. 82, Beyoğlu; and the Neve Shalom Synagogue on Büyük Hendek Caddesi, Şişhane.

Stamps

Stamps can be bought at cigarette/sweet kiosks in resorts and at some souvenir shops. In cities, you can buy them from hotels or post offices.

Tipping

When a 10 or 15 per cent service charge is added to your restaurant bill, you should still leave a further 5 per cent for the waiter. In smaller restaurants, where a service charge is not automatic, leave 10 per cent. Taxi drivers do not expect tips as such, but it is normal to round the fare up. In a Turkish bath the masseurs/masseuses will be delighted with a tip of 50 per cent. Mosque attendants should be given a reasonable tip if they have opened

Windsurfing is popular in all the large resorts

a mosque or *medrese* for you; shoe attendants expect small change.

Toilets
On the whole Turkish plumbing is good. In hotels and *pansiyons* toilets are generally clean and of the conventional sitting-down variety. Toilet paper is something of a rarity in public places, as most Turks prefer to use the water pipe by the cistern. The worst public toilets are on the old ferry steamers that ply up and down the Bosphorus and to the Princes' Islands.

Water sports and sports
Water sports are on the increase on the Aegean and Mediterranean coasts, with most larger resorts such as Fethiye, Alanya, Kuşadası, Bodrum and Marmaris offering windsurfing, water skiing, jet skiing, paragliding etc. Scuba diving is also popular, and professional diving centres, established all along the coast, offer one-day dives as well as five-day courses that lead to internationally recognised qualifications. There are also fully equipped marinas at Istanbul, Çanakkale, Çeşme, Şığacık, Kuşadası, Bodrum, Datça, Marmaris, Göçek, Fethiye, Kalkan, Kaş, Finike, Kemer and Antalya. For more yachting information get in touch with the Istanbul Sailing Club, Fenerbahçe (tel: 0216 336 0633). Though still in its infancy, whitewater rafting is now practised in Turkey. Alternatif Turizm in Istanbul, Bağdat Caddesi 36/8, Kızıltoprak (on the Asian side) (tel: 0216 345 6650 /349 8419) specialises in rafting, offering weekend and week-day packages.

Tennis courts are available at Antalya, Bodrum, Fethiye, Gümbet, İçmeler, Kemer, Kuşadası, Ölüdeniz, Marmaris and Side. Ballooning, cycling and horseriding are alternative means of viewing the tremendous variety of Turkish landscapes. Skiing, hitherto the exclusive preserve of Turks, is now popular with tourists, notably at Uludağ, near Bursa, Turkey's premier ski resort.

Women travellers
As long as they are careful about body language and etiquette, women travellers should encounter few problems. You are less likely to receive unwelcome attention if you are accompanied by a man; if this is not possible, it may be best to travel with Turkish women. Too much eye contact with male strangers is to be avoided; this is frequently misread as encouragement. Images of women in Western films and magazines have fostered the misapprehension that Western women are 'available', so counteract this through careful dress and behaviour. In particular, women walking alone at night, or in pairs, are regarded as inviting attention. If you receive uninvited attention, the best response is to shout *ayip*! (shame on you!) loudly enough for passersby to hear. The culprit may then be shamed into retreat.

There are Turkish Information Offices in Austria, Belgium, Denmark, Finland, France, Germany, Israel, Italy, Japan, Kuwait, the Netherlands, Spain, Sweden, Switzerland, the United Kingdom and the USA.
• **United Kingdom** 170–3 Piccadilly, London W1V 9DD (tel: 0171 629 7771; fax: 0171 491 0773)
• **USA** 821, United Nations Plaza , New York, NY 10017 (tel: (212) 687 2194/5/6; fax: (212) 599 7568) 1717, Massachusetts Avenue NW Suite 306 Washington DC 20036 (tel: (202) 429 98 44; fax (202) 429 5649)

Within Turkey each town has its own tourist office, open the same hours as government offices (see page 177). The airports at Istanbul, Ankara, İzmir, Adana, Trabzon and Dalaman also have tourist offices.

• Istanbul Central Office, Beyoğlu Meşrutiyet Caddesi no. 57/5 tel: 0212 245 6875/243 2928; fax: 252 4346
• Entrance to the Hilton Hotel, Harbiye (tel: 0212 233 0592)
• Karaköy Maritime Station (tel: 0212 249 5776)

• Sultanahmet Square (tel: 0212 518 1802)
• İzmir Büyük Efes Hotel (tel: 0232 489 9278)
• Alsancak Harbour (tel: 0232 484 2148)
• Ankara Central Office, Gazi Mustafa Kemal Bulvarı no. 121, Tandoğan (tel: 0312 488 7007)
• Adana Central Office, Atatürk Caddesi, no. 13 (tel: 0322 351 1323)
• Antalya Central Office, Selçuk Mah, Mermerli Sokak, Ahiyusuf Cami Yanı, Kaleiçi (tel: 0242 247 5042; fax: 247 6298)
• Bodrum Barış Meydanı (tel: 0252 316 1091)
•Bursa Central Office, Fevzi Çakmak Caddesi, Fomara Han Kat 6 (tel: 0224 254 2274/250 5966)
• Marmaris İskele Meydanı no. 2 (tel: 0252 412 1035; fax: 412 7277)
• Side Side Yolu Üzeri (tel: 0242 753 1265; fax: 753 2657)
• Trabzon Central Office, Vilayet Binası Kat 4 (tel: 0462 230 1910; fax: 230 1911)

The Grand Bazaar is one of Istanbul's most popular tourist attractions

HOTELS AND RESTAURANTS

HOTELS AND RESTAURANTS

ACCOMMODATION

Accommodation in Turkey covers the full range, from 5-star Hiltons and Sheratons in the big cities through to simple family *pansiyons* in the towns and villages. Even in these, a private shower and toilet in each room is the norm. Most visitors find standards surprisingly high, and service is always helpful and friendly.

In the following listings accommodation is grouped in three price categories: £££ is expensive, at £120 and above for a double room with breakfast; ££ is moderate at £60–120; and £ is cheap, at £10–60. If no telephone number is given, there is none.

ISTANBUL

Grand hotels

These are Istanbul's top, luxury hotels.

Çırağan Palace Hotel Kempinski (£££) Çırağan (tel: 0212 258 3377; fax: 259 6686). An elaborately restored Ottoman palace in a superb setting on the lower Bosphorus, offering 294 spacious rooms, gourmet cuisine in its many restaurants and a fabulous outdoor swimming-pool on the edge of the Bosphorus. This is probably Istanbul's top hotel.
Conrad Istanbul (£££) Beşiktaş (tel: 0212 227 3000; fax: 259 666/). Stylish new hotel run by Hilton Hotels, set up on a hill in the commercial quarter with wonderful views of the Bosphorus and the Yıldız Gardens. Inside, there's a health club and swimming-pool; outside there's another pool and floodlit tennis courts. Excellent international cuisine. 627 rooms.
Four Seasons Hotel (£££) Sultanahmet (tel: 0212 638 8200; fax: 638 82 10). A one-time prison, but there is nothing penal about the facilities here and the location, between the Aya Sofya and Blue Mosque, is perfect for old town sightseeing.
Swissôtel The Bosphorus (£££) Maçka (tel: 0212 259 0101; fax: 259 0105). Set on the hill above Dolmabahçe Palace, this splendid new hotel offers 600 rooms with fine views, several restaurants and bars, indoor and outdoor pools, shopping arcade, fitness club, tennis, Turkish bath.

Stamboul: the Old City

These hotels are all within walking distance of the main tourist sites, and many are in renovated Ottoman houses.

Ayasofya Pansiyonlar (££) Sultanahmet (tel: 0212 513 3660; fax: 513 3669). Charming group of brightly painted old wooden houses, furnished in Ottoman style, between Topkapı and Aya Sofya. Restaurants, cafés, bars and a Turkish bath. 57 rooms.

Citadel Hotel (££) Kennedy Caddesi 32 (tel: 0212 516 2313; fax: 516 1384). On the coast road overlooking the Sea of Marmara, below Aya Sofya, this excellent hotel offers 31 rooms with traditional atmosphere, superb Turkish cuisine in indoor and outdoor settings, the latter incorporating parts of the city wall.
Halı (£) Klodfarer Caddesi 20, Çemberlitaş (tel: 0212 516 2170; fax: 516 2172). Set close by the Covered Bazaar, this beautifully restored old building offers 35 rooms all with en-suite facilities.
Hippodrome (£) Mimar Mehmetağa Caddesi 17 (tel: 0212 517 6889; fax: 516 0268). Attractive 17-room Ottoman house with a pleasant terrace, close to the Blue Mosque. No restaurant.
İbrahim Paşa (£) Terzihane Sokak. 5 (tel: 0212 518 0394; fax: 518 4457). Small 19-room hotel in a renovated house with a pretty terrace, tucked away in a corner of the Hippodrome close to the Blue Mosque. The hotel runs a café but no restaurant.
Kalyon (££) Sarayburnu (tel: 0212 517 4400; fax: 638 1111). Recently refurbished 1960s motel on the coast road below the Blue Mosque, overlooking the Sea of Marmara. 110 rooms, pleasant sea view, terrace and international cuisine.
Kariye (££) Edirnekapı (tel: 0212 534 8414; fax: 521 6631). This attractive 22-room hotel in a converted Ottoman house, stands in a quiet location just inside the city walls, beside the Kariye Mosque Museum. Excellent restaurant set in a peaceful garden.
Kösk Turkuaz Mansion Hotel (££) Kumkapı (tel: 0212 518 1897; fax: 517 3380). A very attractive 1870s pink and grey mansion, offering 14 rooms, garden, terrace bar and Turkish bath. Five minutes' walk from the Blue Mosque area.
Küçük Ayasofya (££) Şehit Mehmetpaşa Sokak 25, Sultanahmet (tel: 0212 516 1988; fax: 516 8356). Located down the hill from the Blue Mosque near the Sokullu Mehmet Paşa Mosque, this rebuilt Ottoman house has 14 rooms, all with bath; simple decor.
Merit Antique (£££) Laleli (tel: 0212 513 9300; fax: 512 6390). Formerly known as the Ramada, this is one of only a few 5-star hotels in the old city. The building is a restored turn-of-the-century apartment block close to the Grand Bazaar, offering 275 rooms, an indoor heated pool, health club and excellent Turkish and Chinese cuisine.
Pierre Loti Hotel (££) Çemberlitaş (tel: 0212 518 5700; fax: 516 1886). A small 3-star hotel with 36 rooms offering good value. Close to the Grand Bazaar, with an attractive terrace garden fronting the main road. It has a pleasant restaurant.
Poem (££) Akbıyık Caddesi, Terbıyık Sokak 12, Sultanahmet (tel: 0212 517 6836; fax: 529 3807). A pretty, restored Ottoman wooden house with just 8 rooms, some

with sea views. Within walking distance of all the main sights in the old city.
President (£££) Beyazıt (tel: 0212 516 6980; fax: 516 6999). A 4-star hotel close to the Covered Bazaar with 204 rooms and a popular English-style pub.
Sokullu Paşa (£££) Şehit Mehmetpaşa Sokak 5/7, Sultanahmet (tel: 0212 518 1790; fax: 518 1793). An elegant 18th-century mansion with 37 rooms located below the Blue Mosque. The garden has a fountain, the restaurant is in a Byzantine wine cellar, and there is also an original Turkish bath.
Sümengen (££) Mımar Mehmetağa Caddesi, Amiral Tafdil Sokak 21, Sultanahmet (tel: 0212 517 6875; fax: 516 8282). Close to the Blue Mosque with good views to the rear over the Sea of Marmara, this elegant 19th-century house has 30 rooms with en-suite facilities.
Turkoman Hotel (£) Asmalı Çeşme Sokak 2 (tel: 0212 516 2956; fax: 516 2957). 12-room hotel next to the Museum of Turkish and Islamic Art (Ibrahim Pasa Saraylı). Good breakfast-time views over the Hippodrome.
Yeşil Ev (£££) Sultanahmet (tel: 0212 517 6785; fax: 517 6780). In a marvellous location between the Blue Mosque and Aya Sofya, this 20-room hotel in a restored Ottoman house offers a large rear garden with outdoor restaurant and fountain. The most popular (and the most expensive) of the renovated Ottoman hotels.

Beyoğlu and the Bosphorus

These hotels are located either in the European business quarter, a 15-minute taxi ride away from the old city, or on the Bosphorus itself.

Bebek Hotel (££) Bebek (tel: 0212 263 3000; fax: 263 2636). The hotel enjoys the perfect waterside location and stylish terrace bar, but resembles a sleepy guesthouse.
Büyük Londra Hotel (£) Tepebaşı (tel: 0212 245 0670; fax: 245 0671). An 1850s building with a fine façade and an air of faded grandeur. Some of its 54 rooms have fine views of the Golden Horn. Close to (but better value than) the famous Pera Palace.
Büyük Tarabya (£££) Tarabya (tel: 0212 262 1000; fax: 262 2260). Hideous 1960s carbuncle. Once Istanbul's grandest hotel, this 261-room establishment offers good Bosphorus views well away from the city centre. Much used by businessmen.
Elan (£) Meşrutiyet Caddesi 213, Tepebaşi (tel: 0212 252 5449; fax: 249 9326). Comfortable 42-roomed hotel near the American and British Consulates, with views of the Golden Horn. Air conditioned.
Fuat Paşa Hotel (££) Büyükdere (tel: 0212 242 9860; fax: 242 9589). A pretty house on the Bosphorus front at Büyükdere, 30 minutes by taxi from the old city. It offers 51 rooms, indoor and outdoor restaurants and a Turkish bath.

Golden Age I (£££) Topcu Caddesi 22, Taksim (tel: 0212 254 4906; fax: 255 1368). 112 rooms in the heart of the Taksim/ Elmadağ district. Modern and fully equipped with health centre and jacuzzi.
Hidiv Kasrı (££) Çubuklu (tel: 0212 331 2651; fax: 322 3434). Set on the Asian shore overlooking the Bosphorus, this former Khedive's palace sits in splendid isolation, 12km outside the city centre, in its own rose garden and woodland. It has 14 rooms with sumptuous art nouveau décor and a charming restaurant.
Pera Palace (£££) Tepebaşı (tel: 0212 251 4560; fax: 251 4089). The famously grand turn-of-the-century terminus for the Orient Express is now overpriced and overrated. It offers 139 rooms with period furniture, an elegant patisserie and bar.
Sed Hotel (££) Kabataş (tel: 0212 252 2710; fax: 252 4274). A 50-room hotel in the quiet backstreets within walking distance of the Dolmabahçe Palace. Immaculately furnished with marble floors and elegant pillars, it has a boutique feel. Good value buffet restaurant.
Vardar Palace Hotel (££) Sıraselviler Caddesi 54–6, Taksim (tel: 0212 152 2896; fax: 152 1527). Built a century ago in the Levantine-Seljuk style, this refurbished 40-roomed hotel is close to Taksim Square. Modern, functional decoration.

Istanbul environs

Bursa

Çelik Palace (£££) Çekirge (tel: 0224 233 3800; fax: 236 1910). A sumptuous 173-room hotel, the best in Bursa, with its own hot thermal springs, indoor pool, two Turkish baths and shopping centre.
Termal Hotel Gönlüferah (££) Çekirge (tel: 0224 233 9210; fax: 233 9218). A modern 62-room, three-star hotel offering Turkish thermal bath and good restaurant.

Büyükada

Splendid Palas Hotel (££) Büyükada (tel: 0216 382 6950; fax: 382 6775). Less than 100m from the ferry terminus pier, this faded but very atmospheric turn-of-the-century wooden mansion (74 rooms) sits right on the waterfront, with a terrace offering superb views over the other islands. Its twin domes conceal water tanks, essential on an island with no springs or streams.

Çanakkale

Tusan Hotel (££) Güzelyalı (tel: 0286 232 8210). In a wonderful woodland setting with a private beach, this 64-room hotel offers water sports and indoor and outdoor restaurants.
Anzac Hotel (£) Saat Kulesi Meydanı (tel: 0286 217 7777; fax: 217 2018). A simple 27-room hotel in the city centre with pleasant roof bar and restaurant.

HOTELS AND RESTAURANTS

Gelibolu (Gallipoli)

Hotel Oya (££) Miralay Şefik Aker Cad. (tel: 0286 566 0392). Close to the docks, this fairly modern hotel is currently the best in town.

THE AEGEAN

Altınkum

Göçtur Hotel (££) Didim (tel: 0256 813 2740). A modern hotel 2km from the resort centre and 40m from the famous sandy beach, with a pleasant swimming pool, terrace and Turkish bath.

Ayvalık

Chalet Chopin Pension (££) Altınoluk (tel: 0266 396 1044; fax: 396 0697). Set on the Bay of Edremit and well placed for visiting Troy and Pergamum, this extraordinary old millhouse sits on a hillside overlooking the sea. There are only four rooms, traditionally decorated, but the well-known restaurant seats 150 people. There is also a pool.

Cunda Hotel (££) (tel: 0266 327 1598; fax: 327 1943). This small hotel stands right on the sandy beach of Alibey Island, connected to Ayvalık by a narrow spit and small bridge. The owner has his own jetty and boat for exploring the islands in the bay. Simple, good value restaurant.

Behramkale

Assos Behram Hotel (£) İskele (tel: 0286 721 7016; fax: 721 7044). Attractive 20-room stone-built hotel right on the harbourfront, with water sports and indoor and outdoor restaurant.

Assos Eden Beach (££) Kadırga Koyu (tel: 0286 752 7039; fax: 757 2054). 68-room hotel on the beach, with water sports, children's playground, restaurant and café.

Bergama

Berksoy Hotel (£££) İzmir Caddesi, Ilıca Önü (tel: 0232 633 2595; fax: 633 5346). 2km out of town, this is the most comfortable of Bergama's hotels with 57 rooms, a restaurant, bar, tennis court and swimming pool.

Hotel İskender (££) İzmir Caddesi, Ilıca Önü (tel: 0232 633 2123; fax: 633 1245). A standard 3-star hotel in modern premises.

Tusan Motel (£) (tel: 0232 633 1173; fax: 633 1938). A 42-room hotel 8km from the archaeological site, at the junction with the main Çanakkale–İzmir road, with an amusing Roman spa pool. Simple restaurant.

Bodrum

Eldorador TMT Holiday Village (££) (tel: 0252 316 1232; fax: 316 2647). A well-designed holiday complex: 239 rooms and 32 villas on its private beach, 1.5km from Bodrum centre. Offers two pools, water sports and good children's facilities.

Emiko (££) Uslu Sokak Atatürk Caddesi (tel: 0252 316 5560). A Japanese-run *pansiyon* in a good central location not far from the castle. Quiet, reasonably priced.

Manastir Hotel (££) Kumbahçe (tel: 0252 316 2854; fax: 316 2772). On the site of an old monastery, on the hill overlooking the harbour and castle, with two restaurants, a pool with children's section, fitness centre, sauna.

Myndos Hotel (££) (tel: 0252 316 3080; fax: 316 5252). This 72-room hotel 1.5km from the centre of Bodrum is attractively arranged round a pool with children's section. There are indoor and outdoor restaurants, and tennis is available.

Su Hotel (££) 1201 Sokak, Turgutreis Caddesi (tel: 0252 316 6906; fax: 316 7391). A small, quiet hotel with a dozen beautifully furnished rooms, built around a courtyard and swimming pool. No access for cars.

Bodrum Peninsula

Mandarin Pension (£) Gümüşlük. Set in mandarin groves 20km west of Bodrum and just 50m from the sea, this *pansiyon* has 20 village-style rooms. A simple beach bar offers light snacks. The renowned Gümüşlük fish restaurants are a short stroll away.

Secil Hotel (£) Türkbükü. In a fishing village a 30-minute drive from Bodrum, this 20-room family-run hotel offers a large swimming pool and a peaceful setting. The beach is two minutes away. There is a restaurant and also a bar.

Çandarlı

Hotel Diamond (££) Vali Şentürk Caddesi 17 (tel: 0232 673 3893; fax: 673 3894). A very good value, modern, centrally located hotel. Seaside restaurant. Rooms have showers.

Çeşme

Avrupalı Pansiyon (£) Sağ Sok 12 (tel: 0232 712 7039). An unpretentious, friendly establishment with clean rooms, baths, garden.

Çeşme Kervansaray Hotel (££) Çarşı Caddesi 5, (tel: 0232 712 7177; fax: 712 6492). Centrally situated, this historic hotel dates back to the 16th century and the rooms have preserved some of the original vaulting and fireplaces. Can be noisy if you can't find a room at the back.

Dalyan

Göl Hotel (£) (tel: 0252 284 2096; fax: 284 2555). Two minutes from Dalyan marina, this pretty lakeside hotel with basic accommodation has a pool, restaurant and bar. The famous İstuzu beach is 35 minutes away by water taxi.

Sultan Palace (££) (tel: 0252 281 2103). Some 10 minutes upriver from Dalyan, this exceptional and traditional Turkish hotel is totally isolated on its hillside, set in gardens by a large pool. It offers good food and the

by a large pool. It offers good food and the famous turtle beach is 40 minutes away by courtesy water taxi.

Datça

Hotel-Club Dorya (££) İskele Mahallesi (tel: 0252 712 3593; fax: 712 3303). Attractive hotel with a lovely garden. Adequate rooms, swimming pool and a small private beach.
Hotel Mare (££) Yanık Harman Mevkii (tel: 0252 712 3211). 50 room hotel with reasonably priced rooms with sea views and pool – the beach is almost next door.

Dikili

Perla Hotel (££) S. Sami Akbulut Caddesi 97 (tel: 0232 671 4145; fax: 671 4849). A comfortable hotel on the Çandarlı road with uninterrupted sea views

Efes – see Kuşadası and Selçuk

Foça

Club Méditerranée Foça Holiday Village (£££) (tel: 0232 812 1607; fax: 812 2175). A 376-room complex with superb water sports facilities, scuba diving, pool, Turkish bath.
Villa Dedem (£) Sahil Caddesi 66 (tel:0232 812 2838; fax: 812 1700). Seafront hotel with 20 rooms and a restaurant on its top floor.

İzmir

Balçova Thermal Hotel (££) (tel: 0232 259 0102; fax: 259 0829). This 196-room hotel 5km outside İzmir has two thermal swimming pools and a medical rehabilitation centre for rheumatic disorders.
Büyük Efes Hotel (£££) (tel: 0232 484 4300; fax: 441 5695). This luxury hotel, İzmir's best, stands in the city centre in its own gardens, with two outdoor pools and one indoor, five restaurants and a fitness centre.
Hotel Zeybek (££) 1368 Sokak 5 (tel: 0232 489 6694; fax: 483 5020). A modern unpretentious hotel with clean rooms, restaurant and bar in the busy Çankaya district near Fevzipaşa Bulvarı. Related to the Grand Zeybek across the street.
Kaya Hotel (£) Çankaya (tel: 0232 483 9771; fax: 483 9773). A modest 55-room hotel in the centre, with restaurant and lobby bar.

Köyceğiz

Kaunos Hotel (££) Cengiz Topel Caddesi 37 (tel: 0252 262 4884; fax: 262 4836). All 40 rooms in this pleasant hotel have a private shower and a balcony overlooking the lake. Facilities include terrace restaurant and bar.

Kuşadası

Club Kervanseray (££) Atatürk Bulvarı (tel: 0256 614 4115; fax: 614 2423). A converted Ottoman caravanserai in the centre of Kuşadası, with 40 rooms decorated

traditionally and set around the lush central courtyard where the restaurant is situated. Attractive, but tends to be noisy in season.
Golden Bed Pansiyon (£) Aslanlar Çıkmazı (tel: 0256 614 8708). Some rooms in this small, central establishment have balconies with sea views. Breakfast on the terrace.
Hotel Stella (££) Bezirgan Sokak 44 (tel: 0256 614 1632; fax: 614 3787). Only a short walk from the harbour, most of the Stella's rooms have balconies. There is a swimming pool.
Kısmet Hotel (££) Akyarlar Mevkii (tel: 0256 614 2005; fax: 614 4914). Standing on its own small peninsula some 2km from the town, this exclusive hotel set in sub-tropical gardens offers excellent international cuisine. Many heads of state have stayed here, attracted by its seclusion.

Marmaris

Grand Azur and Laguna Azur (£££) Kenan Evren Bulvarı 11 (tel: 0252 412 8201; fax: 412 3530) and Kumluörencik Mevki İçmeler (tel: 0252 455 3710; fax: 455 3622). The Grand Azur is the most prestigious hotel in Marmaris, overlooking a marina and beautiful sandy beach, with lush tropical gardens and a host of restaurants, bars and shops. The Laguna Azur, on a quiet beach with palm trees in İçmeler, is its much smaller sister hotel, with just 64 rooms decorated in art deco style.
Hotel Begonya (££) Hacı Mustafa Sokak 71 (tel: 0252 412 4095; fax: 412 1518). Uncomfortably close to 'Bar Street', but this attractive hotel has a central location, rooms equipped with showers and an excellent breakfast. Open summer only.
Hotel Yavuz (££) Atatürk Caddesi (tel: 0252 412 2937; fax: 412 4112). This 3-star hotel near the harbour has 55 rooms and a small rooftop swimming pool. All rooms have baths, some have balconies with bay views.

Marmaris environs

Doğan Hotel (£). Set on the Bay of Orhaniye, on the west coast of the Bozburun peninsula, this secluded family-run hotel sits right on the beach with pretty gardens, attractive restaurant and Turkish bar. Many boat trips are available for those keen to explore the neighbouring coastline.
Gökçe Hotel (£). Lying off the beaten track on its own farmland, this family-run hotel is a five-minute walk from Turunç and its beach. Excellent restaurant; pool.

Milas

Çınar (£) Kadiağa Caddesi 52 (tel /fax: 0252 512 2102). Cheap, good value rooms, some with balconies – the quietest are at the back.
Sürücü Hotel (£) Atatürk Bulvarı (tel: 0252 512 4001; fax: 512 4000). Small pleasant hotel with café and restaurant, in the south of the town.

195

HOTELS AND RESTAURANTS

Muğla

Grand Brothers Hotel (£££) Açık Pazar Yeri 1, Aydın Yolu (tel: 0252 212 2700; fax: 212 2610). Though a little out of town, this is the only hotel with a swimming pool. You may be able to get a discount on rooms.
Hotel Yalçin (££) Garaj Caddesi 7 (tel: 0252 214 1599; fax: 214 1050). Near the bus station, this old hotel has decent-sized, well-maintained rooms.
Petek Hotel (££) (tel: 0252 214 3135). Muğla's best hotel: a comfortable overnight stop in the centre of town for touring travellers who do not wish to drive down the peninsulas of Bodrum or Marmaris.

Pamukkale

Club Polat's Hotel (£££) (tel: 0258 271 4111; fax: 271 4092). A 225-room hotel in the village of Karahayıt below Pamukkale. Thermal and semi-Olympic pools, indoor and outdoor restaurants, tennis court.
Koçak (££) (tel: 0258 272 2099; fax: 272 2112). A 94-room hotel set up on the plateau, with a fine swimming-pool with children's section, an attractive garden and both indoor and outdoor restaurants.
Özel İdare Pamukale Motel (£) (tel: 0258 272 2024). Set right beside the Roman Baths Museum and the public baths, this 16-room hotel offers the most unusual courtyard pool, once the sacred pool of the Roman baths, now full of fluted classical columns and capitals.

Selçuk

Hotel Kale Han (££) Atatürk Caddesi (tel: 0232 892 6154; fax: 892 2169). A modern hotel, built in the style of a 19th-century farmhouse. All the rooms have private bathrooms, but the main attraction is the garden and outdoor swimming pool.
Hotel Victoria (£) Cengiz Topel Caddesi 4 (tel: 0232 892 3203; fax: 892 3204). An excellent central location with very reasonably priced rooms (some with views of storks' nests) and a good restaurant.
Nur Pansiyon (£) Dere Sok 16, Zafer Mahalle (tel: 0232 892 6595). Just across the railway line from the main street, this friendly *pansiyon* is especially popular with single women travellers. Breakfast (in the attractive garden) as well as other meals is optional.

Sığacık

Burg Pansiyon (£) Atatürk Meydanı 14 (tel: 0232 745 7464). A cheap modern hotel – some of the rooms have showers and harbour views.

THE MEDITERRANEAN

Adana

Büyük Sürmeli Hotel (£££) Özler Caddesi (tel: 0322 352 3600; fax: 352 1945). Probably the best hotel in Adana, 1km from the city centre, with a total of 166 rooms, a pool, nightclub and casino.
Hotel Mercan (£) Ocak Meydanı 5, 39 Sok 29 (tel: 0322 351 2603). Not far from the Atatürk statue, this simple down-to-earth hotel is good value especially as all the rooms are equipped with fans and mosquito netting.
Raşit Ener Motel (£) Yüregir (tel: 0322 321 2758; fax: 321 2775). A fairly modest motel with only 16 rooms. Simple restaurant, pool with children's section and playground as well as a campsite and caravan park.

Alanya

Bedesten Hotel (££) (tel: 0242 512 1234; fax: 513 7934). Standing within the walls of Alanya's hilltop castle, this converted Ottoman market has 20 rooms set around a courtyard. Large pool.
Blue Sky Hotel (£) İskele Caddesi (tel: 0242 513 6487; fax: 512 5402). A pleasant 54-room hotel in the town centre, with a good-sized pool and children's playground. Basic restaurant.
Club Alantur (£££) (tel: 0242 518 1740; fax: 518 1756). Excellent for sports enthusiasts, this hotel, set on the beach 5km outside Alanya, offers one indoor and three outdoor pools, a gym, four tennis courts, mini-golf and a very wide range of water sports, including scuba diving. It has a total of 365 rooms and 12 flats, with four restaurants.
Pansiyon Best (£) Alaaddinoğlu Sok 23 (tel: 0242 511 0171; fax: 513 0446). Near the town museum and the tourist information office, this modest *pansiyon* offers clean rooms and breakfast at reasonable rates.

Anamur

Anemonia Hotel (££) İskele Mah. İnönü Caddesi (tel: 0324 814 4000; fax: 814 1444). Very close to the beach, the hotel has 36 rooms and 6 apartments, several bars and a restaurant.
Hermes Hotel (££) İskele Mah. İnönü Caddesi (tel: 0324 814 3950; fax: 814 3995). A 70-room hotel on the beach; pool with children's section, windsurfing, two restaurants.
Kafka Pansiyon (£) İskele Mah. İnönü Caddesi (tel: 0324 814 2916). A small clean *pansiyon* with 12 rooms, all with shower and WC. Facilities include a café, terrace bar and restaurant.
Star Pensiyon (£) İskele Mah. İnönü Caddesi (tel: 0324 816 4605; fax: 816 4605). All 12 rooms have showers and there is a rooftop terrace with sea views as well as a restaurant.

Antakya

Büyük Antakya Hotel (£££) Atatürk Caddesi (tel: 0326 213 5860; fax: 213 5869). Antakya's best hotel, a modern block in the city centre with 72 rooms, nightclub, casino and indoor and outdoor restaurants. No pool.

Divan Hotel (£) İstiklâl Caddesi 62 (tel: 0326 215 1518). En-suite bathrooms are an important feature of this budget hotel, only a short walk from the river.

Antalya

Argos Hotel (££) Kaleiçi (tel: 0242 247 2012; fax: 241 7557). A very attractively converted Ottoman house in the old quarter above the marina, with 15 rooms, pool, live music and restaurant.

Hotel Ottoman House (££) Mermerli Banyo Sokak 8, Kaleiçi (tel: 0242 247 5718; fax: 242 6630). A welcoming, comfortable hotel with an attractive garden restaurant, café-bar and swimming pool, located in the old quarter.

Lara Hotel (££) Lara Yolu (tel: 0242 323 1460; fax: 323 1449). Set right on the cliff 8km outside Antalya on the Lara road. Attractive pool terrace and two restaurants. Water sports from the beach below.

Marina (££) Kaleiçi (tel: 0242 247 5490; fax: 241 1765). Set in private gardens of date palms and banana trees, this luxurious small hotel was winner of the Best Hotel in Turkey award in 1992. Very comfortable spacious rooms on split level. Excellent restaurant.

Tütav Türkevleri Hotels (££) Kaleiçi (tel: 0242 248 6591; fax: 241 9419). Standing 300m from the old harbour within the walls of the old fort, this group of converted Ottoman wooden houses offers 20 rooms, babysitting, a pool, sauna, indoor and outdoor restaurants, choice of three cafeterias.

Villa Perla (£) Kaleiçi (tel: 0242 248 9793; fax: 241 2917). Charming family-run hotel in a converted Ottoman house, with 16 rooms, private courtyard garden for outdoor eating and small pool.

Fethiye

Anıl Pension (£) Çalış Yolu (tel: 0252 613 1192; fax: 613 1711). Modest 17-room *pansiyon* near Çalış beach, 5km from Fethiye centre, with a small pool and restaurant offering occasional Turkish shows.

Duygu Pension (£) Ordu Caddesi 54 (tel: 0252 614 3563). A welcome is guaranteed in this delightful *pansyion* with spectacular views of the bay from the roof terrace. All rooms equipped with shower and toilet.

Kemal Hotel (£) Geziyolu (tel: 0252 614 5009; fax: 614 5009). Set at the quieter end of the waterfront, by the fishing boats, this simple modern hotel offers 21 rooms, a roof bar, indoor and outdoor restaurants. No pool.

Letoonia Holiday Village (££) (tel: 0252 614 4966; fax: 614 4422). Set on its own peninsula 4km from the centre of Fethiye, this 680-room, 110-villa complex is considered one of the loveliest holiday villages in the

area, offering three sandy beaches, two swimming-pools, three restaurants, three snack bars and the full range of water sports, including scuba diving.

Villa Daffodil (££) Fevzi Çakmak Caddesi 115 (tel: 0252 614 9595; fax: 612 2223). In the style of a traditional ancient Muğla house, this hotel has 15 rooms, a restaurant, bar, swimming pool and sauna. Views of the bay.

Finike

Anadolu Hotel (£) (tel: 0242 855 3804; fax: 855 3805). A pleasant 25-room hotel 2km from the centre, set back from the beach and coast road. Breakfast and simple meals are served on the roof terrace.

İskenderun

Hotel Açıkalın (£) Şehit Pamir Caddesi 13 (tel: 0326 617 3732). A good budget option, in a central location.

Hotel Cabir (£££) Ulucami Caddesi 16 (tel: 0326 612 3391; fax: 612 3393). İskenderun's best hotel – all 35 rooms are clean and comfortable and there is a bar and disco.

Kale

Kale Pensiyon (£) Delightful 7-room family-run *pansiyon* with en-suite shower rooms, opposite the island of Kekova. Shady terrace and veranda. Good cuisine. Speed boat and rowing boat for hire.

Kalkan

Dionysia Hotel and Diva Hotel (£) Cumhurıyet Caddesi (tel: 0242 844 3681, 844 3175; fax: 844 3139). Two attractive small hotels, both with stunning sea views and excellent roof terraces for bars and breakfast. Kalkan centre is five minutes' walk.

Kalamar Hotel (£) (tel: 0242 844 3190; fax: 844 3194). A 68-room hotel with pool and a long stone-paved waterfront with ladders for sea swimming. Kalkan is 1.5km away.

Patara Prince Hotel (££) PK 10 (tel: 0242 844 3920; fax: 844 3930). Immaculately designed hotel of 54 rooms standing within the Club Patara, an ambitious re-creation of a Roman town, complete with triumphal arch, forum and fountains. There is a magnificent balustraded terrace with large pool. Excellent cuisine in four restaurants. A free water taxi takes you across to Kalkan marina 10 minutes away.

Pension Patara (£) Close to the town's shingle beach and tea garden, this pretty *pansiyon* has 10 rooms overlooking the harbour, and an attractive roof terrace on which breakfast is served by the family.

Kaş

Aqua-Park Hotel (£££) Çukurbağ Peninsula (tel: 042 836 1901; fax: 836 1906). This luxurious and exclusive complex of villas and chalet-style rooms spread over the Kaş peninsula is very well-equipped for water sports, with scuba diving, three swimming pools and two water chutes. It has 116 rooms and 24 apartments, and offers a free bus link to Kaş town centre, 5km away.

Club Antiphellos (£) Çukurbağ Peninsula (tel: 0242 836 2651; fax: 836 2654). An attractive hotel with 16 rooms and a pretty pool and terrace, set on an isolated peninsula with access to a rocky beach. It offers water sports and a volleyball court, and has indoor and outdoor restaurants.

Hotel Club Phellos (££) Doğruyol Sok 4 (tel: 0242 836 1953; fax: 836 1890). Air-conditioned rooms, a pool and a central location all make this a good value option.

Me & Di Hotel (££). (tel: 0242 836 1914; fax: 836 1426). Set up on a hillside above the Kaş–Kalkan road, this exclusive 17-room hotel offers excellent, friendly service, a lovely pool in a private courtyard, villa-style rooms, each with its own terrace, pretty gardens and good restaurant.

Medusa (££) Küçükçakıl (tel: 0242 836 1440). Good value as the facilities here include a pool and access to a private rocky beach.

Melisa Pansiyon (£) (tel: 0242 836 1068). Family *pansiyon* in a quiet street near Kaş harbour. 16 good-sized rooms, breakfast on the rooftop terrace. No pool or restaurant.

Kemer

Antalya Renaissance (£££) Beldibi (tel: 0242 824 8431; fax: 824 8430). Modern 5-star hotel in a delightful setting in the resort of Beldibi, between Kemer and Antalya. Its excellent range of water sports from a private beach, large outdoor and indoor pools, tennis courts, fitness centre, Turkish bath, sauna and a range of restaurants and shops make it virtually a self-contained resort in itself.

Beltaş Hotel (££) Beldibi (tel: 0242 824 8192; fax: 824 8344). Well-designed 75-room hotel set in lush gardens with private beach, water sports, pool with children's section, playground, tennis court. Indoor and outdoor restaurants.

Princess Orange (£) Tekirova (tel: 0242 821 4059; fax: 821 1693). Pretty 48-room hotel set round a pool in Tekirova centre, with a cafeteria and outdoor restaurant.

Kız Kalesi

Club Hotel Barbarossa (££) (tel: 0324 523 2364; fax: 523 2090). Comfortable, pleasantly designed hotel with 103 rooms on a private beach 23km from Silifke, with views across to Kız Kalesi. Good pool, water sports, disco, indoor and outdoor restaurants.

Mersin

Mersin Hilton (£££) A. Menderes Bulvari (tel: 0324 326 5000; fax: 74 326 5050). Modern 5-star block 3km from the city centre, with 188 rooms, pool, health bar, tennis courts, gym, disco, casino and two restaurants.

Toros Hotel (£) Atatürk Caddesi 33 (tel: 0324 231 2201; fax: 237 8554). Fine location near the harbour; all rooms have shower and TV.

Ölüdeniz

Club Orka Holiday Village (£££) (tel: 0252 616 6794; fax: 616 6706). A modern complex located in Ovacık (on the road to Fethiye). 32 villas and 44 hotel rooms with all the usual amenities. Facilities include two outdoor swimming pools, bars, restaurants, table tennis and even beach volley ball.

Meri Motel (££) (tel: 0252 616 6060; fax: 616 6456). The best-placed hotel in Ölüdeniz, right on the lagoon, with a private beach ensuring total tranquillity, and 75 rooms climbing up a steep hillside. Not suitable for the elderly or tiny children, the Meri offers a lovely terrace restaurant with live music, windsurfing and playground. No pool.

Patara

Xanthos Hotel (££). Set in beautiful sprawling gardens arranged around a large pool, this attractive hotel has 16 rooms, a lovely terrace and bar area, and a tennis court. Simple restaurant.

Side

Turquoise Hotel (£££) (tel: 0242 756 9330; fax: 756 9345). 5-star luxury complex 3km from the resort centre, in a peaceful beach and forest setting. Huge pool, gym, water sports, tennis courts, children's pool, crèche.

Pamphylia Hotel (££). Standing right on the beach on the southern side of the peninsula, a short walk from the old town centre, this traditional hotel offers an attractive terrace restaurant overlooking the sea, and pretty wooden balconies.

Sevil Pension (£). Friendly family-run *pansiyon* a short walk from the old centre and the main beach. Breakfast only in the courtyard gardens. No pool.

Silifke

Altınorfoz Hotel (££) Susanoglu (tel: 0324 722 4211; fax: 722 4215). 4-star beach complex, 17km from Silifke, with water sports, pool, Turkish bath, nightclub, casino, indoor and outdoor restaurants.

Montana Hotel (££) A 90-room hotel in a spectacular forest setting, 2km from the lagoon and 3km from the beach, offering two splendid pools linked by a cascade, gardens, pool snack bar and restaurant.

THE BLACK SEA

Kilyos

Kilyos Kale Hotel (£) Kale Caddesi (tel: 0212 201 1818; fax: 201 1823). Hotel with 36 rooms and pretty terrace restaurant; clifftop location.

198

Ordu

Belde Hotel (££) (tel: 0452 214 3987; fax: 214 9398). Fine hotel on its own spit of land 1km outside Ordu, with a large pool, Turkish bath, sauna, gym, nightclub, disco, and indoor and outdoor restaurants.

Şile

Degirmen Hotel (£) Plaj Yolu (tel: 0216 711 5048; fax: 711 5248). Beach hotel 60 km from Istanbul in the resort centre, with 76 rooms, disco, restaurant and a jazz bar.

Sinop

Belediye Yuvam Tesisleri (££) (tel: 0368 261 2532). Simple beach hotel with a bar and restaurant.

Trabzon

Özgür Hotel (£) Atatürk Alanı (tel: 0462 321 1319; fax: 321 3952). Simple 45-room hotel in the city centre with a restaurant and bar.
Usta Hotel (££) İskele Caddesi (tel: 0462 326 5700; fax: 322 3793). Central 76-room hotel with a restaurant and bar. Trabzon's best.

RESTAURANTS

ISTANBUL
Grand hotels

All the grand hotels have superb, if very expensive, restaurants that offer a range of international and Turkish cuisine. Those worth singling out are the Çirağan Restaurant for seafood, the Divan for outstanding Turkish and international cuisine, the Dynasty in the Merit Antique for Chinese food, Miyako in the Swissôtel for Japanese food and Monteverdi in the Conrad for classy Italian food.

In the following listings, the price guides are as follows: £ = 500,000–1 millionTL, ££ = 1 million–2 millionTL, £££ = over 2 million TL.

Stamboul: the Old City

Asitane (££) Kariye Hotel, Edirnekapı (tel: 0212 534 8414). Unusual Ottoman cuisine beautifully presented in a tranquil courtyard garden to the accompaniment of classical Turkish music.
Borsa (££) Sirkeci, opposite the railway station (tel: 0212 527 1821). Rated now as the best Turkish restaurant in Istanbul, though it is nothing to look at from the outside. Offers many rare Turkish dishes. Open lunchtime only. Very popular with business people.
Darüzziyafe (££) in the Süleymaniye mosque complex (tel: 0212 511 8414). Located in the courtyard of the original *imaret* (soup kitchen), this unusual restaurant serves authentic Ottoman cuisine. No alcohol. Popular with tour groups.

Gelik (££) Sahilyolu Mobil Karşısı, Ataköy (tel: 0212 560 7282). A large, informal café-restaurant with sea views, very popular with the locals. There is a wide selection of Turkish dishes including spit roasted lamb, doner and *ayran*.
Hamdi Et Lokantası (£) Kalçın Sokak, Eminönü (tel: 0212 528 0390). Unpretentious lunchtime-only restaurant for simple grilled meat dishes. No alcohol served. Closed Sundays.
Havuzlu Lokanta (££) Grand Bazaar (tel: 0212 527 3346). The smartest place in the bazaar, a safe bet for a lunch or coffee break. Simple Turkish food.
Hünkâr (££) Perçin Sokak, Fatih (tel: 0212 631 5944). Friendly place serving an excellent selection of classic Turkish dishes. No credit cards.
Kathisma (£) Yeni Akbıyık Caddesi, Sultanahmet (tel: 0212 518 9710). Old-fashioned décor and Turkish and international cuisine, with tables on three floors and a terrace.
Konyalı (£££) Topkapı Palace (tel: 0212 513 9697). In the fourth court of the Topkapı itself, with good Turkish food and excellent views over the Bosphorus. Arrive early for lunch to beat tour groups.
Küçük Hudadad (£) Kömür Bekir Sokak, Eminönü. Traditional tradesmen's *lokanta* since 1944, in the historic Şapçi Han opposite Yeni Cami. No alcohol served. Excellent soups and stews.
Pandeli (££) Spice Bazaar, Eminönü (tel: 0212 527 3909). Splendid traditional restaurant above the entrance to the Spice Bazaar, decorated from floor to ceiling in Turkish tiles. Excellent Turkish cuisine. Lunch only; closed Sundays.
Rami (££) Utangaç Sokak, Sultanahmet (tel: 0212 517 6593). Next to the Blue Mosque in a restored Ottoman building, with good Turkish cuisine, candlelight and classical music.
Sarniç (£££) Soğukçeşme Sokak, Sultanahmet (tel: 0212 512 4291). A converted Roman cistern, between the Topkapı and Aya Sofya, notable for its architecture rather than the Turkish food. Closed Mondays.
Sedir (££) Telliodalar Sokak, Kumkapı (tel: 0212 516 7222). Good seafood restaurant in this quarter bursting with fish restaurants.
Subaşı (£) Nuru Osmaniye Caddesi, Cağaloğlu. Simple *lokanta* near the Nuru Osmaniye gate of the Grand Bazaar. Just ten tables, delicious home-cooked Turkish food.
Sultanahmet Köftecisi (£) Divanyolu Caddesi, Sultanahmet (tel: 0212 513 1438). On the corner of Aya Sofya square near the Yerebatan Saray, famous for its meatballs and always busy. No alcohol.
Sultan Pub (££) Divanyolu Caddesi, Sultanahmet (tel: 0212 526 6347). One of the classier places around Aya Sofya offering European and Turkish food.

HOTELS AND RESTAURANTS

Ümit Restaurant (£) Nuruosmaniye (tel: 0212 512 9094). Lunchtime only *lokanta* beside the Grand Bazaar, set in the cellar of an antique inn. Clean and attractive; serves traditional Turkish food. No credit cards.

Yesil Ev (£££) Sultanahmet (tel: 0212 517 6786). Well located between Aya Sofya and the Blue Mosque, in a lovely courtyard setting away from the bustle of the streets. Good quality European and Turkish food, though rather overpriced.

Beyoğlu and the Bosphorus

Ali Baba (££) Kireçburnu Caddesi, Kireçburnu (tel: 0212 262 0889). Simple *lokanta* serving good fish and *meze* in a garden beside the Bosphorus. Popular for Sunday lunch.

Anadolu Kavağı (£). This northernmost village on the Asian side of the Bosphorus is full of simple and colourful fish *lokantas*.

Asır (££) Beyoğlu. Next to the police station (tel: 0212 250 0557). Popular Greek restaurant with excellent selection of *meze* and fish. Very smoky.

Baca (£££) Emirğan Yolu, Boyacıköy (tel: 0212 277 0808). Fashionable restaurant offering international cuisine, live music, disco and a terrace with a spectacular view of the Fatih Sultan Mehmet bridge. Reached up a long steep flight of steps.

Borsa Osmanbey (££) Halaskargazi Caddesi, Şair Nigar Sokak 90/1, Osmanbey (tel: 0212 232 4200). Pleasant, popular restaurant open 11–11. Offering many rare classical Turkish dishes.

Café de Paris (££) Mim Kemal Öke Caddesi 19/1, Nişantası (tel: 0212 225 0700). Parisian-style café with a set menu of steak, chips and salad. Generally crowded. Closed Sunday lunch.

Café de Pera (££) Hava Sokak 17/1, Beyoğlu (tel: 0212 249 9598). Open 11.30–midnight. Very good crepes. Popular after the cinema.

Çamlıca Café (££) Şefa Tepesi, Çamlıca. Restored Ottoman pavilions set on Istanbul's highest hill with superb skyline views. Typical Turkish dishes and classical Turkish music.

Çiçek Pasajı (£) İstiklâl Caddesi, Beyoğlu. Collection of small restaurants serving *meze* and meat dishes in the old flower market. Noisy and atmospheric. No credit cards.

Çiftnal (££) Yenimahalle, Ihlamur Yolu 6, Beşiktaş (tel: 0212 261 3129). In a 19th century police station, this restaurant offers grilled Turkish dishes and is open from noon to midnight.

Deep Restaurant (££) Kurabiye Sokak 2, Beyoğlu (tel: 0212 244 0839). An unassuming but friendly Turkish restaurant with a resourceful chef. The prices are reasonable, a factor which attracts the predominantly youthful clientele.

Deniz Park Gazinosu (££) Daire Sokak 9, Yeniköy (tel: 0212 262 0415). With a wonderful terrace offering Bosphorus views, this long-established fish restaurant is owned by a Greek family.

Ece (£££) Tramvay Cad 104, Kuruçeşme (tel: 0212 265 9600). Open 6.00pm till dawn, this old Greek house offers *meze* on the ground floor, a pop music bar on the first floor, and an excellent à la carte restaurant on the top floor.

Façyo (££) Kireçburnu Caddesi, Tarabya (tel: 0212 262 0024). Best fish restaurant in Tarabya, the Bosphorus suburb famous for its nightlife and seaside restaurants.

Four Seasons (££) İstiklâl Caddesi, Tünel (tel: 0212 293 3941). This pleasant restaurant is handy for the consulates and the cinemas, this smallish restaurant has a European atmosphere and good food.

Galata Tower (£££) Kuledibi (tel: 0212 293 1139). Indifferent food accompanied by Turkish music and belly-dancing, but superb location and views. Must book.

Hacıbaba (££) İstiklâl Caddesi, Beyoğlu (tel: 0212 244 1886). *Lokanta* offering Turkish food with a balcony overlooking the courtyard of a Greek church.

Han (£££) Rumeli Hisarı (tel: 0212 265 2968). Good fish restaurant with a terrace overlooking the Bosphorus.

Hidiv Kasrı (the Khedive's Summer Palace) (££) Çubuklu (tel: 0216 331 2651). Splendid restored palace in art deco style overlooking the Bosphorus from the Asian side. Turkish cuisine with live music.

Huzur (Arabin Yeri) (££) Üsküdar (tel: 0216 333 3157). Long-established unpretentious fish restaurant with amazing sunset views of the Asian side of the Istanbul skyline.

Kadife Chalet (££) Kadife Sokak 29, Bahariye, Kadıköy (tel: 0212 437 8596). Open 10.00am till 10.00pm, this pretty restaurant with period décor is set in an Ottoman house and offers Ottoman and international dishes.

Kız Kulesi Deniz Restaurant (££) Salacak Sahil Yolu, Üsküdar (tel: 0216 341 0403). Excellent views towards the old city from Üsküdar across the Bosphorus, with delicious seafood.

Korfez (£££) Kanlıca (tel: 0216 413 4314). Very smart fish restaurant on the Bosphorus, reached by the restaurant's private boat from Rumeli Hisarı.

Liman Lokantası (££) Karaköy (tel: 0212 244 1033). Located above the Turkish Maritime Lines' waiting room, this old classic has good views and excellent food. Lunch only, Monday to Friday.

Rejans (££) Beyoğlu (tel: 0212 244 1610). Opposite San Antonio's church, Istanbul's classic Russian restaurant, now a bit shabby.

Süreyya (£££) İstinye Caddesi, İstinye (tel: 0212 277 5886). One of Istanbul's gastronomic landmarks, serving superb Russian, Turkish and European cuisine. Must book. Closed Sundays.

Ziya (£££) Ortaköy (tel: 0212 261 6005). Under the Bosphorus Bridge, offers Turkish and international cuisine with a fabulous view and tables outdoors in the summer.

Istanbul environs

Bursa
Hünkar Döner Kebab House (£) The best of the well-located clutch of restaurants looking out over the quiet cobbled square of the Yeşil Cami.
Kebapçı İskender (£) Ünlü Cadde 7 (tel: 0224 221 4615). The owner of this café claims to be a direct descendant of the inventor of the kebab.

Büyükada
Büyükada (£) A simple café on the summit of the hill by the Monastery of St George, offering a lunch of cheese, olives and red wine. A long steep path leads up to it from the middle of town.
Many fish restaurants line the promenade, and there are simple kebab houses in the little town square.

Çanakkale
Of the quayside restaurants, **Bizim Entellektüel** (£) has an appetising range of *meze* and fish dishes all reasonably priced. Further inland, the roomy **Trakya** (£) on Demircioğlu Caddesi, claims to be open 24 hours daily.

THE AEGEAN

Ayvalık
The best restaurants in this region are on Ali Bey island just opposite Ayvalık, notably **Artur Restaurant** (££) (tel: 0266 327 1014) and **Günay Restaurant** (££) (tel: 0266 327 1048). On the road west of Ayvalık, beyond Çamlık, the **Şeytan Sofrası** (**Devil's Dining Table**) **Restaurant** (£) has unremarkable food but a spectacular setting overlooking the Gulf of Edremit. Further afield, near Altınoluk on the north of the Gulf of Edremit, the remarkable **Chalet Chopin** (**Değirmen**) (££) (tel: 0266 396 1313; fax: 396 1370) offers delicious Turkish food with live music in a beautiful garden.

Behramkale
There are several good fish restaurants on the harbourfront.

Bergama
There is a string of restaurants along Bankalar Caddesi, between the Red Basilica and the Asklepeion. **Asklepieion Restaurant** (£) İzmir Caddesi 54 (tel: 0232 633 4222) is the best in the town of Bergama.
Berksoy Restaurant (££) İzmir Yolu (tel: 0232 633 2595). Good food from the restaurant of the hotel of the same name.

Bodrum
There are literally hundreds of restaurants in Bodrum. For romantic views of the castle, illuminated at night, try the Turkish restaurants along Cumhuriyet Caddesi, for example **Bistro Stomach News** (££) (tel: 0252 215 3013) or **Kortan Restaurant** (££) (tel: 0252 316 2141). Also on Cumhuriyet Caddesi, at no. 155 is the **Golden Restaurant** (££), offering Chinese and Korean cuisines. Just in front of the castle itself on Kale Caddesi is the **Han Restaurant** (££) (tel: 0252 316 7951), in a converted 18th-century caravanserai. Others to try: **Mausolus Restaurant** (££) (tel: 0252 316 4176) and **Kocadon** (££) (tel: 0252 614 63705), both on Neyzen Tevfik Caddesi.

Çeşme
Körfez Restaurant (£) Yalı Caddesi (tel: 0232 712 6718). A good simple restaurant in the centre.
Sahil Restaurant (££) Cumhuriyet Meydanı (tel: 0232 712 6646). The best of the town's fish restaurants.

Dalyan
Freshwater fish is the speciality here, and there are many restaurants along the riverbank in town, of which you could try **Beyazgül** (££), **Denizatı** (£) and **Begonvil** (££).

Efes (Ephesus)
Bahçesaray Restaurant (£) is an attractive restaurant at Meryemana Kavşağı (tel: 0232 892 3486).
Efes Restaurant (££) (tel: 0232 892 2291). Very conveniently located at the ruins, offering a fair range of adequate if unexciting food.

Foça
Well known for its fish restaurants along the harbourfront, of which the **Ali Baba** (££), the **Bedesten** (£) and the **Palmiye** (££) should be tried first.

İzmir
Altınkapı Restoran (££) 1444 Sokak, Alsancak (tel: 0232 422 56878). Good food, popular in 'arty' circles.
1888 Restaurant (£££) Cumhuriyet Bulvarı, Alsancak (tel: 0232 421 6690). Delicious Mediterranean specialities, notably some fine Jewish dishes. Live music at weekends.
Deniz Restoran (££) Atatürk Caddesi, Kordon (tel: 0232 422 0601). One of the best seafront restaurants, with imaginative *meze* and unbeatable squid.
Hisarönü (££) 1444 Sokak, Alsancak (tel: 0232 464 2705). A modern busy fish restaurant (air-conditioned). The fish selections, including çipura, sea bass and red mullet are illustrated on the table mats.

201

HOTELS AND RESTAURANTS

Kaptan (£) Kemalpaşa Caddesi 39A
(tel: 0232 381 9994). Kebabs, pizzas,
hamburgers and mouthwatering desserts
at reasonable prices are offered by this
modern café-restaurant across the water
from İzmir in Karşıyaka.

Kemal'ın Yeri (££) 1453 Sokak, Alsancak
(tel: 0232 422 3190). A wonderful fish
restaurant with friendly service.

Liman Restoran (££) Atatürk Caddesi,
Kordon (tel: 0232 422 1876). Good seafood
restaurant on the waterfront.

Mask (£££) 1453 Sokak, Alsancak
(tel: 0232 463 0425). An expensive
restaurant with elegant décor, dancing and
good international cuisine.

Meyhane (Bora Yıldırım) (££) 1453 Sokak
(tel: 0232 463 8368). Favoured by locals,
this friendly fish restaurant is in the lively
Alsancak district.

Palet Restoran (£££) Atatürk Caddesi,
Kordon (tel: 0232 421 5786). Expensive,
floating, fish restaurant.

Park Restoran (£££) Kültürpark İçi
(tel: 0232 489 3590). Another plush,
floating expensive restaurant. It offers
good international cuisine with French
leanings.

Vejetaryen Lokantası (£) 1375 Sokak,
Alsancak (tel: 0232 421 7558). Pleasant
vegetarian restaurant.

Kuşadası

A wide range and selection of restaurants is
available here. Try **Ada Restaurant** (££) in a
fine setting on Güvercin island, or
Gondalen Pizza (££) on İnönü Bulvarı 19/2
(tel: 0256 614 5417). Near Sağlık Caddesi at
Emek Sok 4 is the good value **Albatross
Restaurant** (£) and just a few steps from
'Bar Street' is the **1.A Restaurant** (tel: 0256
614 8409). Outside of town in the
Saraydamları district is **Değirmen** (£££)
on Davutlar Caddesi (0256 681 2148) a re-
created old mill, with a fine hilltop setting.

Marmaris

An enormous selection and price range is
available in this popular tourist destination.
The best settings are along the promenade,
especially at dusk. Try **Bamboo Restaurant**
(£) at İçmeler, **Han Restaurant** (£) in front of
Pension Dede in Turunç Bay, **Ayyıldız** (££)
in the old market area, **Turkei** (£££) on Haki
Mustafa Sokağı ('Bar Street'), **Bigma** (££) on
the waterfront, and **Kervansaray** (££) in
Yunus Nadi Caddesi.

Milas

There are plenty of cheap restaurants in the
central Hisarbaşı Hill area, for example
Özcan Kebap Salonu (£).

Muğla

Restaurants congregate around the bazaar
area; alternatively try the hotel restaurant at
the **Yalçın** (££) (tel: 0252 214 1599), just
across the road from the bus station.

Pamukkale

There is not much to choose between the
many restaurants on offer here: location is
probably the deciding factor. The
Kervansaray Hotel (££) offers good food
from its rooftop restaurant. The Gürsöy and
Mustafa restaurants are also worth a try.

Selçuk

Terrace restaurants line the pedestrianised
Çengiz Topel Caddesi:
Firuze (££) (tel: 0232 892 7995). Selection of
mezes and fish. **Seçil** (££) (tel: 0232 891
4902). Includes vegetarian menu. **Seçkin**
(££) (tel: 0232 892 6698) where the food
is nicely presented and the service
unobtrusive.

THE MEDITERRANEAN

Adana

Ağacpınar Tesisleri (£) Ceyhan-Adana Eski
Karayolu 10km. Ağacpınar Koyu (tel: 0322
321 9166). Good restaurant outside town on
the Ceyhan road.

Gözde Restaurant (££) Çifte Minare Camii
Yanı (tel: 0322 453 5501). Pleasant food by
the Çifte Minare Mosque.

Alanya

There is a large selection of *pideci* (pizza
parlours) and small restaurants in the area
behind the east beach near Gazi Paşa
Caddesi. Alternatively, behind the west
beach on Güzelyalı Caddesi, try **Cleopatra**
(££) (tel: 0242 513 7491) and **Öz Duygu** (££)
(tel: 0242 323 18027), which serves
delicious Turkish bread, kebabs and a good
selection of fish.

Anamur

There are a few restaurants around the
main square, the best of which is **Anamur**
(£); others can be found along the waterfront in İskele.

Antakya

Didem Turistik Tesisleri (£) Reyhanlı Yolu
Uzeri (tel: 0326 212 1928). A good range of
Turkish dishes is on offer here.

Saray Restaurant (££) Atatürk Bulvarı 57
(tel: 0326 617 1383). The best place in the
city centre, with Turkish specialities.

Antalya

The best restaurants with the most
enjoyable ambience tend to be found in the
old quarter round the renovated marina
area. One of the most welcoming with good
grilled seafood is **Sunset** (££) Uzun Çarşı
Sokak 19 (tel: 0242 243 9533). Also in Uzun
Çarşı Sokak is **Sirri** (££) (tel: 0242 241 7239),
an attractive garden restaurant, surrounded
by orange trees. **A La Turca's** (£££) Uzun
Çarşı Sokak 48 (tel: 0242 243 1903) also has
a garden and excellent sea bass, but prices
soon mount up.

In addition **La Trattoria** (££) at Fevzi Çakmak Caddesi 3/C (tel: 0242 243 3931), run by a Turkish man and his English wife, serves very good European food in a bistro setting.

Fethiye

Among the wide choice of restaurants along the waterfront are **Rafet** (£) (tel: 0252 614 1106), **Blue Sea** (££) (tel: 0252 614 8734), the roof restaurant in the **Hotel Dededoğlu** (££) (tel: 0252 614 4010), **Çın Restaurant** in the Likya Hotel (tel: 0252 611 2233) and, if you are tiring of Turkish food, try the **Peking** (££) (with Chinese chef) near the Uğur Mumcu Parkı (tel: 0252 612 0706).

Finike

Petek Restaurant (£) in the village centre serves surprisingly good traditional Turkish cuisine.

İskenderun

The side street running parallel to Ulucami Caddesi has a number of cheap restaurants selling stews, kebabs etc. On Ulucami Caddesi itself (no.43) is another good kebab house, the **Hasan Baba** (£).

Kale

Güneyhan Restaurant (£) Saint Nicolas Kilisesi Yani (tel: 0242 871 3810). Well placed beside St Nicholas' Church.

Kalkan

Kalkan is renowned for its excellent cuisine, probably because a number of the hotel and restaurant owners are originally from Istanbul. For that reason prices are on the steep side. Try some of the following: the **Korsan** (££), the **Han** (££), the **Kalkan Han** (££), the restaurant of the **Akın Pansiyon**, the **İlyada** (££) and the **Lipsos** (££).

Kaş

Chez Evy (£££) Terzi Sok 2 (tel: 0242 836 1253) French and Turkish cuisine.
Mercan Restaurant (££) Çarşı İçi, Liman Başı (tel: 0242 836 1209). Good Turkish food in the town centre.
Merkez Restaurant (££) Cumhuriyet Meydanı 18 (tel: 0242 836 1629). Consistently high-standard Turkish cuisine.

Kemer

The best of the many restaurants here are situated round the yachting marina, notably the **Arsemia** (££), the **Ayışığı Tesisleri** (£), the **Duppont** (££), the **Miço** (£), the **Mimosa** (£), the **Sultan Sofrası** (£) and the **Yörük Parkı Restaurant** (££).

Kız Kalesi

Most of the best restaurants in this area are in Narlıkuyu, the village by the caves known as Cennet Cehennem (Heaven and Hell). Look out in particular for the **Deniz** (£), the **Çınaraltı** (££), and the **Lagos** (£).

Mersin

Ali Baba 1 Restaurant (££) Uluçarşı Otopark Girişi Karşısı (tel: 0324 223 3088). A convenient place to eat after shopping, located by the main car park entrance.
Ali Baba-Kordon Restaurant (££) The best place to eat in Mersin, near the Hilton Hotel.
Pizzeria Ocin (££) Bahri Ok İşhanı 39, off Atatürk Caddesi. Rustles up spaghetti, pizzas etc to a young crowd.

Ölüdeniz

Beyaz Yunus Restaurant (££) (tel: 0252 616 6036). The best of the restaurants on the lagoon and beach.

Side

Afrodit Restaurant (££) Old Harbour (tel: 0242 753 1171). A garden terrace restaurant with a good selection of *mezes*.
Bademaltı (££) (tel: 0242 753 1403). A good selection of Turkish dishes.
Toros Restaurant (££) Liman Caddesi (tel: 0242 753 2005). Good Turkish food in front of the old harbour.

Silifke

There are plenty of good places to eat along the coast. In town, try **Piknik Restaurant** (£) İnönü Caddesi 17 (tel: 0324 714 2810) or **Babaoğlu** (£) opposite the bus station.

THE BLACK SEA

Giresun

The three restaurants to sample here are the **Kale** (£), the **Kerasus** (££) and the **Mehmet Efendi** (££).

Ordu

Try some of the good fish restaurants on the seafront, such as the **Midi** (££), the **Gülistan** (££) and the **Sahil Balık** (££).

Samsun

Nothing very exciting here, but try the **Canlı Balık (Küçük Ev)** (££), **Oskar** (£) on Belediye Meydanı, **Cumhuriyet Restaurant** (££) Şey Hamza Sok 3 and the **Altınbalık** (£) for fish.

Sinop

For good eating, look no further than İskele Caddesi and the other streets near the waterfront: **Saray** (£), **Uzun Mehmet** (£), **Akvaryum Balık** (£) and for standard international fare, **Barinak Café** (£).

Trabzon

The best restaurant on the coast is the **Köşk Restaurant** (££) in Akçaabat (tel: 0462 228 3223); the best in town is the **Trabzon** (£) on the main square opposite the Özgür hotel, with a very pleasant ambience and fresh fish specialities; it serves alcohol.

Index

INDEX

ACKNOWLEDGEMENTS

Picture credits

The Automobile Association would like to thank the following photographers, libraries and associations for their assistance in the preparation of this book.

AKG, LONDON 31, 35, 36a
BRUCE COLEMAN LTD 163b (Luiz Claudio Marigo)
DIGITAL WISDOM PUBLISHING LIMITED top map on back cover
MARY EVANS PICTURE LIBRARY 36b, 37a, 37b
THE RONALD GRANT ARCHIVES 118/9, 119
ROBERT HARDING PICTURE LIBRARY 92a
HULTON GETTY 38a, 38b, 39a, 40b, 40c
IMAGES COLOUR LIBRARY front cover
IMPACT PHOTOS 23 (Caroline Penn)
NATURE PHOTOGRAPHERS LTD 162a (E A Janes), 162b (R Tidman), 163a (R Bush)
PICTURES COLOUR LIBRARY 171
POPPERFOTO 13b (Abdurrahman Antakyali - Anatolian, Reuters)
REX FEATURES LTD 41a, 41b, 118
SPECTRUM COLOUR LIBRARY 22a, 22/3, 34b.

All remaining pictures are held in the Association's own library (AA PHOTO LIBRARY) and were taken by Jean François Pin with the exception of the following pages:
P KENWARD 10b, 10c, 11b, 16, 18a, 19a, 19b, 20a, 20b, 26a, 26b, 28a, 28/9, 32a, 33a, 39b, 53, 58a, 60a, 69a, 70, 73a, 73b, 81b, 82b, 86b, 88a, 95b, 102a, 102b, 103a, 121a, 121b, 124/5, 125, 126/7, 127, 128, 130/1, 131, 132, 133, 134a, 134b, 144, 145, 146, 150, 152/3, 153a, 153b, 166/7, 168/9, 170, 172b, 174, 182, 186a
D MITIDERI 10a, 12b, 13a, 27a, 27b, 30b, 33b, 34a, 72b, 135, 155
C SAWYER 11a, 14a, 21a, 44/5, 46, 47, 48, 50, 52, 55a, 57, 62, 63b, 64, 65, 66a, 66b, 67, 68, 71, 74, 75, 87, 93, 94, 95a, 179, 190
T SOUTER back cover (b), 3, 14b, 24a, 24b, 30a, 40a, 49a, 51, 54a, 54b, 55b, 56, 58b, 59a, 59b, 60b, 61, 63a, 69b, 72a, 77, 80, 81a, 85a, 85b, 86a, 88b, 89, 90a, 90b, 90c, 91a, 111c, 172a
R STRANGE 187.

Acknowledgements

Christopher and Melanie Rice would like to acknowledge the assistance of the staff at the Department of Research and Study at Istanbul Chamber of Commerce. They would also like to acknowledge the help given by tourist information staff at Antalya, Muğla, Anamur, Mersin, Alanya, Çanakkale, Selçuk, İzmir, Kuşadası and Köceğiz. The authors and the Automobile Association would like to acknowledge the contribution of Diana Darke, author of *Explorer Turkey*.

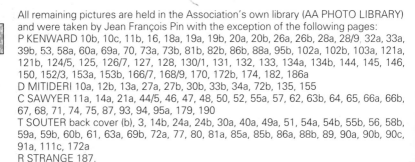

Contributors

Copy editor: Sue Gordon   **Verifier**: Mary Berkmen
Designer: Mike Preedy   **Indexer**: Marie Lorimer